C000110176

The Narrow Smile A Journey
Back To The North West Frontier

Peter Mayne

Nabu Public Domain Reprints:

You are holding a reproduction of an original work published before 1923 that is in the public domain in the United States of America, and possibly other countries. You may freely copy and distribute this work as no entity (individual or corporate) has a copyright on the body of the work. This book may contain prior copyright references, and library stamps (as most of these works were scanned from library copies). These have been scanned and retained as part of the historical artifact.

This book may have occasional imperfections such as missing or blurred pages, poor pictures, errant marks, etc. that were either part of the original artifact, or were introduced by the scanning process. We believe this work is culturally important, and despite the imperfections, have elected to bring it back into print as part of our continuing commitment to the preservation of printed works worldwide. We appreciate your understanding of the imperfections in the preservation process, and hope you enjoy this valuable book.

THE NARROW SMILE

Your eyes are two loaded revolvers
And your narrow smile has destroyed me

PASHTO SONG

PETER MAYNE

THE NARROW SMILE

*A Journey back to the
North-west Frontier*

LONDON
JOHN MURRAY
ALBEMARLE STREET, W.

By the Same Author

THE ALLEYS OF MARRAKESH

"A good book, an interesting book, and one that I
warmly recommend."—HAROLD NICOLSON.   *2nd Printing*

FIRST EDITION .   .   . 1955

Printed in Great Britain by
Wyman & Sons, Ltd., London, Fakenham and Reading
and published by John Murray (Publishers) Ltd.

CONTENTS

*

Part One

CAMERA OBSCURA

page 1

*   *

Part Two

KABUL

page 115

*   *

Part Three

PATHAN—PAKHTUN

page 177

*   *

Part Four

EPILOGUE: KARACHI

page 257

5511856

FOR
T B C C

ILLUSTRATIONS

Between pages 16–17

THE STREET OF THE STORY-TELLERS, PESHAWAR

A FORTIFIED VILLAGE, SHOWING THE *BRUJ*, OR
    WATCH-TOWER

NATHIA GALI   EXPIRING WOODEN HUTS . . .

THE KHYBER PASS OPENS OUT INTO AFGHANISTAN

THE HINDU KUSH—LOOKING NORTH FROM KABUL

TWO RAMS AND A SHEPHERD-BOY

". . . HE LIKES FALCONRY"

NOMADS ON THE MOVE

PAKHTUNS

PATHANS

IN THE HINDU KUSH

A MOUNTAIN VALLEY IN THE HINDU KUSH

THE KOHAT DARRA

★   ★

Between pages viii–1

SKETCH MAP OF THE AUTHOR'S JOURNEY IN
    WEST PAKISTAN AND AFGHANISTAN

SKETCH MAP TO SHOW THE PAKHTUN AREAS

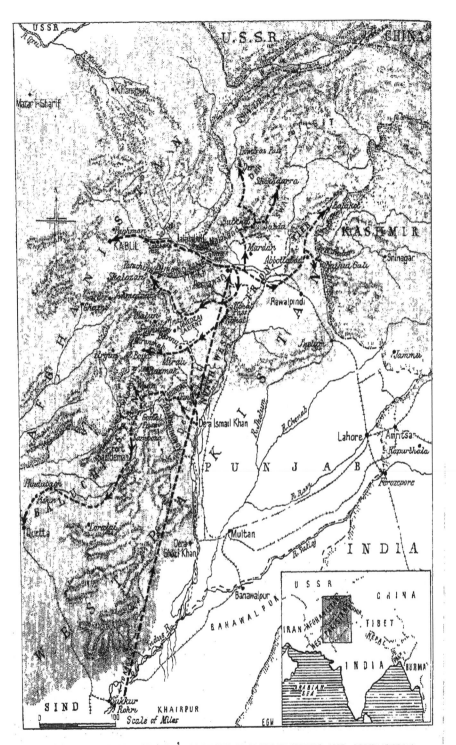

SKETCH MAP OF THE AUTHOR'S JOURNEY IN WEST PAKISTAN AND AFGHANISTAN

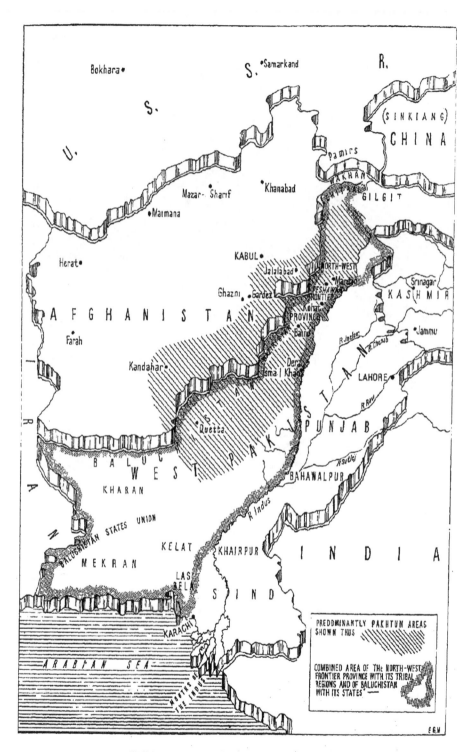

SKETCH MAP TO SHOW THE PAKTUN AREAS

Part 1

CAMERA OBSCURA

Chapter 1

"HE looks quite usual. Much the same as anyone else here, as far as I can see. Perhaps he's a little more . . . sunburnt than most of us, and more handsome, too. He's being a great success, incidentally. Why did you hiss at me like that over the telephone, Peter?"

"I wanted to explain about him, that's why. He was standing right beside me, so I had to hiss."

Daphne waved a hand impatiently. "But why the need to hiss at all? That's what I meant."

"Because . . . Well . . ."

Some new guests were arriving and she had to leave me. The house would soon be full at this rate—a little Hampstead house, nineteenth century, with some fine furniture and a number of good and carefully-chosen pictures. The guests seemed to be mostly people connected in one way or another with painting or books—like our host and hostess. They might be expected to take most things in their stride—even Chainak Khan. Yet I was doubtful, because I knew him and his people too well, I suppose. There was no opportunity to explain things further to Daphne at the moment, however, and anyway Chainak Khan was safely her guest now, and it was true that he was being a success. I could see him through the archway into the next room, leaning up against a book-case, his eyes half closed, talking and purring.

Graham came round with a jug of some mixed drink. "Your friend seems to be a great success," he said. "Thank you for bringing him. Are you ready for some more of this?"

I held out my glass. "Thank you for letting me bring him. I ran into him yesterday. I had no idea he was in England, even."

"What's he doing here?"

"Nothing in particular. He says he's come to have a look at the British in their own country."

"And what does he think of us, now that he's seen?"

"He says that in any case we're nicer in England than we had seemed to him in his country."

"That's a mercy," Graham said, and passed on to the next empty glass. It was in a girl's hand, an arm-chair away.

Yet I did worry a little, because I felt responsible. Chainak was so unpredictable, away from his own homelands: moreover he had the power to charm strangers and liked to use it. The girl in the arm-chair whose glass Graham had just filled turned to me and asked: "Where did you find him? I hear you're responsible."

I was coming in for a lot of reflected glory and it was not, after all, disagreeable.

"I didn't just find him. I've known him and his family for years," I said.

"Where does he come from, then?"

"The nearest big town's Peshawar."

She searched her brain. "That's India, isn't it? No. Pakistan, now. Sorry. Is that right?"

"Quite right. Pakistan. The far north. The North-West Frontier, in fact."

"I see. Kipling."

"And Hollywood Bengal Lancers—but probably that was before your time."

"I remember. A Paythan."

"Well, yes . . . Pathān, anyway. That's what they're called by people who aren't."

"And what are they called by people who are?" she demanded, but went on, without waiting for an answer: "Paythan. A man's handsome by nature, whatever the pronunciation." She gave Chainak an appreciative look through the archway. He was very handsome, but much more Tartar than is usual with the Pathans: Genghiz Khan in his youth, you might think: spruced up and done into an English suit, with a Karakul cap. He was talking nineteen to the dozen in his deceptively-fluent English. God knew where he had picked it up. Not in school, certainly. He had never been to school, except to the little Islamic school in his village where he had learnt the rudiments of the Holy Qoran. He had had to leave in a hurry when he killed his cousin, so that he had had no schooling after the age of ten. I didn't tell the girl this, but it was more than likely that Chainak was

4

telling the group of which he was at present the centre. I could imagine him telling them, as he had told me years before when I first met him. He had only recently returned to his village at that time, after a ten- or twelve-year absence in India. The little cousin's father, Chainak's uncle, had himself died meantime, and Chainak had grown big enough to defend himself. So he had come back at last. "I did it with my slate," he had told me: "*bong* . . . On his head. And then I ran away." When he tells the story now, he generally adds: "Mr. Vincent Sheean has written the story of me and my cousin. You know Mr. Vincent Sheean? He is an American. But as a matter of fact the cousin didn't die. He and me are excellent friends now."

Graham's gin and cider—if that is what it was—was as deceptively fluent as Chainak's English. It just flowed over the tongue and no one guessed what it might be doing inside, in the hidden recesses of the mind, so smooth, so honey-smooth.

"Graham tells me you're just off to the East," the girl was saying.

I said yes, I was making a trip to Pakistan, but only for a few months. I added that Chainak had promised to help me brush up the language during the week or so that remained before I left. It needed brushing up too. I hadn't spoken it for years.

"Hindustani?"

"No. It's called Pashto."

"Oh."

People are either bored or impressed if anyone claims to speak an outlandish language. This one was bored, and I can't really blame her.

"He looks like a prince," she said. "Is he?"

"The Pathans are inclined to look like princes—but none of them are. They're mostly peasants. Sturdy individualists. They don't even have leaders in the proper sense of the word, let alone princes."

"Sturdy, anyway. Let's go over and join them, shall we?"

I took her over to the group where Chainak was in the middle of saying: "All right. I will tell you." Then he saw us coming and broke off for a moment to say, "Hullo, Peter. I am telling them about that ridiculous man who threatened me." It was obvious that he liked the look of the girl with me, and he gave her a glance I've seen him use before. He knows exactly the effect he can make, given favourable circumstances. He made a little space for her beside him, up against the book-case. "I'm telling these ladies and this gentleman a story of London," he went on. "Peter knows it's true."

"I don't *know* that it's true. I wasn't there. But it has a true sound."

"Isn't that enough?" asked the man in the group.

"Not at all enough!" Chainak remarked firmly. "This story is true like on the Holy Qoran—or, for you Christians, like on your Bible. It is about me and a man meeting in a street of South Kensington. Nobody had told me that South Kensington is a dangerous place at night. The man said something, and I replied something polite, and then he said something about girls—and I said about last buses and how to get home after, and he said not at all necessary, and I thought a bit and then said 'After all, no thank you for your trouble', and he became annoyed—because I expect he thought he was now losing the prize—and suddenly he pulled something dark from his pocket in that small and empty street which he had explained as a short cut to some other place, and he said fiercely: 'Come on! You'd better hand over your wallet!' Very fierce. But he was quite little and soft-looking—like a fierce mouse."

Chainak was making his eyes flash. His audience obviously wished to believe him and I suspect that they did. I believe the story myself. He does not play tricks with the truth, as a rule: at least I have never caught him out.

"What did you do?" the man asked.

"I? I said like this. I said: 'Young man. Murder to you is a fairy's tale. Amongst my people we are forced to kill each other because of . . .' What is it, Peter? What is the expression? Oh yes, because of our rudimentary social system. So I said: 'We are quite accustomed to it, as a matter of fact.'"

He had hardened his voice, no doubt reproducing the tone he had used at this strange encounter, his eyes closing like slits, which emphasized the Tartar look I have already commented upon. His lips curled up from his teeth as he continued:

"I said: 'If you are not gone while I count to seven, *I* will murder *you*.' And I made some motions with my hands." Chainak looked down at his hands contemplatively.

"And then?"

"That's the end of the story, I think," Chainak said.

"He went away?"

6

"Of course."

People looked at each other, wondering whether to believe after all.

"I am learning Cockney," Chainak remarked in a new voice, the story being finished. "And also Scotch."

"How nice," one of the girls said. "What can you say in Cockney?"

"Oh, many things. I shall have to think—and then I shall put something Cockney into the conversation, shall I?"

"Yes. That would be very pleasant. And Scotch?"

"About Scotch I don't have to think, because so far I have only learnt one sentence and that is 'durrrty buggerrr'."

"Interesting," the girl commented, unmoved: and the man put in: "You shouldn't say 'Scotch', you know. You should say 'Scots'."

"He shouldn't say 'durrrty buggerrr' either, I think."

"I have a friend that I meet in a pub. He is Scotch and he is always saying it. He is from the Venice of the North. Have you been there, Peter?"

"You mean Edinburgh? Yes. But it is the Athens of the North. Not Venice."

He turned to the girl beside him. "Athens. Very well. My Scotch friend says that they have built their Athens in Edinburgh."

"Dear Auld Reekie," she said, smiling.

"You are confusing everything for me. What is Auld Reekie?"

"Auld Reekie? Edinburgh. Smoke-smelly, it means, I think. The Scotch cover their Parthenon with wisps of it."

Chainak was confused again. "What do they cover it with, did you say?"

"Wisps of smelly smoke."

The other man in the group laughed and broke in: "Parthenon is Greek for 'House of the Virgin'. But the one in Edinburgh doesn't look very much like the real one in Greece, to be honest. Probably the climate was wrong, and Sir Walter Scott. But it was brave of them to try."

"Ah. Virgins," Chainak said. "We people very much appreciate virgins. You don't seem to have many in London, if I may say so."

"The virgins are not for the visitors—that's the explanation."

"I'm told that until recently all your women were kept locked up. Is that true?" One of the girls was busily changing the subject.

"Not in the least true. How could they do their work in the fields if they were kept locked up? Or bring the water? Of course they work in the house too and if ever we take them to Peshawar—Peshawar is our big city, like London for you—they put on their *burqa*—the *burqa* is the big white cotton thing, covering everything from the head to the feet—they put these things on so that those miserable city-men shall not be able to see them. Because our women are modest, you see."

"But I have read that the women of Pakistan are all coming out of seclusion to take their part in the life of the nation."

"Oh, I see. But you are talking about something quite different. *I* am talking about our Pathan women—not about the down-country townspeople, and the rich nawabs and their women. Our Pathan women prefer to remain chattels, like God intended."

With a slight edge to her patience the girl started to explain about the position of women in the modern world, and Chainak listened politely. When she had made her point, he said:

"I see now. The sexes are the same in spite of what my eyes tell me. And if other men look at my wife and she looks at them, I may shoot neither her nor them. Is that what you mean? On the contrary it is my duty to shoot. My wife is for having my babies: that's what God has given her breasts and a womb for—and also strong arms for working in the fields. Only in time of fighting she can come and mix with outside men—who are then too busy shooting to look at her in that way. At such times she can bring food and ammunition to me and the other men, too: yes, and she can shoot. Straight— *t-hung*! . . . in the heart. If you were a Pathan woman, madam," he went on irritably, "your husband would beat you on the wedding-night, and you would have to defend your stomach—but if he could get your belt off, then you'd be finished. It would be shameful if you screamed or cried. All the other ladies would be listening outside the room, laughing together and saying: 'Listen! She's having a bad time.' In due course they would be allowed to enter the room so that they could report to everyone that . . . nature had had its way. It's just plain nature. London, and all this . . ." he finished up, with a sweeping gesture of his arm, "is not nature at all."

The girl had the grace to laugh and agreed that all this was not really nature. Unfortunately Pathans do not share the polite western convention about giving in so that talk may remain on a pleasant, friendly level. Chainak must have decided to give her one more

8

smack, just to point the moral. He said: "And so, madam, if you do not care about nature, you had better not go to bed with a Pathan."

There was silence for a moment—for a little longer, perhaps, than was quite comfortable. Chainak was unaware of it.

"What we Pathans lack, of course," he resumed meditatively, "is education—though it is spreading more and more now. I told you how I had had to run away? Well, that was a pity. I have done my best to learn something from people I have met, of course, but I lack schooling, and schooling is good. I must tell you that I find many things in London that would be good for my people, too. I like, for example, your policemen, and I frequently have conversations with them. They are kind to the public—though sometimes, I am told, this is not so. But as a rule they are kind, and behave like servants of the public, which is what they are. With us this is not the case. I will explain some day, if we meet again. Red peppers up the rectum, and other things. They have learnt all sorts of tricks, our police, but the real Pathan does not torture his prisoners. Sometimes it may be necessary to cut off a finger to send to the prisoner's relatives, if they are slow with the ransom-money for example. But such a thing would only happen when the prisoner is mean and refuses to write the proper letter to his relatives, explaining the need to be generous. Such prisoners are always rich, naturally—that is why they have become prisoners. In these cases he must pay for his meanness by losing a finger, and then another, if need be. But there is less kidnapping now that the Hindus have gone." He paused, thinking about this side effect of partition, I dare say. It wasn't very common, but some of the Hindus were rich, and it was always a possibility to be considered. He went on: "Now, with enemies, it is a different thing. We always kill the enemy prisoner before we allow the women to insult the body. You notice the difference? Shall I tell you how the women insult the bodies?"

I felt it might be better to stop short of these details. So I said:

"We've got an early start tomorrow, Chainak. It's getting late."

In fact we were making for North Wales on the following day. I wanted him to see something of Britain other than a big city, and North Wales in spring, with its rhododendrons and azaleas, would be a good counterblast to London. I was going in any case, because I had friends I wanted to see before leaving for the East. And apart from all else I thought that if Chainak really got going he might say

B

something that his audience would be quite unable to stomach, even though they would try to hide the fact. He would enjoy shocking them directly he discovered that he could. However the girl with the militant feminist views had questions she was determined to put to him.

"Don't take him away," she said to me. "Just a few more minutes. Listen, Mr. Chainak Khan. . . ."

"You may call me Chainak."

"All right. Listen, Chainak. I'd like to know about marriages. Do the parents arrange everything in your country? Does the bride-groom have any say in the matter, or the bride? Can they meet and get to know each other before they are married?"

"But I told you! The girls don't go about veiled in our villages. You can see them there. I had seen my wife often. She was from a house in the same village. A sort of cousin's house. I had often looked at her from behind trees. If I had been living in the village when we were both children, then I could also have talked to her before. But she was big by the time I came back to the village and I had not known her before because she is several years younger than me. So I could only look at her secretly. I also sent her written messages, but she could not read. She was very beautiful. I was pleased to marry her."

"I suppose it is possible that marriage like that can be happy."

"Naturally. The wives love the husbands, and the husbands love the wives if they are beautiful and while they are still young. Later the wives have the babies to love them, so everyone is contented. It becomes difficult for the wives if they don't have any babies, as you can understand. Or if they only have girl-babies."

"And what if it is the husband's fault that there are no babies?" the girl asked him.

"The husband's fault . . . ? Let's stop talking about this, shall we? I shall now tell you something bad, because I find that I am telling you only the good things about us. The worst thing is the way we have to kill each other because of *badi*. How do you say *badi*, Peter? Blood-feud? Yes, because of blood-feud. In this way the blood-feud goes on from father to son, on and on—or brothers and cousins, any of the men in the family against any of the men in the other family with whom there is this feud. And in my family, for instance, there are now no men left except me and an old one who is too old for fighting, or even to work properly. Sometimes we have a truce, when we reap the crops, or when there is some bigger fight between our tribe and some other tribe. But I must say that it is a very bad thing indeed. You see I am a Pathan who has been away from his village for a long time and I have been able to see that in some things the habits of others are better than ours. This killing is very tiresome. Imagine! I have come to England on a visit, and now I must quickly go back because of this business of no men left. Two of my male relatives were killed a week ago, and I have this news now—by air-mail letter. Our enemies in the next village have got to a very strong position. They have gone ahead. I must do something about it, for the sake of the honour of our family, and for my own honour. The others would like to get me as well, because that would completely finish us, unless my wife gives me a son in time. I must go back and see, *Insha'Allah,* that she has a son quick. I have a place booked in a ship in ten days from now."

The tone of his voice, hitherto mocking, had become filled with a deep seriousness. I knew he meant what he was saying—but for the outside world it must lack reasonable plausibility, like a piece of fiction that doesn't quite come off.

"Well, well," said the other man in the group. "I have often wondered what Pathans might be. Now we know."

"I have talked too much, and not well," Chainak said quietly. "My people are better than me. If you want to know about us, you must come to our country and then you will know."

*   *   *

The following week or ten days were, for me, filled with the anguish of having forgotten Pashto. It had slipped out of my head, leaving no apparent trace. Perhaps my struggles with Arabic during the several years that I had been away from the Pathans had been responsible, in part. Pashto, for all that it contains a good many Arabic words and has a script resembling Arabic but with certain additional letters, is completely dissimilar in its structure. It belongs to the Indo-European group of languages. All the time we were in Wales, Chainak refused to talk anything else to me. He told me endless stories, sang songs, infuriated the other people at Portmeirion with the unceasing gutturals of his language. Towards the end of our visit I was beginning to remember again. You can't ever quite forget a language once you have really learnt it, after all. We played darts in Pashto, and, in particular, Chainak grew ecstatic over a Camera Obscura.

"*Hagha der mazedar shai dai!*" he exclaimed approvingly.

"Yes, it is good. But I doubt if they make them any more. Edwardian children used to be taken to see them on the pier at Brighton."

"Speak in Pashto! I shan't talk to you unless you reply in Pashto!"

"How can I talk about Edwardians and piers in Pashto? You've never had either."

"What do you want to say about this Camera Ob . . . about this thing?" he asked patiently, in Pashto.

"I want to say . . . Look! Chainak, look! Jim's come out on to the terrace. How close he seems!"

"How innocent! It's nice to be watching him when he doesn't know."

The Camera Obscura at Portmeirion is mounted on top of a solitary tower dominating the main block of hotel buildings and the terrace in front of them. All this is practically at the level of the estuary. Immediately behind the hotel block the cliffs rise precipitously. It is wonderfully beautiful. Concealed there, in the turret, and leaning over the concave table on which the Camera Obscura projects the image of whatever section of the surrounding landscape happens to be in the adjustable line of vision, we could see every detail of the terrace, two hundred yards away; Jim himself, in tweeds and a doggy sort of cap; his parrot circling in the mild spring air above his head, presumably screaming. It only stops screaming when it perches on Jim's shoulder or a tree. Then there was an old woman, a guest at the hotel, we supposed, though we did not recognize her. A goggling child who watched the parrot. An immense mimosa that festoons itself along the hotel-front—and, behind, the cliffs rising sheer. Chainak was feverishly working the two handles that control the mechanism. The image on the sand-table went wheeling up into the air with the parrot—the cliffs, trees clinging to it, cottages clinging to it too, the campanile—and, always, the parrot circling and (presumably) screaming. Jim had been left far below.

"If I had my sling . . ."

"Your what . . .?" I didn't know the word, so he repeated it in English.

"Sling. And a nice round stone. Pretty plump grey-and-pink bird. We don't have that colour, do we? Only green."

We looked up from the table into the shadows of the turret. The concave lens of the mechanism was turning slowly above us and, when I glanced down again, the parrot had disappeared from the image on the table.

"It's gone."

"There's writing on this handle, Peter. Can you read it?"

I lit a match and read: "Barr and Stroud. 1918."

"Is that the name of the people who make it?"

"I expect so."

"I would like to ask about one for me."

"We'll find out from Jim. I dare say he'll know."

"Come on. Let's go and ask him. I must have one for the village. Can't you imagine how useful? After all, we've got the *bruj*"— *bruj* means watch-tower—"so all we'll need is the looking-glass and this—this table-thing. It will be most convenient, I think."

*   *   *

Back in London, on the eve of my departure for Pakistan, Chainak made me dial a telephone number, but it was not a success.

"Is that Barr and Stroud? It is? May I speak to the gentleman concerned with Cameras Obscura, please?" I waited while someone called to someone else, far away at the other end of the line. Chainak nodded encouragingly to me.

"Don't forget to say about how to fix 'the loot'," he said.

The man was back on the line now.

"What exactly do you want to know, sir?"

"I wanted to inquire about Cameras Obscura. Do you still make them. You wouldn't have a second-hand one, by any chance?"

"I'm afraid not," the man said, "but I'll make certain. Where would you want us to mount it? We shall need all the details, of course. The site, and so on."

"Well, actually," I admitted, "it's not for me. I'm inquiring on behalf of a friend who's only temporarily in London."

"Would it be for an amusement park? Or perhaps for the seaside?"

"No. Not an amusement park. Nor for the seaside, really."

"You know," the man put in, in a chatty voice, "we haven't had an inquiry for a Camera Obscura for longer than I can remember off-hand. In the past there'd be an occasional inquiry, from proprietors of amusement parks and the like. But in recent years, I can't recall..."

"It isn't exactly the same, in this case. It's for a friend of mine who lives in the foothills, fairly open country to his south and east, but rising to the north of the village, and he thinks it would be a great convenience to him."

"Yes?" the man said, to encourage me. I suppose there must have been a hint of uncertainty in my voice.

"It's for his watch-tower, as a matter of fact. He's got a watch-tower already, you see. So it ought to be quite an easy matter..."

"I see."

I turned to Chainak and reported.

"Good," he said. "Now tell him about 'the loot'."

"No. Wait a moment. We must jolly him along slowly to begin with. Leave it to me." I took my hand off the mouthpiece again and continued:

"The position is this. We've been visiting Portmeirion recently... Hm? Portmeirion. North Wales. Surely you must know. Yes... No, certainly not! I suppose some people might call it strange, but I call it wonderful—yes... yes, the *hotel*. Many, many more than three stars—but that's not the point. The thing is that they've got one of your 1918 models at Portmeirion and it would have done splendidly for my friend's needs. Can you supply one like it, and for how much? What? But I thought I had told you. He needs it in order to avoid having to keep a man permanently on duty in the watch-tower." I was getting to the point now, and rushed nervously ahead with what I was compelled to say: "There's a shortage of men in the village at present, and my friend thought that if he had a Camera Obscura he could make his women sit round the observation-table, doing their household chores, grinding corn or whatever it was, and at the same time they could keep an eye on the table, and twiddle the knobs. The exact site? Does it really make all that difference? Well, there's an orchard alongside the tower, and then a bit of land they plant with sugar-cane, and another village quite close by, and fields of maize. And, to the north, mountains. But actually it would be more for observing the other village than anything else."

14

The man at the other end of the line was strangely silent. I even wondered if he had left the telephone. Chainak jogged my elbow and said:

"Why don't you ask him about fixing 'the loot'?" And then he said it in English for fear that I had not understood. He need not have bothered. I knew what it was all about. The Sten-gun, which he generally calls 'the loot' because it was 'taken' in Kashmir. But the conversation was already embarrassing enough without embarking upon this final complication before I must. Anyway, the man did not seem to have clearly understood thus far, yet.

"Am I to understand, sir," the man now asked from the shocked incredulity of his desk, "that your friend wants the Camera Obscura for observing the neighbours?"

Chainak was getting impatient.

"What does he say, what does he say? Give me the telephone, Peter!"

He tugged at the cord, and at my arm.

"Let go, Chainak. You'll ruin everything. You won't know how to jolly . . ."

"Give it to me!"

Chainak took it. I had done my best, and now stood back in a resigned sort of way.

"I want," said Chainak in crystal English into the mouthpiece, but with a certain authority, "I want this Camera Ob . . . in order that my women can watch the neighbours carefully, as well as do their household work. Have you understood up to this? Good. Next. I want to know if you can arrange a place for the Sten-gun—which I have got—on top of the tower—which I have got too—in such a way that it will turn with the looking-glass and so that it can be fired at the neighbours, if necessary, when their picture comes on to the little table? Please tell me, without any more fussing, if this is possible for you. If it is not possible, then I shall waste no more time in placing my business elsewhere."

Chainak looked round at me proudly. I could hear a little voice squeaking in the ear-piece.

"Listen, Chainak. He's saying something."

Chainak returned his attention to the telephone.

"Oh. Ah, yes. Yes? Please say that again. Slowly."

The man said it again, and a black cloud came down over Chainak's face. He paused for a second, considering his reply—but there was a click in the ear-piece that even I could hear, and so, by the grace of God, it was too late for replies.

Chainak was furious. "Peter! Peter! Please get the number again. I have something to say to that man."

People outside Pathan-country don't seem able to understand the Pathan point of view. That's the trouble.

THE STREET OF THE STORY-TELLERS, PESHAWAR

The first three words on the banner stretched across the street are English—though in vernacular script· GRAND CLEARANCE SALE—the last three are in the vernacular—*Kapra aur boot*—which here would mean·"Clothes and footwear"

A FORTIFIED VILLAGE, SHOWING THE BRUJ, OR WATCH-TOWER

NATHIA GALI. EXPIRING WOODEN HUTS

THE KHYBER PASS OPENS OUT INTO AFGHANISTAN

Pakistan's frontier-post, Torkham, is in the clump of trees, in the middle-distance.

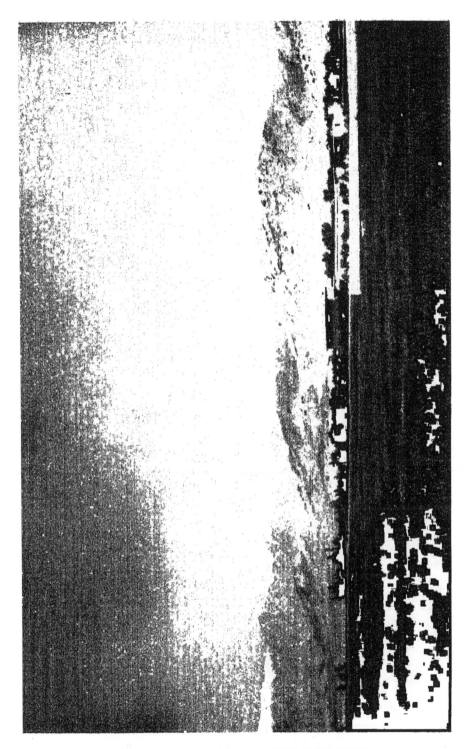

THE HINDU KUSH—LOOKING NORTH FROM KABUL

TWO RAMS AND A SHEPHERD-BOY

" HE LIKES FALCONRY"

NOMADS ON THE MOVE

PAKHTUNS

PATHANS

IN THE HINDU KUSH

A MOUNTAIN VALLEY IN THE HINDU KUSH

THE KOHAT DARRA

Chapter 2

PATHANS . . . I was on the way back to their mountains. I had
stayed in Karachi only as long as it took to renew old and happy
contacts and had then started northwards, over the Sind desert
that comes lapping up against the city like the surf of a tideless
and exhausted sea.

I travelled in a sleepy old aeroplane, a Bristol Freighter fitted with
a few seats. It was flying on a Royal Pakistan Air Force assignment,
but they had been kind enough to take me as a passenger. Most
of the space was monopolized by a dismantled glider and, alongside
it, with their instructor, sat the young men who were to be taught
to glide it They were, I think, members of a University Officers'
Training Corps of some kind, and I saw that they were excited, and
they kept looking with fondness and pride at the red-painted fuselage
of their craft. I tried to read, but I couldn't—the aeroplane was
making too much noise, snoring its way through the air, grunting,
seemingly only half awake. It was too early in the day for the bad
flying conditions that must be expected when the sun really got going:
as soon as the desert had had time to stoke up its furnaces, the hot
air would rise and wait around for such as us, and toss us about as if
we were a dead leaf. I could see nothing through my windows
except a little rectangle of sand and scrub, perhaps as much as five
hundred of the many thousands of square miles of identical sand and
scrub. I had no wish to give them more than a glance. Unable to
read, I sat and ruminated.

Four hours later we would reach Peshawar, someone had said, and
I supposed it would prove to be true. Peshawar, with the forbidding
defiles of the Khyber Pass to the west of it. Four hours, four years . . .
It was already four years since I had last been in Pakistan. I had
lived in Karachi at that period. Now I was that much older, and the
aeroplane too. The pilot looked young, very young—a handsome
brown face, hair black and glistening under his cap. I took him to

be a Punjabi. He seemed alert enough, but would even he be able to keep the engines awake enough . . . ?

No British in this aeroplane but me. Most of the British had left Pakistan in 1947, when independence came. But a fairly solid group of British business-men had stayed on in Karachi after partition (and were there still), and a nucleus of British officers of the old Government of India had accepted contracts under the new Government of Pakistan who were short of trained administrators and secretariat men. I had myself served Pakistan for the first two years of her existence. I still felt that I partly belonged to this country.

I remembered the excitement when 'freedom' became a reality. Throughout the provinces of Pakistan it could be felt, almost palpably, a tremendous enthusiasm in this same air. The future had hung suspended in it as if it were a crock of gold—heavy, frangible, and full of promise. Yet to much of the outside world Pakistan had seemed a threat, rather than a promise: and to the Hindus of India it was the negation of all they had longed and toiled for—it was the vivisection of the body of Hindustan.

What had mattered here, however, was the Pakistanis, with the new flags flying, the green and the white and the crescent moon, and the infant star it protected. Today, nearly six years later, much of the promise had been fulfilled, even if it had been accompanied by a bloody flux that would have destroyed a creature less determined to live and grow big.

It was good to be back. This time I was here with a motive strictly personal and limited: I had come to visit friends in the mountains that lurk like wolves on the borders of Pakistan and Afghanistan. Pathans. I had first been to their country before the war: and then, during the war, with a commission in the Royal Air Force, I had been seconded to the Government of India for work connected with 'air' aspects of Pathan country. For some years I had lived close to the tribesmen and, as far as the pattern of my personal life was concerned, I had had time to develop a deep love for them as people. I wanted to see them again, particularly certain of them whom I still thought of as friends.

Gigantic rocks showed themselves in my window now, away to the north. The beginnings of Baluchistan. We were getting on. There was a river below, its bed three times as wide as the channel

winding its way down the length of it to the Arabian Sea. Mohen-
jadaro was somewhere down there too, with its Indus Valley civilization still part-buried under the debris of millennia: and the huge, grey
rocks to the north, rapidly growing from cliffs to hills to mountains
now, would be Bugti country, for me no more than fragments of
map-knowledge. I had never been there, and all I could remember
about the Bugtis was that they were a Baluchi tribe, of Biblical sim-
plicity, and that from a nineteenth-century pioneer-administrator's
point of view they had had the one supreme merit—they bowed to
the unquestioned authority of their chieftain. The benefits of nineteenth-century progress, as the great Sandeman well knew (though
he was still a young man, and not great at all, when he first met the
Bugtis), were more easily demonstrable to an audience of one, than to
a whole tribe of doubting, suspicious and violent tribesmen. As it
happened, the Bugtis placidly entered the British fold behind their
tumandar,[1] who had seen the light and decided that it would be better
to offer his allegiance to the British in return for an allowance, than
pay fief to his overlord, the Khan of Kelat. It does not happen like
that with the tribal-region Pathans, who don't care about chieftains
or other people's enlightenment.[2]

It was not long before the mountains of the 'independent' Pathans
were visible through my window, tier upon tier towards the horizon.
From this height Afghanistan was probably visible too, but there was
too much cloud to be sure which range marked the frontier. On
the map it is clear enough, boldly and definitively the Durand Line.
It is a newish frontier in terms of politics, and not really a frontier at
all in terms of any other science. It was drawn in 1893, and it ought
to matter a lot, but when it comes to problems of everyday life in
those mountains, it counts for less. The Pathan tribes who straddle
it ignore it in their daily business. It is no more than a symbol.
History has taught them to use politics and its symbols much as they
use their rifles—to train on their opponents when it suits them, but
otherwise to be slung over the shoulder and disregarded.

The term Pathan is the Indian mispronunciation of the name the

[1] A Baluchi chieftain.

[2] There have been exceptions amongst the Pathans, all the same. For
example, the Turis who inhabit the Kurram Valley. The Turis come into
my narrative later.

Pathans give themselves—Pakhtūn.[1] Who these people are is another matter. The *Encyclopaedia Britannica* admits how difficult it is to trace clear references to them earlier than the eleventh century A D. Some modern historians in the East are less chicken-hearted: they say that the Pakhtun tribes of today are the direct descendants of a people mentioned by Herodotus in the fifth century before Christ—the Pakti.

The fact of the matter is that nobody really knows. Until the seventeenth or eighteenth centuries the Pakhtuns were known only to themselves—to the outside world they were a barbaric and violent people inhabiting the border country of what was, almost equally vaguely, called Afghanistan. They are sometimes referred to as Afghans, rather than Pakhtuns. No trained anthropologist ever studied them. It would be interesting to discover exactly what makes them fierce and ruthless, as well as something definite about their origins—but inquirers would meet with obstacles as frustrating to the science they profess as Pakhtun knives and rifles might be menacing to their lives. It is not permissible even to look at a Pakhtun woman, let alone talk to her: and a fundamental requirement of anthropological field-work is, naturally, the observation and questioning of the women. A number of distinguished men have come in contact with Pakhtuns and have written about them—but none has been an anthropologist.

So who are the Pakhtuns? How can we be sure, when even the historians differ amongst themselves so truculently? Still, from my point of view, the uncertainties do offer an advantage—that I can choose to believe what I choose to believe.

I choose to believe those who say that none of the Pakhtun tribes is indigenous to the country it now occupies. Broadly speaking the Pakhtuns inhabit the North-West Frontier Province of Pakistan and the tribal regions to north and west of the provincial administrative boundaries. There are important groups of them in the Southern

---

[1] There are regional variations in the way the letter of the vernacular script is pronounced. The more easterly tribes make the *kh* hard, as in the Scottish word 'loch': the westerly tribes soften it to *sh*, as in the English word 'lush'. Pakhtūn—Pashtūn: Pekhāwar—Peshāwar. I shall stick to the most usual English rendering in each case. I shall write Pashto, for the language, for example, and then with complete disregard for consistency, Pakhtun, for the man who speaks that language.

and Eastern Provinces of Afghanistan, beyond the Durand Line. They spill over into Baluchistan.

There is evidence to show that they are extremely varied in origin. It is assumed that they came at various periods on the different waves of migration that have carried the people of Central Asia and Persia and the Middle East thousands of miles from their original homelands. There have been men to support the theory that the lost tribes of Israel are to be found amongst the Pakhtuns. But whatever the case, it seems unlikely that any of these tribes was other than weak when it first came—for no one, not being an aboriginal, could have settled here of his own free choice. It is hard, cruel country on the whole, despite its cultivable valleys.

There seems to have been no cartographer's finality about tribal boundaries. The Pakhtuns were essentially nomadic peoples. There would be eternal inter-tribal fighting—over water, grazing grounds and the like. There would be mutual and continuing distrust. There would be a tendency for tribes occupying the valleys in relative ease, to grow relatively soft. Such a tribe, as it grew softer, would be raided by its tougher, highland neighbours. It might even be expelled from its cultivable valley in time, and take to the hills itself as the only available alternative. But whatever the case some convention had to be adopted to regulate inter-tribal affairs and to make possible the seasonal movements from summer- to winter-grazings in that country of extreme heat and cold. Fighting was all very well, but there had to be some limit. Indeed, in the course of time a rudimentary code was adopted, and it still holds today. It is called Pakhtunwali—the Pakhtun Code, and it has its heart in three categorical imperatives:

To give food and shelter to all who demand it.

To grant asylum to all in need of it.

To retaliate against any form of attack.

Pakhtunwali is not without nobility, even if it springs from violence and mistrust.

'Ah, would that the Pakhtuns could agree amongst themselves! Would that some understanding were theirs!' This was the lament of a Pashto poet of the seventeenth century. His name was Khushal Khan, and he was a member of the important Khattak tribe. He had personal reasons for lamenting, of course: he had been imprisoned by the Moghul Emperor Aurangzeb, and on his eventual escape, he did his utmost to organize the tribes in opposition to the man who had wronged him. Poor Khushal Khan, he failed, because the Pakhtun tribes did not unite in his time, any more than they do today, except in a cause that offered immediate concrete, certain and shareable reward. Khushal Khan's cause had no such appeal for anyone except Khushal Khan himself. There is seldom concord even amongst the members of a Pakhtun family, so how could there be concord in the larger unit of the village, or the hamlet, or the section of the tribe— let alone within a tribe as a whole, or amongst the Pakhtuns as a whole? You cannot expect concord unless the individual advantage of each member of the unit is demonstrably the same. The Pakhtuns have no one to speak for them, since each man speaks for himself—no leaders, since no man admits the superiority of another man—and they all go their own ways in consequence. It is true that Khushal Khan Khattak, had been a 'leader' of a sort—the sort that foreigners have tried to invent for the Pakhtuns. He had been subsidized by the Emperor Shah Jehan (Aurangzeb's predecessor on the Moghul throne). To the extent that he had been able at that time to buy them with Moghul gold, Khushal Khan had had Pakhtun mercenaries to follow him. But later, as fugitive from a Moghul prison, with no gold at all, he could produce no claim to 'leadership' that even his son Behram cared to recognize. In fact Behram accepted Moghul money for taking up arms against his father.

It was not to be so very different two hundred years later, when the British reached Pakhtun country. The maliks, or headmen, through whom the British hoped to control Pakhtun country, were obeyed by the tribes they were supposed to represent only to the point where the British had power to enforce obedience, or that it suited individual pockets to obey. It was madness for Government to count upon undertakings given by maliks in the name of a Pakhtun tribe (as they could in the case of the Baluchi tribes, for example), and ridiculous to brand as disloyalty a Pakhtun's failure to play the political game according to rules laid down by foreigners. The tribes play the political game instead of football, and with unorthodox brilliance.

From earliest recorded history invaders had come through the passes and defiles of Pakhtun country on their way to India, that prize for the greedy. They were content to get through as quickly as they could, of course. There was nothing worth taking in those barren hills, but the tribes ignored the fact that none of these invaders had seriously considered overrunning and subduing them: they recalled only that everyone had failed to do so. And with each successive failure, their almost paranoiac arrogance increased, till they came to believe themselves invincible.

It is obvious, of course, that the plainsman tribes were not invincible at all—some of them were encircled and subdued by the Sikhs in the early nineteenth century, and the rest by the British in the second half of the century. It should be equally obvious that the toughest and most formidable of the Pakhtuns can claim these distinctions solely because their mountains are difficult of access. It is these inaccessibles who have kept alive the tradition of invincibility. Does some special virtue lie hidden beneath the poverty which accompanies the 'invincibility' of the élite, I wonder? The élite themselves have come to think so, and their belief is tacitly shared by the Pathan plainsmen. So real is this feeling that I am tempted to reserve the term Pakhtun for the independent tribes of 'invincibles', and to let the term Pathan stand for those who, by the accident of geography, politics and the ambitions of empire-builders, have been encircled and subdued and who, as a result, are more prosperous than they have ever been before.

By the turn of the century it all looked quite nice on paper—a sort of Neapolitan ice-cream, three layers, each with its distinctive political colour, yet all of the same general ingredients. You had the British-administered North-West Frontier Province, peopled by Pathans. Next you had the 'independent' Pakhtun tribal regions, a 'protectorate' lying as a buffer between the N-W.F.P. and the Durand Line frontier of Afghanistan. And beyond the Durand Line you had Pakhtuns again, as triumphantly uncontrolled by Kabul as their brothers-in-Pakhtunwali were uncontrolled by the British. The situation had not changed basically by 1947, so far as the most important and intractable of the tribes were concerned—for example the Wazirs, the Mahsuds, the Afridis and the Mohmands on the British side of the fontier, and all the Afghanistan Pakhtuns on the far side of it.

In 1947, when Pakistan came into existence, the Pakhtuns still held their topographical trumps. Probably they were still uncertain of Pakistan's strength and determination, but they were realists. They sent their emissaries to make polite speeches to the newcomer-Pakistanis and, in return, were promised the continuance of the allowances and benefits they had been receiving from the British. At the same time,

23

because it was traditional for them to visit Kabul as well, members of the same tribes crossed the Durand Line to renew expressions of good-will with the Afghan throne. Both Karachi and Kabul knew what the Pakhtuns meant by such protestations, though it would have been silly to expect either to publicize their knowledge. The Pakhtuns knew too. Their tribesmen returned to their mountains, bearing gifts from both sides, and they must have told themselves over their cups of green tea that the *status quo* had been satisfactorily assured.

Chapter 3

IT was already the end of May, and Karachi had been unpleasantly hot. To make matters worse it was the Muslim month of fasting —Ramzan.[1] Of course in a big (over a million), modern (fretwork concrete with *bidonville* undertones) city like Karachi, religious observance is apt to be less strict than in village communities, but feelings that varied between the self-conscious martyrdom of those who fasted, and the guilt of those who did not, had been sensible in the atmosphere, and the atmosphere itself had been charged with almost 100 per cent humidity, and I dislike Karachi anyway. So I had leapt at the opportunity of this lumbering flight to the north where it would be cooler, and drier, at present. The alternative to flying would be about forty hours in the train.

The Bristol Freighter behaved like the ageing but conscientious pack-animal it was. In spite of 'fatigue', it carried us up and over the spine of mountains that divides the Derajat from the Peshawar Vale, and exactly four hours from the take-off, it put its ears forward and stuck out its fore-legs to brake the force of the landing. The landing was as smooth as a mill-stream. I was relieved, and the Glider instructor crossed himself sketchily and sighed. He was a Pole, I think. Peshawar, and on time at that. We all smiled at each other as we taxied in to where a group of people was waiting.

It was possible that I would be met, but I was uncertain. I had telegraphed to my host, and I had also written to some other Pathan friends, so there might be someone there to welcome me. Everybody seemed to know everybody else, but I saw no one I recognized and stood around, a little lost perhaps. I watched them drag my luggage out of the open nose of the aircraft. A big suit-case, a little one, a bed-roll, a typewriter, and a zip-bag which gaped permanently since

---

[1] The particular letter of the Arabic alphabet that gives the *d* of Ramadan in Western Islam, gives *z* in the East: thus—Ramzan.

the zipper lost a tooth. Then a Pathan came up to ask me my name.
I told him, and we both consulted a note he held in his hand. It
was indeed addressed to me—by my host Nawabzada Muhammed
Farid Khan, with instructions as to what I should do: rather confusing
—luggage one way, me another, lunch alone because of the fast for
Muslims, and how was I? Relieved and happy, as a matter of fact.
It was a disturbing business, this return to what had once seemed
home.

It all looked much the same on the surface, though one of the
airstrips was new, and a new airport building, a little removed from
the shack alongside the Air Force hangars that had served in the past.
Peshawar is a small town, but it is the biggest in the North-West
Frontier Province, and is strategically important. It deserved its
expanding airport. It was evidently getting grander. But the air
was the same as ever: shining and ice-coloured, like a pane of glass
under the sun—itself cool to the touch, but carrying within itself the
knowledge of heat beyond, yet dry and invigorating. Away to the
north and west the foothills shimmered under their transparent veiling
of heat. The silhouette of the mountains on the skyline was blurred,
as the contours of an ageing face lose the sharp focus of youth. For
anyone who knew where to look the deceptively-easy entrance to the
Khyber Pass could be seen in the west, not ten miles distant, hills
sloping down smoothly to each side of it and in the centre a strange
little tumulus.

The man with Muhammed Farid Khan's note bustled about with
authority. He was in the uniform of the Frontier Constabulary,
exceedingly smart and business-like. Farid Khan commanded this
admirable corps at the time. As his orderly and I started towards the
barrier I became conscious of a big hand waving, a round face under a
khulla and *patkai*,[1] cotton trousers called *partūg* that fell in folds and
closed in near the ankles, this big hand waving and a voice, all gutturals, shouting something I couldn't yet hear. The gutturals ceased
and the voice concentrated on my name:

"Peter sahib, Peter sahib!"

"Fateh!"

I put down the zip-bag and we embraced each other. Then he

---

[1] The stiff conical cap, decorated with gold thread, and the turban which is
wound round it.

introduced me to his two companions, reminding me of their names which had slipped out of my mind, and people started pushing from behind in the blocked exit barrier.

"I didn't recognize you at first," Fateh said, looking me over. "How thin you are!"

"You look different too. What's the matter? You look sad."

This is not the traditional way to greet an old friend, but Fateh is a privileged person for me, and I for him.

". . . and these?" He indicated my jeans. They had seemed very appropriate to travel in, but if you looked closely they were not very elegant, of course. "People will think you are poor. Haven't you got a suit?"

Farid Khan's orderly nodded, in agreement with Fateh. Hadn't I got a suit? But Fateh's companions had got going with the conventions meanwhile.

"May you not become tired. Welcome . . . in peace. Live in happiness . . .": and I was replying: "Welcome . . . And you? Live in happiness . . ."

"Live in happiness. Come at all times—in peace. May you never become old."

During this exchange, which provides a convenient opportunity for deciding what you want to say next, we were all examining each other more carefully. Were we much changed? Had we become tired and old after all, in spite of these well-mannered protestations?

"Do you mind moving on, please, sir?" an official was saying in English.

"Oh! I'm sorry." I picked up my zip-bag and Fateh snatched it from me and handed it to one of the others to carry.

It was Muhammed Farid Khan's jeep, but Fateh treated it as if it were his own, motioning the others into the back, and me into the seat beside the driver. The orderly was dealing with my luggage. We set off. They wanted to stop at their favourite tea-shop, but presumably Farid Khan was waiting, and so I said no, we went through all the formulae of leave-taking and would probably have parted quite soon if the tea-shop proprietor had not come out to delay matters. And then a tonga-driver. A tonga is a two-wheeled dog-cart, plying for hire. Here in Peshawar they are proud of the ponies that draw them.

"A new pony," the man said. "New this year. I take her out in the mornings. You'll see the old one you used to know, this evening. Shall we go driving this evening? I offer you a drive without paying. I've got a new son, as well. I have two sons now."

"Perhaps not this evening. Some other evening. A new son? Only one more in all these years?"

"Well . . . Two more daughters also."

"Never mind," I said. I had clambered back into the jeep.

"May you meet good on your way," they said, and we shook hands all round, all over again, a double hand-clasp, after which you should carry your right hand to your heart.

I was happy once more, now. Such little unimportant things can make a man happy. It is enough, quite often, to see friendly faces again, to remember and be remembered. Roads that seemed friendly in the past, houses unchanged (except for the name-plates of their occupants), the trees in full elaborate leaf. We drove past the Company Bagh—in the towns dating from the nineteenth century there is always a Company Bagh, a public garden named after the British East India Company. On down roads set with rose bushes and pomegranates, trim grass verges well kept, peepul trees, neem trees, bungalows white under the sun—the same loving roads, but somehow empty. I wanted to see people moving, preferably friends, of course, but anyone would have done, and there was nobody about because it was midday, summer, and Ramzan. Even so, an impression of a deeper emptiness persisted. The jeep had a little pennant on its bonnet, flap-flapping. I suppose I was really only trying to cover up a vague, sudden feeling of distress when I changed the subject of my thoughts and said to the driver:

"You shouldn't use the little flag when the general sahib is not in the jeep, you know."

"Does it not please you, then? I thought it would please you, the little flag."

*   *   *

Muhammed Farid Khan—the *Border-Genail* as they call the officer commanding the Frontier Constabulary—was wonderfully unchanged: smiling, fair-complexioned as an Anglo-Saxon, speaking

English as if it were his native tongue, completely Pathan for all that, and far too young to be a general, you might think. But Pakistan is a young country, and in England the younger Pitt had been Prime Minister at twenty-four. Muhammed Farid and another man, Muhammed Khan, sat watching me eat my lunch, while a servant went to my room to unpack my luggage.

"Don't let him unpack more than I shall need for today, Farid," I said. "I shall be going up to Nathia Gali tomorrow, *Insha' Allah.*"

Farid glanced at Muhammed and then turned back towards me with a look of relief on his face. But it was not till several sentences later that he said, as if it were just a nice piece of news: "Sayeed and his family arrive tomorrow. He's been transferred to Peshawar. They'll all be staying with me till their house is ready. Won't you be here to see him? You *must* stay to see him."

I suddenly realized that it would have been very awkward for Farid if I had not already announced my intention to leave the next day. The Sayeeds—a whole family of them—might just squeeze into Farid's spare rooms if the womenfolk overflowed into the quarters screened away for Farid's wife (who keeps strict purdah), but only just. So I smiled and said:

"Lucky for you that I'm going, in that case." And they both laughed.

Hospitality is, of course, a duty—for three days, in any case—even if you don't like your guest, even if he has invited himself, even if he is your enemy. You can't turn him out, once he's in. Farid must consequently have been much relieved that I was going of my own free will.

"I only got your telegram last night, so there was no time to warn you. But you'll be back and stay with me on your return from Nathia Gali, of course."

"Yes. Later on, I hope."

"Sarfaraz is coming to dinner tonight. You'll be in to dinner? I thought you'd like to see him again."

"Excellent. I very much want to see him."

"And some others," Muhammed said. "You know them all"

"By the way," Farid broke in. "Did that old bandit turn up at the airport? He came round to me last night to ask if I knew when you were arriving, and I told him, today."

"Fateh, you mean? Yes. He was there. I thought he looked a bit sad."

"Perhaps he is a little. We've had to stop the smuggling."

"He used my car at first, do you remember? I must have been very naïve in those early days."

Farid laughed. "I didn't know you knew. And I didn't like to tell you at the time—though I should have, because it would have meant impounding your car if he had been caught at it. It was easier when he started using his own car."

"I told him it was very improper to use mine, directly I knew what was happening, and he promised he wouldn't do so again. In *my* car, I mean."

Poor Fateh. Of course they got him in the end—when he shot up the frontier guard. His business at that period, apart from being my driver, was smuggling cloth over the border. Contraband, in quite small quantities, but profitable while it lasted, and he had been able to buy a second-hand car of his own after a while. I don't think anybody minded the smuggling much, but from my point of view, as a government servant at the time, it looked bad perhaps. The Chief of Police had said to me: "I hear they've got your man." 'They': not 'We'. It made it sound less personal, I suppose. "It was inevitable, one day. But it would be quite in order for you to do what you can to help him. I quite see that you can't let him down, and after all it was his own car. Not as if he still used yours."

I did help Fateh to the best of my ability—but they kept him in prison, sensibly refusing bail, till the case came up. I wondered what he did for a living now. I had forgotten to ask him, in the pleasure of seeing him again at all.

"They've closed the whore-shops," Muhammed said, giving me the news.

"Poor whores. What else?"

"Well, Turabaz has married again—at sixty, or whatever it is. And Rahman's got himself involved with a singer so that nearly all his money's gone. And that young man who used to run a fancy-goods shop has surprised everyone by marrying and giving his wife three vigorous sons in succession. And what else? There must be lots to tell you, but it's all gone out of my head for the moment."

"I'm glad you're here again," Farid said. "Look! You haven't taken any of that." He pointed to one of the many dishes that covered the table for my solitary meal: it was a Persian dish, meat pounded to paste smooth as silk, rolled into balls and covered with a creamy sauce. I had missed it, in the confusion of other delicacies. Farid feeds his guests elaborately and well.

"I must get back to my work," Muhammed said. "But we'll be seeing each other again this evening. I'll be here too."

Farid had dinner served in the garden that evening. Sarfaraz was there—surely more than seventy now! Also Muhammed Khan and two or three others. They were all old friends and, since one or two of them spoke no English, conversation was in Pashto.

"You've quite forgotten it!" someone said. I was rather hurt, because I had been telling myself that Chainak's coaching had brought it half-way back to fluency. Moreover the others often lapsed into Persian, which I don't speak at all. So I said:

"Stick to Pashto, whatever you may think of mine—or I shall speak in English, to annoy you."

Persian is a snob accomplishment amongst educated Pathans.

In spite of his age and weight Sarfaraz enjoyed a six-foot sprightliness that laughed at time. Youth continued to sing within him, and snatches of its song came bubbling up through his lips whenever there was a pause in the conversation. Persian songs, at that. Even if I can't speak Persian, I can recognize such essential words as Love and Passion. These he sang about. Then he said that he was writing his memoirs or, in any case, that he was thinking of doing so. The trouble was the awful and seemingly-endless boredom of writing them down, so many years of them—and the longer he lived and the longer he delayed, the longer would the boredom of writing continue. He thought it might be best if he could find some person to whom he could dictate his naughty old life.

"Some *young* person?" Farid suggested maliciously.

". . . some beautiful young person, no doubt," Sarfaraz said. And I said:

"But if the young person is too beautiful, perhaps the book will never get finished."

"Or even started. . . ."

Sarfaraz chuckled. This is the sort of amiable pleasantry that old men in these parts enjoy. I doubt, even, if it is confined to Pathans. It seems to suggest eternal spring in the loins. I would have liked to say something of the sort, but I couldn't remember the Pashto for loins. 'Heart' (which I could have used instead) would have been so much less appropriate. Loins: it is the sort of word that dictionaries are apt to be bad about, and the only Pashto dictionary I still possessed was little more than a phrase-book, printed in Amritsar with a triumphant disregard for the nuances. I looked up the word later and found it—not under 'loins', as it happened, but under 'lions', though I am unlikely to be believed by anyone who has never seen what an Amritsar lexicographer, typesetter and proof-reader can together do with the English language. It said:

'LIONS, to gird up. *mla taral.*'

But '*mla*', as I knew, is ordinarily 'back', in English: and I don't think that it is in his back that Sarfaraz keeps his eternal spring. There was another entry, too:

'LIONS, side of. *tashi.*'

A side of lions? Beef, yes—or a pride of lions. But it couldn't be that either. Sarfaraz would have enjoyed loins-talk, but he seemed content enough with the conversation as it was, and he had already gone off into his wheezy old giggle again:

"Poor little beautiful young person! What a time in store, when I start the memoirs!"

*   *   *

I was unable to leave for Nathia Gali the next day, as things turned out. So I moved to an hotel. Everyone who has ever been to Peshawar must know Deans Hotel. It is the sort of place that has grown up from a small central core to which extra rooms have added themselves, like branches to a tree. But eventually there must have seemed room for no more branches, and so additional blocks of rooms took root, rather as the suckers of a banian tree will take root, still connected to the parent bole, but enjoying a semi-independence. There had been no further banian-suckers since I was last there, and it was all much the same as before—but emptier.

In the dining-room the punkahs still whirred overhead as if they would drop their wings into the soup, like flying-ants in their season. The pictures on the walls had been changed, however. There used to be two separate engravings of the same picture, called 'Wedding in Morocco'. I had particularly noticed this in the old days just because there were two identical pictures on adjacent walls. Having settled in Morocco myself since then, I looked for them now, but they had both disappeared. In their places were photographs of Churchill and Eisenhower, and dotted about on the other walls were British and American architectural glories bathed in technicolor or something almost as beautiful. Evidently the British and American Information Services had been battling for space, and had dead-heated. The food was the same to the point where one wondered how they had contrived to keep it warm all these years. The waiters greeted me as if I too had been on the hot-plate ever since we had last met. When one of the waiters, up-graded now from the bell-hop he had been, said to me with evident surprise: "How old you've grown!" I was rather taken aback.

"Everybody gets old if God does not take him too soon," the head butler said, noticing my change of expression, I dare say. He was himself almost motionless with years.

In the late afternoon I went walking through the Company Bagh and my feet suddenly remembered the water-course with its tricky crossing, the stone on the near bank, the oleander-root on the far side that would afford a foothold if you started off with the left foot and jumped for it. It was like remembering a piece of jargon in a foreign language, complete and familiar as in the days when one was accustomed to using it. Everything was the same as it used to be, except for an emptiness and an oldness. My eyes noticed only the recognized things: the unfamiliar things didn't count at all: and it was not until I realized this that I knew I must stop and readjust myself to today. The continuity of my life had been broken.

The whites had gone. Of course that was the most striking symbol of change. Not that the whites had been other than quite ordinary whites for the most part, but their going had necessarily changed the character of the place. Peshawar is two: the old city, walled and fortified, the great southern market for Central Asia—as Marrakesh is the northern market for the Sahara; and then the new 'cantonment' area, holding the garrison of regular troops, shops, a cinema or two for American or British movies, and the Club, and the bungalows of the whites. The Cantonment had been alive with whites—administrators, soldiers, their wives, white children with ayahs in attendance, and yapping bands of the dogs the whites kept, spaniels, fox-terriers, dachshunds, setters and the rest of them. The Pathans in their villages round about kept two kinds of dog—*buldang* and *bulterr*, breeds which had been more than sniffed at by a bulldog or a bull-terrier in previous generations, and still preserved excellent and profitable fighting qualities. Dog-fights were quite a feature of holiday afternoons, away in some tree-screened hollow where the disapproving whites would not notice. Why should the whites mind so much? Nobody could understand this. Did the whites not chase the jackal and throw him to their own dogs if they could catch him? Hunting the 'jack' (in default of foxes) was decent: that was why. There was always the possibility of a fall and a broken neck: a sanctified cold-blood sport, whereas those awful dogs . . . and to cut the miserable creature's ears off so that its adversary should be denied an ear-hold . . . not nice, not nice. So the *buldangs* or the *bulterrs* used to be pitted against each other in some hidden, tree-screened hollow, far from where the jackal enjoyed being chased, and the whites, rightly, enjoyed chasing it.

The Cantonment which had been alive with whites now seemed dead, and not only because the whites had gone. I was not yet ready for the collapse of an image. I needed a moment for my own transition to the present. The club, the Officers' Club—it was there in its accustomed place on The Mall, and it was strangely bigger than I had expected to find it. One sees the past through a magnifying-glass, and perhaps I was looking at the present through the same magnifying-glass and was startled by what I saw. So big, so empty—a ribbon-development fortress, and dead. . . .

"Things have changed," said a bar-boy, his beard flecked with grey now and festooning over his chest. He was playing with a cigar-box. "No more tiffin at four."

"Sad," I said. "And no more blood and guts? Do you remember?"

I was thinking how sometimes someone would run amok and shoot comparative strangers in the street, and how a romantic lover had come raging into the Cantonment and had carried off his love from a tea-shop and shot down his pursuers as he galloped his pony and trap through the gates to outlawry. Out through the barbed-wire perimeter. Flowers behind the ear and ripped-up stomachs.

"No more new members to buy the cigar," he said sadly, pressing a button at the side of the box. It was terrible to see the old trick working for so forlorn an audience. The lid creaked open on a spring that had lost its youth, and a very large male organ, wooden and unconvincing, reared up dutifully. Most of its paint was gone now.

"How sad," I said.

How sad! The antlered skulls nodded sadly round the walls of the empty room. In hunting-pink the pink-faced Masters of Hounds gazed sadly from as many as twenty, thirty picture-frames. The bar-boy closed the lid down on its treasure.

"No more," he said.

But we were talking about different things. The disintegration of the club was for me no more than the disintegration of a memory, for him it was the fading of his very life. The club servants had for years made a corner in the Peshawar whites, and had liked them in a fatherly, slightly patronizing way, treating them like possessions for their own exclusive use, as if they too were clip-eared *buldangs* and *bulterrs*. It had been a shock when the whites packed up and went, and never came back. Indeed life was changed for two or three of the villages around Peshawar from which the club believed they chose their staff. Of course the club did nothing of the kind. The villagers chose themselves, and monopolized the club appointments, and were quite ready to deal with any outsider who trespassed on their preserves. Life amongst the Pathans had changed in other, more general, ways too—in ways far more fundamental, from what I had read and been told. But my informants had not been Pathans. It was said that the tribes, the real Pakhtuns, had changed too, and that they behaved like lambs since the whites left. I was not yet quite ready to believe it.

Was blood-letting in the new era strictly controlled according to the Queensberry Rules of the Feud-game? Did everyone walk in an aura of sweetness and light at other times? I wanted to know. But the bar-boy would know nothing beyond a radius of five miles from the city of Peshawar. It was no use asking him.

Had it all changed so much, I thought to myself as I stared round at those silly, nodding, antlered skulls, and then again at the bar-boy and his cigar-box.

*   *   *

"I haven't got a house in Peshawar any more," Fateh complained. "I haven't got anything now—neither house, nor punkahs, nor car, nor friends. Nothing."

He had come with a friend who had once been in the police, I think, and had later been Fateh's associate in the smuggling business. I knew the man and did not like him much, but the fiction of friendliness had to be maintained since he was Fateh's man. They were fetching me from the hotel in order to visit other friends and drink green tea, *qawa*. It ought to mean 'coffee'—the word is approximately the Arabic word for 'coffee'—but they use it for green tea. I had put on a gaberdine suit to please Fateh and do him honour. But I couldn't let his complaint pass quite without comment.

"But Fateh, what do you expect? All your glory came from that smuggling, didn't it? I know perfectly well that the salary I used to pay you made little or no difference. You can't run your own car on —how much was it? Forty rupees, fifty, a month? In fact you could scarcely have put food into your family's stomach for that, even in those days."

"Since you went away," he said with pleasurable gloom, "my life has been removed from me, and they have given me nothing in return. Can you imagine, I have to drive a lorry now? Me—who am accustomed to my own car, and a house here in Peshawar, as well as the property in the village, I have to get up at five in the morning to clean that horrible lorry! My sons have to go out to work, too, and I have to perform this horrible work myself. And what do I get out of it? Nothing, nothing, nothing!"

"Since the British went away . . ." said his friend.

"But it's not the fault of the British, nor of the Pakistanis, after all."

"Then whose, Peter sahib? Did they not impound my car and leave it to rot, there in the sun and rain?"

"That was before, Fateh. I remember that time. It was when I was here myself. On the whole you were extremely lucky to have lost nothing but your car—and, of course, the load of cloth. You might have had to serve a long jail sentence. And I can't help adding that I was lucky that you didn't lose *my* car for me, instead."

Fateh smiled placatingly. "Yes, that was rather bad of me, in the early time, wasn't it? But directly I could afford to buy my own car, I bought it, didn't I? And didn't I fill your tank up with petrol too?"

"Military petrol."

"Of course. Where could I get other petrol for you? It was wartime."

"And I made you siphon all the petrol out again. I ought to have laid a charge against you."

"A charge? But you were my sahib!"

"Never mind. It's all in the past now. I suppose you siphoned it out and sold it to someone."

"It was he who siphoned it out," Fateh said, nodding towards his friend. "I dislike the taste of petrol."

I smiled and said: "I am happy to see you again, Fateh."

But Fateh didn't smile. He said: "Oh Peter sahib, you look so poor and thin! When I got your letter I told everyone—'Peter sahib is coming back like a sultan, probably with a fine new car, and of course he will wish me to be his driver again.' What will they think now? You look better today than yesterday, but I can see now that it is only show, really. I saw the truth at the moment of your arriving."

I suppose he was referring to my jeans again. Pathans allow themselves to wear any old clothes that come handy and find no shame in it—though they like to have a smart clean outfit ready for festivals. But for the whites, it was different. The whites set certain standards for themselves, and the Pathans insisted that they keep to them. This went not only for clothes, but also in such matters as honesty, trustworthiness, truthfulness and other facets of what the British are pleased to regard as the bedrock of their national character. But for the moment Fateh had a particular problem in mind: the fact that I had failed him.

"It's true that I can't help you, Fateh," I admitted.

"I don't want you to help me. I just wanted you to know that the world has changed for me."

"You know, of course," put in the ex-policeman, "that it doesn't even rain in Peshawar any more—since the British went?"

The Tonga-driver who had spoken to me the day before had said the same thing—'it doesn't even rain any more . . .' An extravagant image that would appeal to a man dependent upon Providence. It would be useless to try to make Fateh understand in his present mood. I tried, a little. I pointed to the remarkable advance that the N-W.F.P. had been making since partition—to industrial projects which are not merely charming Ten-Year-Plans but working realities, to the increase in education, to increased hydro-electric power.

"They've got electric light in many of the villages round about now," I said.

"Pah! Electric light."

So then I told him that the whole world was in a mess, and that he was probably better off in Peshawar than he would be elsewhere. "It doesn't rain anywhere any more," I said.

"That's exactly what I was saying—you have betrayed me, the Pakistanis have allowed my motor-car to rot in the sun and . . . in the sun, I mean, and it is me and the poors who suffer. Others," he added darkly, "grow fat."

"You grew fat yourself once—from the smuggling." I patted his shoulder but he brushed my hand away.

"Where are the days when I had a punkah over my head, and friends who loved me? And the motor-car?"

I was growing bored with all this. It had gone on long enough and, hoping to end up on a proper moral note, I said:

"Gone, gone for ever, with a bundle of smuggled cloth! Poor Fateh."

He stopped, looked me straight in the eyes and murmured furiously: "They had no judicial proof."

Judicial proof. This was the first phrase in English that I had ever heard him use, and what's more he used it quite correctly. It is exactly what had happened. Fateh was guilty without a shadow of doubt. His alleged offence had been committed within the administered district, just short of the tribal regions boundary, and he had been tried by the normal civil courts. He was put into jail while the charges were framed, and the charges failed because they were not proven. Perjured witnesses, destruction of evidence. How could you expect a Pathan to subscribe to the concept that an attempted misdemeanour came near to representing the offence itself? Had Fateh's bullets hit the frontier guard? No, unfortunately they had missed—excitement, probably, and rather shameful at that, considering how short the range was. Had he actually smuggled the goods over the border? No, he had not: yet they had taken his car, and the cloth, had tried to prove that the cloth was stolen and not even his own, and even there they had ignominiously failed. In fact every one of the witnesses at the trial had gone so far as to say that it wasn't even Fateh in the car, but someone else who had escaped and never been identified, and the court had been unable to disprove that, too! It was a monstrous negation of justice that his motor-car and the cloth had not been at once restored to him with a fitting apology and compensation.

It was also, for me, rather alarming to hear Fateh reacting to the events as if he considered himself greatly injured. But we had reached our destination, and I was able to avoid further comment.

"Will Gul Khan be there?" I asked as we went in. It was a little house in the old city, up in the welter of alleyways behind the Kissa Kahani bazaar.

"No."

Our host had come out to meet us. "*Puh kher raghalai,* Peter sahib. After so long. Is all well with you? Come at all times. May you live in happiness."

"And is all well with you? Live in happiness. The house? And the children? God be praised, Abdullah Khan."

We embraced in the formal way, arms about each other's shoulders, the head laid first to the left of the other's neck, then to the right, and then to the left again.

"Come in. Ghulam Muhammed Khan is here too."

"I am glad. And Gul Khan? I had hoped . . ."

"My brother? No."

There were several others there, apart from Ghulam Muhammed Khan, in the narrow room with mattresses along the wall. They gave me green tea. Fateh went at once to the chillum and set about lighting it. A chillum is a simplified sort of water-pipe, a hubble-bubble, and it isn't the sort of thing you can carry about with you. Fateh can scarcely move a hundred yards without a smoke, so he was now filling the pottery container with 'charas' and setting a light to it. His hand was cupped round the mouthpiece, his lips pressed against his hand, and with each puff the glowing 'charas' seemed to sink more firmly into the container and, as the suction was released, a little wriggle of smoke came out of the cup and dissipated itself in the air. He inhaled once or twice and then passed the chillum on to some-one else.

"Gul Khan is dead," Abdullah Khan said in a flat voice. "They killed him three days ago."

"They . . . ?" In the sudden shocked blankness of my mind I was trying to remember who 'they' might be. Obviously it had been the usual thing, all over again, another chapter in a blood-feud, endless and without meaning. "They? Do you mean Roshan and Mahboob and that family?"

"Yes. That family. There were four of them there, and they got Gul Khan in the sugar-cane. You remember our village? Yes, well, on this side of our village, after you've passed Roshan Khan's village, and the dry river-bed—the *khwar*. You remember it?—there's that big open part and after that our sugar-cane begins."

I could picture the place now. It was up towards Mohmand country, but within the administrative border still. Sugar-cane. High and concealing.

"Then they left him and went away," Abdullah Khan concluded.

"Who found him?"

"The women. It was the women It was dusk and they were coming home to the village. They found him and started shouting, and then Sadiq came running. Sadiq? You know him of course."

"Yes. I know him." Sadiq. The third brother. I had known him quite well: a big, heavy, pleasant man. "Was Gul Khan still alive?"

"Sadiq bent over Gul Khan but he didn't touch him or anything. He could see that he was quite dead. Sadiq just stood there, the women say, and the words must have been going round in his head, but he was silent. Gul Khan's face was all shot away, the women say. I didn't see. I was away from Peshawar. I only came back yesterday, and he was already buried. In this hot summer-time, you see . . ." He looked vaguely across the room at the far wall, and then he said: "He had wounds in his stomach too. Then, so the women say, Sadiq's face closed itself—you know, like a tobacco plant in the evening—and he bent down and very softly he took Gul Khan's handkerchief out of his pocket and put it into his own, not saying a word. And then he went away. He didn't even need to ask who had done it. He knew it was one of the brothers—Roshan or Mahboob."

"He was crying inside and didn't wish to speak," someone said.

"Yes, I expect so," I said. "Poor Gul Khan . . . I wish . . ."

*   *   *

I was sitting in the garden of the hotel after dinner with a Scotch and soda. Fateh had promised to find out if he could where Sadiq was to be found. I wanted to see him. Gul Khan was one of the friends I had so much hoped to see again. It would be something to see Sadiq, and speak to him, if he would speak of it at all. I told myself that this was only an incident in what must be accepted amongst Pathans as a perfectly normal sequence of events, but it didn't help much. I was in no mood for casual conversation, and annoyed when a stranger at an adjacent table—the only other man on the lawn—started to talk to me across the narrow, intervening space. If I had had a book that I could have pretended to read, or a piece of paper on which to make any sort of protective doodles, it would have been easier. As it was I could find no excuse this side of incivility for not responding, and I found myself saying "yes, English", in answer to his preliminary probe. He was a Pakistani: quite an agreeable-looking man, in a linen suit, a collar and tie, and the other accoutrements of western living, but he was not content with the half-smile I had given him before I turned my head away. He got going with the probe again, deeper this time. I was presumably a tourist? No? A business-man? Pakistan welcomed foreign traders. Not a business-man either? Then what, if he might ask? I had to reply now. I said that I made a precarious living by writing.

"Ah," he said, relieved to have got to the facts at last. "I see. A journalist."

"Not a journalist."

"Then . . .?"

I didn't really want to talk to him at all, so it seemed more than usually difficult to explain what kind of a writer I could claim to be. I said, as briefly as possible, that I had spent some years in the border country here, and had wanted to visit it again."

"Then you *are* a journalist?"

"I assure you I am not. I shall do my best to cover expenses by writing something—but not journalism."

"I see," he commented without conviction. "What will you write about?"

"Pakhtuns, I think. Something about Pakhtuns."

"What do you know about Pakhtuns?" He was smiling slyly.

I answered, with the deliberate intention of annoying: "Enough to fill a book, I hope."

He paused for a moment before he spoke again. I think perhaps I had annoyed him, but if so he had evidently decided that it wasn't

D

41

worth quarrelling about and in this he was better mannered than I had been. He said: "If I can help you, I'd be glad to. I'm a Pakhtun myself, and there may be things I can tell you that would be useful."

I looked more closely at him: this little man with the thin face and the hands of a town-mouse.

"Yes," he said. "I'm an authentic Pakhtun, but your surprise doesn't surprise me. Pakhtuns aren't all thick-set, savage bandits who live in the mountains—though that's the way the world is inclined to see us. But if you've lived here you ought to know that yourself."

I said: "Yes, I do know that. But... I'm sure you won't think me rude if I suggest that the distinction between the two kinds of Pakhtun is one of your problems here."

"If you know that too, then you know more than many Pakistanis. What perhaps you don't know is that most educated Pakhtuns—like myself, if I may say so—recognize the gulf that education places between us and the tribal people from whom we have sprung: and also the fact that, for the time being, we educated Pakhtuns are at a grave disadvantage *vis-à-vis* our own tribes. I was educated in England, as a matter of fact. It's very strange. Had you realized that you have an exact parallel to our problem in your public schools? Had you thought of the relative positions in the schoolboy hierarchy occupied by, say, the captain of the football team and the rather mingy boy with spectacles who has won a scholarship to the University? It's a question of time and development, of course. When the schooldays are over, English boys with spectacles and scholarships discover that it is now their turn to shine. The situation is so commonplace in England that nobody troubles to think about it, but here . . ." He gestured into the shadows. "Here it will take some years yet. Mind you, I think it will be easier now that the British have gone. Your people did a remarkable job in many ways, but forgive me if I say that on these frontiers the British were both vacillating and incurably romantic, and did much—though with the best intentions, I dare say—to uphold the snobbery of the tribal sports-field. Naturally it wasn't quite the same—it was military expeditions instead of cricket and football, and 'Do honour to the good loser', so that they often let him leave the field in the belief that he had in fact won, and not lost at all! But you weren't up against schoolboys here: you were up against the most hard-headed of realists who would shamelessly turn your rules against you, if it suited them, or disregard them if they didn't." He started to laugh quietly, and then became serious again. "Our task now—I mean the task of the educated Pakhtuns—is to persuade our tribesmen, against all the evidence of their conditioned reflexes, that it would profit them to become like us. By profit I mean, of course, material benefit—money, if you like—not some vague moral and intellectual advancement. And the strangest thing of all is that it seems to be starting to work."

I had listened with attention, but I wanted to get his terms of reference quite straight, so I asked him: "Are you from the tribal areas, or the administered districts?"

"Would it make much difference?"

"Yes, I think it would."

"Why?"

"Because the tribal Pakhtuns are snobs—unlikely to accept the example of men in the administered districts, however educated and able, because ... Well, because ..."

"... because they consider themselves superior to men of the administered districts?"

"Yes."

"If it helps you to believe what I am saying, let me tell you that I *am* from the tribal areas," he said smilingly. He told me his tribe and section.

"Highlanders and Lowlanders," I commented. "It's the same pattern pretty well everywhere in the world, perhaps."

"Yes, if you like. It certainly happened that way in Scotland. The Highland clans held out longer than the Lowlanders, but even they came in with England when they saw that it was worth their while. And, really, when you look at a list of the men who control the fortunes of the United Kingdom, it's surprising the number of Scotsmen who figure on it. Are you Scottish? No? Will you be surprised in a few years' time to find that the fortunes of Pakistan are largely controlled by Pakhtuns?"

"I shall not be surprised at all."

Beyond my companion I could see Fateh Khan coming across the lawn towards us, and before even he had reached me he had started saying, as if the other man didn't exist at all:

"Sadiq isn't in his village, they say. And no one has seen him in Peshawar. They don't know where he is."

"They're sure he isn't in his village?"

"Quite sure."

The other man was getting up from his table. He said: "So you speak some Pashto."

I said: "Yes."

"Perhaps you would like my card. I live in Karachi. If you should be coming there, why not ring me up?"

I thanked him and took his card and we said good-bye to each other, and while he was probably still in ear-shot Fateh was asking: "What does he want, that city-man?"

I suppose I wasn't listening properly, as I watched the man disappear across the lawn, so neatly shod. I turned to Fateh again.

"Fateh. Please do something for me. I'm going to Nathia Gali tomorrow, *Insha'Allah,* but I expect to be back here again soon. Try to find Sadiq, will you? And tell him I very much want to see him —because of Gul Khan."

"Yes—but what was he saying to you, Peter sahib, that city-man?"

A strange snobbery—and I have been more than touched with it myself. Formal education and well-pressed suits do not surmount the Pakhtun hierarchy. Some day perhaps they will—but it seems to me that Pakhtunwali must die first. Meanwhile the snob-scale still starts from the other end. The élite of the tribal regions still look down upon the men of the villages inside the administered border: the villager looks down upon the men who live on the outskirts of the towns—a town like Peshawar, for example—the men who 'commute' daily, to and from work in the town. The 'commuter' looks down upon the small-time city-dweller who is probably not Pakhtun at all, and—with a sudden flick of the social tail-end—the small-time city-dweller looks up to the cultured townsman, civilized, educated, envied, to the man who had just left us, who has climbed another sort of snob-ladder, towards a different and entirely foreign objective.

"That man?" I asked. "Oh, just talking. Nothing particular. What else have you got to tell me, Fateh?"

"Nothing particular. Only a little. But about Gul Khan, a man says that there was a boy there. In the sugar-cane. The boy was waiting with his sling for the birds to come at sunset—and he saw the killing. He says that the men were Roshan and Mahboob, and Omar Khan. Do you know Omar? That man with one eye bad. And there was a fourth man but the boy didn't see properly because he was hidden behind the others. Perhaps he was only there for a guard, to warn the others if anybody came. He didn't do any shooting, the boy said." Fateh, paused, collecting his thoughts, and then went on: "They killed Gul Khan in this way. They..." And he started to give me the details, but I didn't want to hear.

Chapter 4

NATHIA GALI. Why had I ever come to such a place? I ought to have known by now that the glories of nature are not enough—at least, the vertical glories are not enough: for Nathia Gali is perched on a nine-thousand foot hill-tip with Nanga Parbat for neighbour to remind us how little we are. A spine of rock divides the east from the west precipices of Nathia Gali, Blue Fir and Chir woods decorate it, and a couple of peaks complete it to north and south. If you leave your lodging you must go up, or go down, or pick your way along the spine like a high-wire walker.

But my question is no more than a rhetorical plaint, because I know perfectly well why I had come to Nathia Gali—solely because the government of the North-West Frontier Province of Pakistan enthrones itself there each summer.

I had come to see the Governor and the Chief Secretary to Government, and to get the necessary permits to visit the Pakhtun tribal areas. I had not meant to stay longer than it would take to get these permits, but two circumstances, both outside my control, held me there for upwards of a week. The first was the moon herself. She was still busy with the fourth lunar month of the Muslim calendar, Ramzan, and a week of the fast remained to be completed. It was obvious to anyone, no matter how impatient, that a visitor could not hope for a very friendly reception from the Pakhtuns until they could return to their daily routine and feeding-hours. That was one good reason. The second was less good—a disinclination to face the journey down again. I don't suffer more than ordinarily from vertigo, but the combination of five-thousand foot ledges which hereabouts pass for roads, and the driving technique of the men who man the 'bus-service' to a horizontal world, were too much for me twice in the course of a few days. Coming here had been cruel enough, but you cannot make much speed on a one-in-four up-gradient. Going down would be different. From my lodging—a chir-wood hut—I could watch the birds volplaning into the valleys with easy grace, and remember that they had wings to do it with, whereas buses have not.

I stayed for the first few days with an English family I have known for a long time—husband, wife, two girls around eleven and twelve now, their woman guest (English, too) and her baby, three ponies, three dogs, an umbrella-stand stiff with hunting-crops, slip-leashes, yak-tail fly-whisks and other reminders of horse and hound—and a dome-shaped lawn overlooking the Himalayas. As you sit on this lawn you have the impression that if the world spins any faster, you will be shot off into space. After a day or two, however, the sensation becomes less disagreeably exciting than it was at first. Contrary to all expectations, the laws of gravity apply here too, despite the lightness in the head. It must be the exhausted heaviness of the legs.

I would have liked to stay on with this hospitable family for the length of my Nathia Gali visit, but the need to get on with some writing overcame my pleasure at being part of their home, and I moved to the chir-wood hut. I used to go back to them every day before lunch for a tankard of beer, and to take my share in the recurrent task of stopping the baby's pram from going over the edge. The pram had a sort of brake, and the baby's mother, Betty, used to put little stones under the wheels sometimes, as an extra precaution, but the deep valleys called . . .

"One of these days," Betty would say, and then couldn't bring herself to say more. So she just moaned: ". . . oh my poor little baby. . . ."

Solitude is good, and much of most days I spent alone. God knows there was solitude enough! Nothing moves in those mountains except birds, and monkeys that hoot-hoot-hoot amongst the wild strawberry-beds. The local people are few, impoverished and unsympathetic, and it is difficult to feel pity for them other than as a purely abstract emotion. They are morose and ugly; thin, craggy creatures with moustaches that droop like plants that have somehow failed to strike. They are of a tribe called Malchi, with sad little hearts, and eyes that reflect the doom of the world. Perhaps they are good people. I don't know. But they are cringing, and I cannot feel any warmth towards them. Their origin is uncertain and the experts disagree, just as they disagree over the origins of the various Pakhtun tribes. Anyway the Malchi are not Pakhtun or Pathan, and as a matter of fact the whole of this mountainous area and the Hazara valleys to the north of it were only lumped in with the true Pakhtun country of the north-west, in order to provide a summer hill-resort for the government of the new province at the beginning of this century. Not a bad reason for drawing a boundary line, I dare say. Probably the mild servility of the Malchi people suggested their country for a hill-station rather than any of the wooded, well-watered areas of true Pakhtun country. There are such, here and there.

Whatever the case, the Malchi people live in huts of mud and stone, with a roof formed of mud and fir-branches, plastered over. Most of them that I saw inhabited the nearest valley, five thousand feet below: and, from above, it was for all the world as if their valley were a golf-course, and their dwellings tee-ing grounds for a dotty confusion of trick holes. They contrive to terrace little fields for their crops—which are mostly maize—but few of them raise sufficient to feed themselves for more than three months of the year. This is much the same case as with the Pakhtuns, but whereas the Pakhtuns are accustomed to raiding their richer neighbours, the Malchi are not. For nine months of the year they must find employment somewhere, somehow. Their old women and babies are driven up the sheer mountainside to the settlement to beg, when Government is in summer residence. They beg incessantly, being in genuine need and also, partly, because it suits their temperament. They would come and sit immediately outside the window of my hut, and beg: and when I gave them something, they would look at the little coin despairingly. To have come so far, for *this* . . .

Since the Malchis have wives and babies, I must assume that they also have some sort of sex-life, but I doubt if it can be more than an infrequent and joyless ritual.

So, for the moment, I was dangling my legs over the precipices of Nathia Gali, filled with impatience to be gone. I would take a walk each day, in one of the two possible directions, starting off quite often through the little bazaar. It is a collection of expiring wooden huts, some of them dangerously two-storied. One late afternoon I was hailed by a stranger.

"*Cherta zai?*"

48

It was a man with a long, bearded face, not Malchi. I had seen him a few days before, standing a couple of yards distant while I asked someone something. The man I had spoken to that day was a Pakhtun, an obvious Khattak with a round face, bobbed hair and the uniform of the Frontier Corps. Probably he was a member of the Governor's bodyguard, off-duty, no shoulder-tabs: just taking the air and longing for sundown and the chillum that would then be permissible. I hadn't particularly noticed the long-faced, bearded man that day, but I looked at him now.

"*Cherta zai?*" he repeated. "Where are you going? Come and sit with me. Drink some tea."

I couldn't exactly place him, with his sharp features. He had an untidy black turban through which his long black hair crept in strands. He spoke Pashto with the vowels of Kandahar or Waziristan.

"I can't stop now. Anyway, it isn't time to have tea. What tribe are you?"

"*Mujh? Wazir yum. Mohmit Khel.*" Mohmit Khel is one of the tribal sections of the Wazirs.

He turned and clapped his hands together to summon the tea-shop servant. It was a tumbledown shack of a place, with a lot of battered old tea-pots, blue enamel mostly, hanging on a wall. There were two or three tables, and one or two somnolent-looking clients.

"Sit here," the Wazir said. "Eat cake." He said the word in English: ca-ak, with a long, flat vowel. "And tea—the first."

I sat down and we talked. It was almost at once obvious that he took me for an officer of the Frontier Corps. This corps is to the tribal regions what the Frontier Constabulary is to the administered districts—a highly mobile and highly trained body of men. He had heard me talk to the Khattak sepoy of this corps the other day, and probably he hoped I would prove to belong to the Tochi Scouts, the unit of the Frontier Corps that operates in his native North Waziristan. In the past it had been officered by the British. He would have liked this to be true, in any case, since it would have provided some link between me and his country. I would have liked to be able to say it was true, too: the 'Tochis' have an immense reputation on the Frontier—but do many people know about them in the outside world?

"No. I'm not in the 'Tochi'," I admitted.

"But you are British and you speak Pashto. You can speak some Waziri Pashto too. How are you not 'Tochi'?"

"I had Wazir friends. They taught me something."

"Wazir friends? Who?" he asked, in the full expectation that he would know them, but he didn't wait for me to tell him. Instead he hurried on to his next question, which was even more important:

"Have you been to Mir Ali?"

Mir Ali. A village in the Tochi Valley, away in Waziristan.

I said yes, I had been there.

"Ah-h. . . . My village. You have been there. What is your *tankhwah?*"

"My pay? I haven't any pay."

"No pay? Then how do you live?"

I laughed and said that hospitable people gave me tea—and ca-ak.

"Eat it," he ordered.

"Not yet, because I'm waiting for the Azan so that we can eat together when you break your fast."

"Good. But tea and cake are not enough for food. Where is your motor-car?"

Across the village street in another rickety-rackety tea-shop some-one was starting to light his chillum. Then, in the shop alongside us others lit up too. I hadn't heard the Azan—the call of the muezzin.

"Is it time, then? The Azan?"

"Ah! Now we can eat. Start! Eat the cake. There. Take that bit—the fat bit. If we were in Mir Ali we would eat a sheep tonight. Oh, it would be splendid . . . there in our village! Will you stay with me?"

Why was he so friendly, so insistently friendly? Perhaps for him the fact of my knowing his village was enough; I was nearer to him than anyone else here. Perhaps he could never go back to his dear Mir Ali because of something he had done. I didn't ask him, but it is likely that he was an exile from his tribe, alone here in this miserable place, and that anyone at all, me for example, who would speak to him in Waziri Pashto and had seen sweet, far Mir Ali with its cluster of disintegrating homesteads and the fine proud watch-tower—anyone with such qualifications was a friend. He took my hand.

"Will you go there again, *Insha'Allah?*"

"To . . .?" I nodded, and then mimicked the whine of a bullet fired in mountain country—*tak—toooong*!—at least this is the sound the Pakhtuns say it makes, and it is accurate enough.

He shook his head from side to side, saying 'tch-tch'. "Not if I am with you."

"But you won't be with me."

He smiled sadly. "Eat more ca-ak. *Dagha*. That bit. Take that. *Da Wakhla!*"

"*Da wakhla?* Like the poor *ush?*"

He smiled again. "You know that?"

"Everybody knows that, surely."

"Yes, of course."

All the Pakhtuns know it, anyway.

When the animals were herded together into the Ark, it seems that Noah took the precaution of confiscating the sexual organs of all the male creatures, because he could not risk further overcrowding in an Ark already filled to capacity. God knew how long it would be before the flood subsided. These trophies, then, were put carefully aside against the day of disembarkation. When the day came in the fullness of God's time, Noah stood himself at the head of the gang-plank and, good organizer that he was, returned to each his property as he went by. The couples must have smiled happily and have thanked him for his kindness, till finally only the donkey and the camel—the *ush*—were left. Perhaps Noah was exhausted by his labours, but whatever the case he seems to have been guilty of care-lessness, and the donkey had kicked up his heels and disappeared in the dust of his own delight before it was realized that he had made off with what properly belonged to the camel. And when Noah, with some diffidence, offered the camel the last remaining trophy, the camel turned up his nose in a manner that everyone who has seen a camel could identify, and stalked down the gang-plank in disgust. His disgust was understandable, of course, but Noah was a practical man, and even if the little mistake was his, there was nothing he could now do to put matters right. So he shouted after the camel, and again the camel said no, over his shoulder, and Noah shouted again, angry now, because an irrevocable mistake is something you must make the best of. But the camel was already at some distance and refused even to look round. Noah was really angry by this time, and threw the thing viciously after the camel.

"*Da wakhla!*" Noah shouted. "Take that!"—and it hooked itself on backwards.

It was neither Noah's fault, nor the camel's. It was simply one of those unhappy facts of nature that must be put up with.

"Anyhow," the Wazir said to me, "this is a big piece of ca-ak that I am offering to you and you should not refuse." For a moment he was silent, looking me up and down. Then he said: "You must grow a beard and say that you are the nephew of the Amir Amanullah."

I laughed then. More than one 'stranger' has arrived in Waziristan in the past twenty years and demanded not only sanctuary among the tribes, but also help in recovering the Afghan throne for King Amanullah who was forced to abandon it and flee in 1929.

"I shall say that I am a mad *ferangi*," I said. *Ferangi* means Frank, but it is used for any sort of foreigner.

"You are *ferangi* and your eyes are mad with brain."

My eyes. They are small and sharp with something other than brain—flint or madness, perhaps. Simple people are very conscious of eyes, and others have said to me, "Your eyes shine like . . ." but they hesitate over the exact metaphor, as a rule. I don't mind, but sometimes I wish that I could veil them. The best I can do is to screw them up and peep out through the slits.

'You are *ferangi*'—a foreigner. . . . I suddenly felt lost. I didn't belong any more. Was that why I sat there so willingly with the outcast Wazir? Because he made me feel that time had not moved on, carrying me away, away on an unseen flood, down the dry watercourses of his native Waziristan?

Waziristan. In the back of my mind was the official-looking tour-programme that Government would certainly expect me to present for their approval. I wondered how much of it would be approved, and how much I would have passed myself if I had been the official, and someone else the man who demanded special permits, special facilities.

"I hope to go to Mir Ali," I said to the Wazir.

"Grow your beard first."

"For respectability?"

"You don't wear a moustache, even. People will not respect you if you have neither moustache nor motor-car."

*   *   *

The Governor

I was very pleased to see the Governor again. As the Honourable Khwaja Shahabuddin he had been Minister for Refugees and Rehabilitation in the Government of Pakistan in the early days after partition. I had served as Deputy Secretary to Government in that Ministry, and consequently I knew Shahabuddin well. I both liked and respected him. He is of the Nawab of Dacca's family, a Bengal Muslim, that is to say. On the face of it, this mild and gentlemanly Bengali Muslim would not be the obvious choice for Governor of a Province peopled with the violent Pathans: still less might he seem the man to deal with the even more violent 'independent' Pakhtuns of the tribal areas. His appointment as Governor carried with it both responsibilities—that for the administered districts, and in his special capacity as Agent to the Governor-General of Pakistan, for all matters relating to the no-man's-land of the Pakhtuns. Yet, if a Bengali were not considered the best choice, then a man of what other province would be more suitable, other qualifications being equal? Certainly not a Pathan, whose local affiliations would make it difficult, if not impossible, for him to steer clear of internal Pathan politics. Certainly not a man from Baluchistan because the Pakhtuns would not readily accept such a one. Certainly not a Punjabi, or a Sindi, because the arrogant northerners regard these excellent men as their inferiors. Why not a Bengali, after all? He would be so far removed in character and political geography from the Pakhtuns, that he would probably stand a better chance of succeeding than a man from any other province. Shahabuddin had, in fact, succeeded remarkably well. He had learnt Pashto sufficiently to make his formal addresses to the people: he was honest, hard-working, trusted. He was also well-bred, with a good clear brain. The Pakhtuns liked him.

Khwaja Shahabuddin was as charming as ever. Apart from his work his main interests are his family and his home, so that Governor's House, Nathia Gali, during his summer residence there, has all the atmosphere of a 'home'. It rises from a knoll a little below the level of the spine of Nathia Gali, with all the splendour that an earlier public works department architect had been able to give it: the commuter's dream, a comfy little suburban house blown up to the size of a castle. It was warm with the feeling of Shahabuddin's family life. His grandchildren played contentedly with orderlies sufficiently domesticated to have put their fire-arms aside on the grass, temporarily. There were Siamese cats and rose bushes, and Shahabuddin with a friendly welcome, asking me about Morocco. I asked him, in my turn, about the tribal areas. He spoke of them as if they too formed part of a domestic interior, and I am sure that he felt this to be true. I could have my permits, he said, and I could go where I pleased—all I had to do was to present my tour-programme to his Chief Secretary, to whom he would be speaking himself on the subject.

"I particularly want to visit various friends. That would mean going to their villages and staying with them. I suppose that will be all right?" I asked him.

"Why not? Anything you like. Naturally the local political officer must be the final judge of what is practicable at the time of your visit to his agency. The monsoon will have broken by then. Rains sometimes block the roads—and occasionally there may be little quarrels amongst the tribes themselves"—he smiled at the idea— "which would make it difficult for them to receive visitors. But send in your programme and we'll do the very best we can for you. I am sure," he went on, "that you'll find things very different from the old British days. We've been able to remove all the regular army garrisons, for one thing. Of course Pakistan, as a free Muslim state, has that tremendous advantage over a Christian government. The tribes today can regard our government as their own—and they do. There's been a change of heart. Yes. Things have advanced a good deal, though there's a lot more to be done. Education. The tribal-area schools have been enormously increased, and the tribesmen are asking for still more. They're starting to come on now."

"Yes. I've heard so. It will be very interesting to me to see."

"Come and see me on the 'Id day," he suggested. "I would have liked to entertain you before that, but it's difficult, during the fast." Shahabuddin is a very strict and orthodox Muslim. But the feast of the 'Id ul-Fitr would mark the end of the fast. "You're staying in Nathia Gali till the 'Id, aren't you? Come then, please."

I said that I would, with pleasure.

The Chief Secretary was equally welcoming. He is an old friend, too. And within a day or two I had had the formal reply to my request: I was to go where I pleased, subject only to my dates suiting the political agents concerned, so that proper arrangements could be made. I was very content with this. Moving about in the tribal areas is not much like travel elsewhere. Sometimes it would involve escorts, or the provision of transport. It would have been useless to say that friends amongst the tribesmen would look after me, and to remind Government that if you are the guest of a Pakhtun, he will consider it his duty to see that no possible harm comes to you. It could be that the enemy of your host would find in your visit the perfect opportunity for shooting you in order to bring shame upon the man whose duty it was to protect you. A government servant would naturally prefer to avoid any such little risk by reserving the right of veto, according to the local situation at the time. So, all things considered, I was being granted more than a visitor has the right to expect. I was suitably grateful.

Chapter 5

WHEN the man jumped up to greet me—it was at the entrance to the Grand Hotel in Abbottabad: I had that moment arrived from Nathia Gali (with a prayer of thanksgiving for my arrival) and I had seen him squatting at the entrance, his arms stretched forward over his knees—I had not been able to think of his name. I knew that I knew him more than just simply by sight, and guessed that he was a Khalil or Mohmand from one of the villages near Peshawar, and by the time he had finished with the formal greeting and I had signed the hotel register, I had remembered his name.

"Abdul Qadir Khan!"

If mere acquaintances meet in a far place to which both are strangers, a false intimacy springs up, and a witness to the meeting might suppose that the two of them were long-lost friends. I didn't feel that Abdul Qadir Khan was a long-lost friend, but I was pleased to see him, all the same. I not only knew his name now, but could place him—at least I thought so: a friend, or possibly a relation, of Fateh Khan's. So, to confirm this, I said: "I saw Fateh in Peshawar."

"Fateh Khan? You mean Fateh Khan from Fulana Kili?"—and then I knew that I had been wrong after all. No matter.

Abdul Qadir was asking: "Have you come here on leave? Where are you stationed now?"

Abbottabad is a small town in the foothills of the Hazara District, north of Nathia Gali, and some hundred and twenty miles east of Peshawar. It is the headquarters of the district, and quite pleasant in its quiet, peaceful way. The people are not Pathan, though some of them speak Pashto. Their language is called Hindko. I supposed that Abdul Qadir had some job here. Obviously, from his question, he had telescoped the seven or eight years since we could have met into a negligible absence on my part—a temporary transfer from the Frontier, perhaps, or a long visit to England. I was climbing the stairs behind a porter, and Abdul Qadir was coming up behind me. We had reached the first floor by now and, outside the room I had been allotted, a very old hotel room-bearer was taking charge of my luggage from the porter.

"Give those to me," Abdul Qadir said to the porter, managing to wrest my typewriter from the room-bearer at the same time. Then, turning to me, he said: "Haven't you got a bearer, then? No? Then I will be your bearer."

I looked at him. I hadn't engaged a servant because I didn't think I wanted one: and even if I had wanted one I would not have chosen a Pathan. And if it had been a Pathan it would not have been Abdul Qadir. A good bearer necessarily has some trace of servility in his make-up, and a good Pathan has none in his. So it follows that a good bearer is apt to be a bad Pathan. Quite possibly Abdul Qadir was a good bearer. Perhaps I was doing him an injustice, but from the little that I could recall, he was one of the 'commuters' and had picked up too many of the city back-street tricks.

Poor man, he looked wretched. It was not so much that he seemed undernourished or ill, or even just poor. He appeared ill at ease. But he paid no attention to me when I said that I didn't want a bearer, and himself told the room-bearer that we had no need of his services.

"I mean it," I said. "I don't want anyone at all. I'm only staying till the morning. Then I'm off to visit friends. Their men can look after me." I turned to the old man and said that he could go, because I wasn't unpacking my suit-case. The old man left us. We were alone now.

"Only tonight . . . ?" Abdul Qadir was nervous.

"What's the matter? Is something wrong?"

"Nothing."

"Just poor?"—and I fished something out of my pocket to give to him. It wasn't very much.

"I don't want that," he said, but he took it. "I want to be with you."

It was touching, in a way—if it was to be believed. But I didn't believe it. He needed a job, doubtless, and that was a different thing. He had been bearer to a British officer before. It had come back to me now. It was at that officer's house that I had frequently seen him and talked to him.

"Can't you get a job in Peshawar?"

B

"Nowadays? Nothing. The Pakistanis don't want Pathan bearers."

I could not blame them, but I didn't say so. Meanwhile a piratical look had come over Abdul Qadir's face, as he said: "They are afraid of Pathans."

I laughed at the idea of people being afraid of Abdul Qadir, but no doubt he himself was content to think I shared his triumph at the fear he and the other Pathans engendered.

"You can't manage without a bearer," he then added. "And if you're not stationed in Peshawar any more, never mind. I'll come with you wherever you are."

I said again that it was out of the question. I said it with a smile, but firmly, so that he should know it was useless to continue. He watched me for a moment and then slowly the pirate, the romantic brigand, faded from his face.

". . . then what can I do?" he burst out, in sudden, shrill distress.

It was rather horrible. I had to say something.

"Do? Why, go back to your village, of course. You've got your house and your wife and children, haven't you? Yes, well, go back to them, and work on your land. You can keep your eyes open for a job in Peshawar meanwhile, if that's what you want: and you've friends at the club and all over Peshawar who will keep their eyes open for you, too."

"I don't want to work on the land," he muttered, with rather more self-control.

"Then I don't know what to suggest. I can't help you myself. I'm only in Pakistan for a short visit. There's nothing else for you but to go back to the village."

"I . . . I don't want to."

"Why not? Trouble?"

There's always trouble. Pathans have to accept that fact.

"No, but . . ."

He had something on his mind. I would have preferred not to hear what it was, for fear it should involve me in more than sympathy —but I couldn't cut short the conversation at such a point.

"What have you done, Abdul Qadir?"

He swallowed. He was making a special effort. It even seemed as if he were acting a little scene, as much to impress himself as to impress me, because he then said, with another up-surge of arrogance: "You say you've just come from Peshawar. Well. You must have heard. They told you Gul Khan has been killed?"

I nodded.

"I shot him." Abdul Qadir was a good deal bolder now, as befitted the man who had murdered Gul Khan.

"I was told it was Roshan." I kept my voice quiet, I think. "Roshan, surely, or was it Mahboob? Not Omar. Who did the killing?"

"People don't say it was me, then?" he asked quickly.

"Was it you?" But immediately I had asked my question I knew that I had made a tactical mistake. I hurried on to cover it up with words, before Abdul Qadir's pride forced him to say again that it was he. I said: "They all think it was Roshan—or possibly Mahboob. Omar Khan was there too, they say. I believe you can go back to the village all right."

"What can you know . . .?"

Gul Khan with his face blown to pieces and his stomach open, lying there under his ragged little tomb of stones outside the village. . . . I had not thought about it for some days now. I stood watching Abdul Qadir's face. I was instinctively sure that he had not done it, or any part of it—and there was the boy-witness's evidence to support me. Abdul Qadir was out of character as a killer—out of character as a Pathan at all. A dominant gene had been inattentive at the time of his conception, perhaps. But whether he had done it or not, I didn't like him, and I didn't want to be with him any longer.

"You can go back to your village quite safely, I think," I heard myself saying to him, and I thought, without saying it, that he could in fact go back with as much safety as there can ever be for a man whose family is involved in a blood-feud. It just goes on and on, as Chainak Khan had said to those people in London, accumulating blood and hate, and even if you don't get the big-shots, you can get the easy small-fry—Abdul Qadir, for example. The big-shots might count ten points a head, and the small-fry, say, two or three points. It all went towards the score, and there was never any finality about the score.

A little worm of guilt was moving inside me when he left. I ought to have done something—but what, and for how long? Perhaps a school-teacher feels like this towards a pupil who somehow cannot hold his own amongst his fellows. I stood at my upstairs window and saw Abdul Qadir plodding drearily down the drive to the road. He turned and looked up in my direction, and I stepped quickly back into the room so that he should not see me standing there, watching.

*   *   *   **

I remember getting up at least an hour earlier than I had to—the bus was due to leave at seven—because of my feeling of guilt towards Abdul Qadir. I was afraid that after all it might be he who brought my pot of morning tea and drew my curtains back, rather than the old room-bearer. I was afraid that, sensing his advantage over me, he would make another attempt to trap me into taking him with me, to safety. I had deliberately avoided telling where I was bound for, of course, but it would be unlikely that he would sit around at the bus station. He would naturally suppose that I was travelling in my own car—all 'whites' have cars. It is axiomatic. So he would come to the hotel, and early at that.

I was therefore up practically with the summer sun, as if I were a conspirator. I had difficulty in finding a tonga to carry me and my luggage to the bus stop, but I did find one, and was relieved not to see Abdul Qadir as we stumbled sleepily through the little, still-sleeping town. I did see him once again, but for the moment I was free of him.

I had a long wait at the bus station. People were lying about against the veranda railings, asleep still, as they had probably been all night long in their vigil against morning and the start of their journey. The bus was going up the Kaghan valley, as far as the road was motorable for heavy transport. Government were busy opening up the Kaghan to tourist traffic, and the project involved building roads where only tracks had existed hitherto. It is beautiful country high up the valley, many many miles from the nearest Pakhtun snipers (if such things still existed)—and with great good sense they were employing an irregular body of Pakhtun tribesmen as road-makers. The British had done the same, as a matter of fact, in another part of the country. The tribesmen concerned were Mahsuds: they had been organized into a battalion, uniformed but unarmed, and officered by their own men. Much as violent and exhausting games are organized in western colleges to inculcate the manly virtues and to foster the team spirit, and perhaps to keep the mind off sex by diverting the energies elsewhere, so these Mahsud Pakhtuns were being kept busy with pick and shovel, and being paid for it, as a respectable and indeed useful alternative to raiding their neighbours. In any case it is obvious that unless the Pakhtuns' energies can be usefully diverted and rewarded, they will continue to take what they want by raiding. They, can, theoretically, be screened off from their prey in the administered districts, provided a sufficiently powerful force is stationed along their borders to keep the peace. But such a course in no way answers the problem of what the Pakhtuns are to put in their stomachs.

The Mahsuds, the Pakhtun tribe providing this body of road-builders in the Kaghan valley, inhabit the mountainous central tract of Waziristan. As a tribe their fighting strength is traditionally put at 18,000. Actually the number is considerably more. People who come into contact with them either love or loathe them. It is difficult to keep a dispassionate balance in one's attitude. I love them. I did not know Mir Badshah who was Commanding Officer of the Mahsud battalion working up at Balakot, but I knew him by reputation, and knew some of his family and many of his Mahsud friends. To that extent he knew of me, too. He had seemed happy to welcome me, when I had telephoned through to the nearest police post to inquire from him if I could come and stay for a few days. I was on my way to visit him, that morning.

I sat myself in the bus and waited. The sun was well up by now, and the other prospective passengers were lolling about, taking tea, a scruffy lot on the whole. The two front benches, described as 'First Class', were already half filled. I was in the second row, up against a window. No sign of a driver yet, or of anyone to control the seating. A man in a bedraggled turban clambered in, followed by a group of women like big, blousy White Wyandottes in their *burqas*. Probably under all those folds of heavy white cotton cloth they were quite small: possibly pretty, too. But veiled in this way against the predatory stares of strangers, they were entirely unattractive. Some twelve to fifteen yards of heavy cotton are draped from a dowdy little white cotton cap, and the cap itself is cut into the semblance of a crown with points and decorations. A Frontier Government Handbook for tourists lyrically describes it as 'the beautifully crocheted cap . . . to rest on the head', and it is possible that to anyone conditioned to the idea of beauty concealed beneath this hideous garment, the garment itself becomes beautiful. My own feeling is that nothing could have been better designed to discourage the interest of strangers. In came the White Wyandottes, four of them, lugging three visible children, and clutching at least a further three under the folds of their *burqas*. They slumped themselves down beside me on the bench, and I could feel the warm spread of flesh against me. It was not unpleasant, but the Wyandottes themselves perhaps felt otherwise: they immediately began to cast apprehensive looks in my direction, as if they sniffed rape, or the desire to rape, in the air. I looked straight ahead of me, disregarding their man's half-suggested appeal that I move myself elsewhere. The only other seat available in these two front rows was next to a fattish, uniformed passenger, and I preferred to stay where I was—if it could be called a true preference. I had no *burqa* in which to withdraw myself. I had to do the best I could with my thoughts.

Mahsuds. In terms of pure congenital intelligence, this tribe is said to rate the highest of all the Pakhtuns, whereas in numbers they are smallest of the important tribes. Their neighbours to the north are the Utmanzai Wazirs, and to the south and south-west, the Ahmedzai Wazirs. Some writers even link the Mahsuds with the Wazirs, calling the two together Darwesh Khel, but as in matters of tribal origins and relationships the tribes themselves disagree, I see no reason why I should not accept the finding that most closely accords with my own inexpert observation. So, for me, the Mahsuds and the Wazirs are distinct and separate tribes. Certainly they are very different in character, and they fight together incessantly—though that proves nothing. Howell, in his book called *Mijh*—which means 'I', the first personal pronoun, and is consequently the most important word in the Mahsud Pashto vocabulary—rates their intelligence high. He talks of their ingenuity and persistence, and of how plausible they can be in argument, and of their recklessness of the results of individual action, and of the lack of tribal cohesion that follows too—and this in spite of their discipline in the field. He sketches in a picture of a people fanatical, tough, independent, fearless—and to be feared. Howell was writing in 1931, when the British still had a further sixteen years of their time on this Frontier to run. He allows himself a prophecy of the two possible alternatives, in the future of the Mahsuds. 'The old welter may continue,' he says, 'and the Mahsuds throw in

their lot with the inhabitants of Afghanistan—or they may be trained
to take their place in the federation of India. . . .' In 1931, the federation of India was the goal. No one had at that time considered the
possibility of partition. I had heard that the Pakistanis were training
the Mahsuds to take their place in the state of Pakistan, and wondered
what the Mahsuds would consider to be their place.

The bus had started, somewhat behind schedule, but not much:
just long enough for a group of passengers who had not hitherto
thought about tea, to start thinking about it, and to get out to brew
and drink it. But we started, and the movement of the bus, after so
long a period of blessed immobility, was enough to wake some of the
babies. The bus was suddenly filled with their wailing, so their
mothers scrabbled about under their *burqas*, freeing their breasts, I
suppose. In any case the wailings ceased soon after. The woman
next to me threw up the vizor of her *burqa* for air—it was only then
that I saw she was an old woman. Then she quickly popped back
again, and started waving her arms about as if the smoke of my
cigarette had contaminated her. I could hear her grumbling inside
her folds, but the man with them took no notice, and neither did I.
As a matter of fact smoking was not permitted, and there was a notice
to that effect, alongside the notice about not spitting. But I declined
to be the only man who observed both ordinances.

Abbottabad with its sugar-loaf hills had been left behind, and the
country was opening up: to the south the mountain formation that
carries Nathia Gali, another such formation to the eastward in the
direction we were taking, and a long, steady staircase of foothills to
the north, stretching to Swat Kohistan. It was very green, and very,
very hot. I had never been to Balakot and hoped that its greater
altitude might mean it would be cooler. One of the women in the
second row suddenly whipped a baby out of her *burqa*, handed it to
her next-door neighbour, threw up her vizor and started to vomit.
She was a young girl, and very quiet about it. She had managed to
open her legs—a movement which transmitted itself all along the
line till it reached me in the form of a little jolt from the woman
next to me. The girl was being sick on to the floor, between her
knees. No one took any notice at all. I lit another cigarette, deciding
that I had established a right to it. There must be limits to the demands
that one passenger can make upon another.

"Look!" said the fattish man in uniform conversationally,

leaning over his neighbours in order to speak to me. "Look! Mansehra."

I nodded and smiled politely. Mansehra? What of it? Was there not enough going on immediately round us to hold the attention? Mansehra. A little town on a knoll. Very pretty.

Mansehra, and a stop for tea and gossip. Then another little townlet. And another—Garhi Habibullah, right in the valley of a big, bundling river. There had been a lot of fighting here when the Kashmir war was on. It looked peaceful enough now, and when some-one showed me bomb damage—Indian bombs, Pakistani damage—I could not be so very impressed by the shack in ruins. I suppose I was thinking of London, or Hamburg that I had seen not so long before, or, on the same scale as Garhi Habibullah, of some little village in the tribal areas after a warning has gone unheeded. Or perhaps of Gul Khan with his face shot away. Garhi Habibullah, far down in its ravine, with the snow-waters roaring by. It was quite peaceful at present, and though the tea was thick and oversweet, it was welcome. The White Wyandottes had got out and were being shepherded under a walnut-tree. I hoped they would not be going any farther.

Chapter 6

I DON'T know what the time was: perhaps two hours later, and perhaps we had already travelled forty miles beyond Garhi Habibullah over rough, un-metalled roads. The mountains to north and west of us had been climbing more quickly than we could, and at a steadily increasing pace, whereas we were compelled to jink backwards and forwards, following the contours of a hill here, forcing boldly through a cutting there, often losing height as we slipped down to cross a tributary stream and up again, stomach in the throat, on the far side. The river continued to the south-west of us, pale, tumbling, broken water. The valley was wider here for a moment—and rather dull, to be quite honest, without colour and almost treeless—but it was closing in again. After a while we passed an encampment of obvious Pakhtuns and I shouted to the driver, but he waved gaily and shouted back to me 'Not yet!', though I could see a flag flapping from a roughly-cut flag-pole, and the Mahsud battalion insignia on it. It was evidently a detachment of the battalion, and somebody explained that my host, Major Mir Badshah, was to be found farther up the valley, in the main camp.

When we came to it, there was no sign of life. The camp seemed deserted. There was a single whitewashed hut, near the roadway: apart from that, nothing but tents, one of them fronted by a pattern of kerosene cans from which greenery sprouted aimlessly—Battalion Headquarters, with its garden in front of it. Below the escarpment on which the camp was set, I could see a narrow band of cultivation, rice fields, and then the river still there, but narrower hereabouts, so that the water had become fiercer and still more broken. The bus stopped and a sentry came out from the shadows of the cottage. And then people came out of the cottage itself and greeted me formally. The formal Pakhtun smile does not show any teeth. They took my baggage, one man to each piece, and I said good-bye to the driver and to the other passengers. The White Wyandottes could not be expected to make any gestures, but their man bowed from his seat. I turned to follow my host's men.

It was a little cottage, built in the Mahsud manner, though some three hundred miles from the nearest true Mahsud village. Its door and windows faced the river. It had a carcass of axe-hewn timber, framework for a single, rectangular room. The corners and other vertical wall-members were pine-trunks, tied together across the length and width with similar timbers. The walls were mud, pure and simple, supporting nothing more formidable than their own weight. They were held firm to the wooden carcass at ceiling level. The roofing was branch-wood, laid over with a criss-cross of twigs, or straw or anything that had been handy, and the whole bound with mud, whitewashed. It was quite solid, and the thickness of the mud walls would keep it cool in spite of the considerable midday heat. It would be warm in winter, too, as I knew.

For furniture there were two beds at the far end of the room, side by side, with no interval between them, and bright with a huge cotton cover. A couple of wooden chairs and a table with an embroidered cloth on it had been set up in front of the empty fireplace. There was an Afghan carpet, from somewhere north of Herat, stretched over the entire floor-space which still left a good deal over to be doubled back under itself at one end. It was of the traditional dark clarety red, with red and black 'elephant's foot' patterning, with white and a little blue. Why 'elephant's foot' here, where elephants don't belong—though one at least of India's invaders has used elephants in his baggage-train? The design suggests the big, fubsy puds of an elephant, and the trade description has stuck. A group of three or four men was squatting on the carpet, in the biggish open space just inside the door. A table-cloth has been spread between them, and dishes of food stood ready.

"Have you eaten yet? Sit down and eat with us."

A man had brought a basin and ewer and stood waiting to pour water over my hand. You must eat with the fingers of the right hand exclusively, and even if you think they are clean, it is proper to go through the motions of washing them. I did so and squatted on the carpet with the others.

"Badshah sahib is coming," they said, and in a minute or two he came.

He is a spare, middle-aged man, hard as a nail, one-eyed, but his

66

one eye has a brightness like that of the gleaming torch with which an oculist stares deep into the retina of your own eyes. Mir Badshah Sahib stared into mine as he welcomed me and sat down with us. He did not eat, but he watched me as I ate, and occasionally picked out a special piece of chicken and handed it to me. They all wore the baggy, cotton pantaloons called *partug*, and long shirts, *korta*, hanging outside to just below the knee. They all wore turbans of some sort, the majority the bulky black type affected by the Mahsuds, with a fringe very often—though Mir Badshah and one other man had the gold-thread *khulla* round which a neater, tighter turban is wound, the *loongi*.

I am accustomed to the questioning that follows the welcome due to a stranger and submitted to it readily enough. We had never met before, though I knew of Mir Badshah. He is a Mal Khel Mahsud and, since the war (which in these regions means the Kashmir war, and not World War II), has become perhaps the best-known personality of all the Mahsuds. I noticed that when he was speaking, the others remained silent. Two of his sons were there: Alam Jan about twenty, and tough-looking, and another a good deal younger; and there was a little girl sitting in the background watching us. They said she was Nek Bibi, Mir Badshah's daughter. She was about seven or eight, with a highly intelligent face, and she proved to be the only female creature in the camp, except chickens. It would be normal for Mir Badshah's children not to speak much in these circumstances, but amongst grown Pakhtun men it is common for everyone, young and old, neophyte or experienced, to talk across no matter whom, to interrupt and comment as they please and without hindrance. It seemed that Mir Badshah had more personal control over his people than is usual. I told him about myself in answer to his questions, and about Morocco, about the great Pasha of Marrakesh—el-Glaoui whom Mir Badshah in some ways resembles. Mir Badshah nodded approvingly.

"I have come back here to see my friends again," I explained.

"I have been told that you write things. Will you write about your friends?"

"I think so. I would like to."

"Of course," he said. It seemed altogether reasonable to them that I should wish to write about Pakhtun friends.

Everything closed down in the heat of the afternoon. Three

thousand feet or so above sea-level cannot do much to domesticate a north-Pakistani summer. The men worked on the road till something after ten o'clock and then broke off. The rest of the day was theirs, to do with as they pleased, except for those detailed for guard duties. There was little doubt that the midday meal was normally taken a good deal earlier than we had had it that day. My bus had been late. Immediately we had eaten, there was a move.

"You would like to sleep?" Mir Badshah asked me, indicating the beds at the far end of the room. I nodded and said "thank you".

I lay down on the smaller of the two beds and Mir Badshah, with the bodyguard good manners of the Pakhtun host, lay down on the bed next to mine. You don't leave a guest to sleep in solitude. The others left us, and we talked for a while. He is a very shrewd man: and a courageous man, too. He had been a subedar-major—equivalent to a company sergeant-major—in the old Indian Army, and had served in France in the Kaiser War. Mahsuds had been recruited at that period, evidently. When I first came across the Mahsuds, recruiting had stopped. The Mahsuds are inclined to be over-exuberant, perhaps. Mir Badshah seemed to like the British. Pakhtuns often do, as a matter of fact, and the British like them. Pakhtuns are able to feel that the British are their equals, and that makes for an easy relationship, whether as friends or enemies—for it never prevented the outbreak of serious fighting, of course. But 'friend' is not really the word I am looking for: a Pakhtun can never make a friend of a man from whom he has something either to gain or to fear. Administrators must be excluded from the category of friends for both reasons: soldiers, and officers of the irregular armed forces, must be excluded because they are dangerous. Such men the Pakhtuns can admire (if they are admirable) but they can never be their friends because the relationship must always remain linked with the Pakhtun advantage or the reverse. But they tended to like the British, and they did not despise them except when the British were insufficiently tough. Contrary to what everyone seems to believe, I do not think that the Pakhtuns are fanatically Muslim, men to whom the very idea of an infidel is hateful—though they are happy that the outside world should believe this. It would have been better had the British been Muslims, of course, and the fact of a common religion offers the present Pakistan Government a very real advantage, but it is not enough in itself. The Pakhtuns are Pakhtuns first, and Muslims afterwards—just as the British were British first and Christians afterwards. The Moghuls were Muslims: and when the Pakhtuns wanted to oppose these Moghul brothers-in-Islam (which they did constantly) they eased their consciences by coining a handy term 'Moghulwali' to represent the allegedly mock-Islamic code of the Moghuls. Pakhtunwali was, and is, their own. But the Pakistanis are wiser than the Moghuls ever were in their handling of the Pakhtun tribes—at least I was beginning to think so.

We lay and chatted for a while, the silent intervals lengthening gradually till Mir Badshah fell asleep. He kept turning in his sleep —he was not well at the time: some intestinal trouble, I gathered— and I felt uneasy because it was clear that he would normally have taken his siesta in his own tent, with his own people round him. After a while he heaved over, and I could see that he was awake again. So I said:

"Why don't you rest in your own tent, Mir Badshah sahib? You needn't worry about me."

I think he would have gone, but someone was coming into the cottage, a man in a heavy black turban, full-bearded, two fingerwidths of his moustache shaved clean in the middle of his upper lip. He was handsome, and I saw that he was a mullah. Islam knows no priesthood, but the mullahs, who are instructed in the Qoran, are the equivalent of a lay-brotherhood. He sat down near us. Mir Badshah half raised himself in greeting, and I made polite gestures from my bed too. They talked quietly together, the two of them, not bringing me into the conversation—which was nevertheless about me.

". . . English . . . Yes, he speaks Pashto. I don't know. For some days probably. No, he does no work, he just writes things, he just moves around. He has no money, no car, no family, he is unarmed, he just moves around. He lives with the Moors in Morocco, el-Moghreb, far away . . . but he was here with the Pakhtuns before, but I didn't know him before. . . ."

The mullah was asking questions, so quietly that I could not clearly follow them, but I could guess their import from Mir Badshah's replies: nor did it strike me as strange that they should discuss me in my own half-hearing. The mullah wanted to know, and it would have seemed indelicate to him to question me when there was someone else present who knew the answers.

"He speaks Arabic," Mir Badshah was saying.

"Only a little," I put in quickly. "The Moghrebi Arabic."

But it was enough for the mullah, who wanted to recite some verses from the Qoran, which was the only Arabic he knew. I did not understand, and that gave him an advantage that pleased him, so he kept smiling at me and nodding. He sat there, nodding as he told the ninety-nine beads of his rosary—little dried wooden berries, strung on a cord with a lozenge of turned wood to mark the hundredth, unknowable name of Allah. Click-click, the little berry beads, and the still, hot air around us . . .

"When are you coming to Waziristan?" the mullah asked. suddenly.

"Later, I hope. I want to go to Afghanistan first."

"Oh? I didn't know." Mir Badshah was surprised. "Are you going to Afghanistan, then? Kabul?"

"I hope so. I'm waiting for my visa. The Afghans have to decide first to give me permission, so that my passport can be stamped by them."

"But since you are so friendly with Pakistan, I wonder if . . ."

"Exactly. Perhaps the Afghans will refuse to let me go."

The mullah smiled at Mir Badshah, and then towards me.

I said :"The Pakhtuns are friendly with the Afghans *and* with the Pakistanis" And the mullah smiled again.

"Will you go to India too?" Mir Badshah asked slyly.

"No. I have only come to see Pakhtuns, this time."

"There are many Pakhtuns in India. Hundreds, thousands . . ."

"When a Pakhtun leaves his mountains to live in some other country, he ceases to be a Pakhtun quite quickly, I think."

It interested me to see their reaction to such an impertinent statement. They laughed with their lips closed. I was encouraged, and anxious to confirm what I felt to be the truth, so I went on:

"They become what the Indians call Pathans."

"Pathans. Hm-m . . ." The mullah looked away and said: "They become kings sometimes."

"Well, it's true that Pakhtuns have become Pathan kings in India." I started laughing now and said: "You'd better teach your people Urdu." Urdu is the principal Pakistani language, the official language of the country, though English is used for government and international purposes.

70

A walk in the country

"The Pakistanis will have to learn Pashto," the mullah remarked, examining the beads of his rosary again. "Mahsud Pashto, I think, would be best. . . ."

*　　　　　*　　　　　*

Down below, in the paddy-fields that bordered the river, someone was singing: a loud strident voice, reduced in volume by the raging of the river-waters and the distance. Light as its impact might be upon our ears, yet I knew that it was a full, rich sound. It ceased for a moment and a chorus followed—just a short passage—and then the solo started again. I wandered forward across the narrow plateau on which the camp was set, and looked down over the paddy. A group of Hazarawal villagers was transplanting the young rice from what must have served as a 'nursery' to its final home near-by. They were hock-deep in water, bending over the rice-tufts and uprooting them. Beyond the river the first mountains of Kashmir rose in their receding planes. The air was quite still. In the camp some movement had started, now that the heat of afternoon had passed. It was very satisfying to me to be with Pakhtuns again. Nek Bibi, Mir Badshah's daughter, stood some yards away in her pink rayon pyjamas, with her silk shirt hanging outside them. She was shy, a little, and stood tugging at her green bead necklace, or combing her hair with her fingers. Her brothers were apt to tease her: I had noticed this. She was probably lonely here, with no other children, and perhaps she wondered if I would play with her. She didn't like to ask, but when I wandered past her and held out my hand, she took it without saying anything and came too. I wasn't going anywhere in particular, just wandering. Alam Jan, the elder brother, came out of a tent and joined us. He suggested that we fire a few bursts with a new sub-machine-gun his father had, and Nek Bibi looked pleased, but when it came to the point we couldn't find it, and perhaps Alam Jan didn't want to ask him where it was. So we had to change the plan, and decided to walk down to the detachment whose camp I had seen as I had passed by in the bus earlier in the day.

"It's only two miles," he said.

We started off, Nek Bibi running ahead, and then lagging, and talking all the time, as Alam Jan and I talked together. He was interesting to me, and a very likeable, well-mannered young man, apart from the fact that I wanted to know how he planned his future. He belonged to a new generation of 'educated' Pakhtun tribesmen— but his was an education in the arts of war, which might divide him less sharply from his people in the Waziristan mountains than a formal University training. He was finishing his time at the Pakistan Military Academy—Sandhurst, West Point, the equivalent of these— and he would probably take a regular commission. He liked military history, it seemed: he was a good shot, he liked the open air. Nek Bibi darted back and forth like a shuttlecock, her necklace flying.

"You must go back, Nek Bibi," Alam Jan said.

"No."

"Yes."

"No."

He smacked her. "Yes!"

She looked furiously at him and he smiled. Then he patted her and said yes again.

"I want to come with you and the *ferangi*."

"If you like the *ferangi*, then you can become his daughter and he will take you away with him. Do you want that?"

"If he is a *ferangi*, I can't be his daughter."

"Oh yes you can. *Ferangis* have daughters too."

"But not me."

"Do you want her for a daughter?" he asked me.

"I don't think so," I said.

Then she turned to me seriously. "Do you say your——?" But after all she didn't like to ask so important a question of me direct, and she turned back to Alam Jan. "Ask him. Does he pray?"

I said: "Yes."

"Which way does he turn when he prays?"

I thought rapidly. In the west we turn to the east. In the east Christians turn to . . .: I couldn't be certain, after all. Do Christians turn towards Jerusalem, whatever point of the compass that may represent to them? I racked my brain for the answer, but she wouldn't wait.

"Which way?" she demanded, addressing me personally this time.

"That way," I decided, pointing across the river to the range of mountains in the east.

"Kashmir . . .?" She was incredulous. Alam Jan laughed.
"Well . . ."

"Badshah sahib was fighting there," she said, thinking of something else now. She called her father by his name, in this manner. "He has *taghme*, many. Two new *taghme*. No one else has these two. Some have one, some have the other one. No one else has these two new *taghme* for Kashmir."

"Is that true?" I asked Alam Jan. "What are these two new medals that Nek Bibi is talking about?"

Alam Jan's English is excellent. Nek Bibi didn't speak a word of it. So conversation was in English or Pashto, as required.

"She talks about the special medals struck for the Kashmir war. The Fakhri-i-Kashmir, and the Hillal-i-Kashmir. Father has both. That is true. Two other Pakhtuns have both, as well as father. Only two others, however, and I expect that Nek Bibi would like him to be the only man to have both. The Mahsuds were the best fighters in Kashmir. Of course you know that."

"I've heard nothing, except tea-shop gossip."

"Do you know Rap Khan?"

"Rap Khan . . .? I don't think so. Which section of the Mahsuds?"

"Bahlolzai Mahsud. He's malik of the section. He's with us here in Balakot. We'll see him at the detachment. NEK BIBI! Go! Didn't you hear me? Go back home!"

Poor little Nek Bibi, she turned sadly and wandered back the way we had come. The light was already dying—it must have been later than I had realized. She went slowly and sorrowfully away from us, and then—suddenly—as if some pleasant thing had come into her head, she started to skip down the road, pyjamas ballooning, her necklace jumping about round her neck, away, away, through air thickening with dusk, back to the camp and whatever it was that it had suddenly occurred to her to do.

They weren't expecting us at the detachment. The men were sitting about on their string beds, smoking and chatting together. Some got up, stiffening to attention as we approached, others stayed as they were, and it had no importance either way. We joined them and the haphazard arrangement of charpoys was reorganized into a hollow square, with about thirty of us together. Alam Jan gave them a brief biography so that they should know who I was and what I

F

was doing there. They were unsurprised, but glad that I could speak Pashto because that made things easier, and better.

I found myself on a charpoy with two or three others, formally seated to begin with, our legs dangling over the side. Quite inadequate cushions, stuffed with gravel surely, tended to keep us from slithering into the sagging, corded centre. As the atmosphere thawed we edged into greater comfort, if less formality. I had slipped off my shoes and drawn my legs up on to the bed, my elbow sharing a cushion with someone else's. Rap Khan came over, sent by Alam Jan, I suppose. Tall, curly bobbed hair, with a twist of it arranged so that it came up under each ear-lobe: loose limbs, and eyes that smiled in an amused way. We spoke of this and that, and after a while he was as relaxed as the rest of us on the bed.

"Rap Khan was first over the rope bridge," someone said. It was obviously important. They were anxious for me to know about it, and to repeat the names of those who were with him. Kashmir, of course. The Holy War, *Jehad*, the war against the infidel Dogra-Hindu Maharajah of Kashmir, the bulk of whose subjects were down-trodden, poverty-stricken Muslims. It is a long story, the Pakhtuns tell it in their way, and the Indians who, at the request of the Maharajah—and in return for his formal accession to India without which, it seems, it would have been highly improper for the Indians to interfere—flew troops in to save him and beat off the Pakhtuns, tell it in their way. No one, however, is likely to dispute the fact that the Maharajah's repression of his Muslim subjects, notably the Sudhans in the mountains of Poonch, caused them finally to rise against him in self-preservation: and most people feel that they were amply justified. The Sudhans may not have been wise, because they were virtually unarmed, whereas the Maharajah had his own trained army, and used it ruthlessly against them. But their desire to free themselves of the Maharajah's despotism, and if necessary to die as an alternative, is understandable.

But it is a long story and seven years old now, and for more than six of the seven years the United Nations have tried to clear up the mess. As far as the Pakhtun tribes were concerned, it began with *Jehad*, a war in the name of Allah. The Qoran says: "Verily those who believe . . . and those who wage war in God's name: these may hope for God's mercy, for God is forgiving and merciful." And again: "Fight them, then, that there should be no sedition, and that

74

the religion may be wholly God's . . . and know that whenever ye seize anything as a spoil, to God belongs a fifth thereof. . . ." Nearer home, in man-made Pashto verse, Khushal Khan the Khattak had written more than three hundred years before: "An army should be urged by pride and hope of plunder . . ." He would have liked to invest his war against the Moghul Aurangzeb with the aura of *Jehad* —but somehow or other the Pakhtuns did not see it that way, and he complained bitterly against them—"Those troops of mine were but serving for their bread," he cried. But in Kashmir it was *Jehad*, all right. Loot—this is the reward of Holy War in this life, sanctioned by the Qoran itself, just as 'gardens beneath which waters flow' are the reward for the faithful in the world to come.

The Pakhtun tribes who took part in Kashmir were not sponsored by the governments of Pakistan or of Afghanistan (tribes from both countries took part)—they believed themselves actuated by the highest of motives, *Jehad*. Plunder and loot were their legitimate rewards, and they took them with both hands—women, arms, anything. If they had not stopped to loot they might well have taken Srinagar, capital of Kashmir, before the Indians flew their troops in. It has been said that Pakistan loosed the Pakhtuns on Kashmir, but it can be shown that they worked hard to prevent the declaration of *Jehad* and even managed to postpone the tribal invasion for a while. It need not surprise anyone that the Pakistan Government could not prevent it—any more than could the Afghan Government. The Indians who protest so vehemently against Pakistan say nothing about the Afghans, incidentally. The fact is that in October, 1947, the Pakistan army scarcely existed, except on paper, and it would have required considerable organization and force of arms to hold the Pakhtuns back, once they rose and came surging through the North-West Frontier Province on their way to Kashmir.

The Pakhtuns certainly took violent, barbaric and profitable part in the Kashmir war, and there is little doubt that individual and highly-placed Pakistanis helped them as they made for the battle areas. Amongst the foremost of the tribes were the Mahsuds, and foremost amongst the Mahsuds were perhaps Major Mir Badshah himself, and such men as Rap Khan who sat beside me on the charpoy, smiling and happy as his companions told me of his exploits. It was strange to hear such details divorced from their context, strange to hear this epic of Mahsud gallantry and to be given a list, in descending

75

order of bravery and achievement, of the other tribes who had fought too. I could not help noting that the Mahsuds' traditional foes—the Wazirs, their next-door neighbours in the mountains of Waziristan—were not even allowed to figure. It was strange that the tribe accorded second place in valour after the Mahsuds were not even Pakhtuns at all—but the Sudhans, the Muslims who had risen against the Maharajah of Kashmir's oppression.[1] And yet, is it strange? This 'honours list' started—like charity—at home, with the Mahsuds, descended by way of foreigners with whom no comparisons need be feared, through the lesser tribes of Pakhtuns to whom a Mahsud could afford to give a patronizing pat, to faint praise at the tail-end of honour of the real competitors in the hierarchy of Pakhtun 'invincibles'—the Afridis, for example.

The muezzin gave the call to prayer, and men got up to wander over to a rough, mud-boundaried suggestion of a praying-place, lining up with a discipline they reserve for God and battle. Rap Khan had slipped off the charpoy and had laid his mat on the ground beside us. You can pray anywhere: in the middle of a market-place, if you like. I stayed where I was, quietly: and when it was all finished they came back and the talk began again. Stories, little separated anecdotes—the stoking of a fire in some mountain hide-out, for example, and the setting of a big cauldron over it, watched by two Hindu soldiers that a Mahsud party had ambushed and captured. The Mahsud captors said nothing to their captives: they just went on patiently with the stoking of the fire till one of the Hindus asked, with some anxiety, what they were about.

"We're hungry. We haven't eaten for days, so we're lucky to have caught you. Which of you would like to go first?"

But they let one of the Hindus escape, deliberately. In such ways as this, the Mahsuds say, stories of the Mahsud devils would spread through the ranks of the Hindu forces, stories of how the devils had long furry ears and fed on human flesh.

Rap Khan laughed contentedly at the recollection. No one spoke of the wretched Christian missionaries at Baramula, a woman amongst

---

[1] The Sudhans in earlier days, I am told, claimed Rajput origins—that is to say kinship before conversion to Islam with the bravest and finest of the Hindu martial clans. Today, since the Kashmir war, there is a tendency for the Sudhans to claim kinship with the 'Durrani' Abdali Afghans, Pakhtuns who have been Muslims for centuries.

them, that tribesmen had murdered and thrown down a well. Not that the incident must be presumed to have shocked the Pakhtuns —war is war, and women as well as men who get involved in it are apt to be killed one way or another—not that it was the Mahsuds who had done it, as a matter of fact. They told me only of things that their memories relished, and most easily retained.

It was quite dark, and still the happy talk continued till Alam Jan rose and beckoned to me. A small party walked with us to the road.

"Come again. Come tomorrow. At all times," Rap Khan said.

Horrors are not limited to these peoples. Men have thrown their victims down wells in other countries, too. You can read about monsters in most of our Sunday papers in the west, since this sort of this is considered suitable Sunday reading. And in some ways, it is true, we manage things better in the west than the Pakhtuns do, because we can enrich our horrors with neuroses, and that makes them all the more palatable—rapes and maimings, slobbering hysteria and other elements to chill the spine pleasurably. The Pakhtuns are apt to miss the finer points of horror: they kill quickly, and neatly too if they are using a rifle. A knife is different.

Dinner was ready when we got back. 'Shna' was there. I had forgotten to mention him: I have never known his real name because everyone calls him Shna for his steel-blue eyes. He was evidently driving a truck for the battalion now. I had known him years before. He introduced a friend of his—Rehmat Khan, a small man, button-bright. That evening both of them were helping with the service of the meal. They and the others squatted around, or stood around, waving their hands to keep non-existent flies out of the food, watching each mouthful as it went down and making encouraging noises so that we should eat more. Amongst people who are traditionally hungry, great steaming dishes of food and insistence on overeating are the marks of hospitality.

We were only six at the meal. We fed in the open, outside the cottage, and for some reason dinner was presented in a western manner, with table and chairs. The glasses, filled with snow-water from the river, stood at the left of each place because the left hand is used for drinking when the fingers of the right are greasy with food. The man beside me was a subedar-major—an enormous Bahlolzai Mahsud with the gentle movements that very powerful men allow

77

themselves to make.   Alam Jan was with us, of course, and his younger
brother, and one of Mir Badshah's officers, a very likeable Afridi called
Shahzada Khan.

Mir Badshah presided.   He seemed unnaturally quiet.

"Are you sick, Mir Badshah sahib?" I asked him.

"A little . . .   If I should go away tomorrow . . .   I have to visit a
doctor, and there is no doctor here.   You will be all right?   My
sons will look after you.   You must stay.   They will do everything
for you that I would have liked to do myself."

Nobody commented on his sickness.   Conversation continued.
My neighbour, the Subedar-Major Wadi Khan, spoke seldom, and
never to me, yet I had no impression that this was an unfriendliness.
Shahzada Khan, the Kuki Khel Afridi—and the only non-Mahsud
amongst us, except myself—was gay and entertaining.   The others
were inclined to chaff him, and he took it all in excellent humour
They chaffed him specially about his cousin—one Wali Khan, Kuki
Khel Afridi, the most important of all the Afridi maliks, or headmen.
The chaffing had a complicated back history, mixed up with 'Pashtunistan' which is complicated in itself and something I understood
even less well at that time than I do today.

It appeared that Malik Wali Khan had quarrelled with the Pakistan
authorities.   The quarrel had attached itself to some more or less
trifling incident—I suspect that it arose from lack of experience and
tact on the part of the youthful Pakistani officer who was at the time
charged with the handling of Afridi affairs.   He and Wali Khan, in
any case, had not seen eye to eye, and Wali Khan had carried his
angry protests too far.   It was at a time when Pashtunistan—that
campaign for the Land of the Pakhtuns as an independent and sovereign
state—was most violently in the air: perhaps I should say, rather,
most violently *on* the air, for it was a great deal more ranted about
over the Kabul Radio than ever it seems to have been on actual
Pakhtun tribal soil.   The Afghan Government had taken it upon
themselves to champion the Pakhtun cause against the Pakistanis,
whom they depicted as the oppressors of the Pakhtuns.   I heard a
lot more about this later: for the moment I only knew that Pashtunistan was presumed to be desirable for the Pakhtuns, and that Wali
Khan, mishandled by whoever it was, had decamped to Kabul like a
sullen schoolboy.   The Afghan Government had received him with
open arms and had nominated him as some sort of Pashtunistani

leader. That was all right for Wali Khan, and seems to have provided him with a monthly allowance at least equivalent to the Pakistani allowance he had been receiving before he decamped. But quite soon Wali Khan found that he was also expected to do something for this new sovereign state—something specific. He was required to gather together a tribal *lashkar* (as they call an irregular 'army' of tribesmen), and lead it to the Kohat Pass, with luck even to the River Indus, there to plant a series of Pashtunistani flags, as living evidence that Pashtunistan existed and that the Indus marked its south-eastern frontiers. The whole idea, of which this was to be a symbol, was that the Pakhtuns proposed to secede from Pakistan. No one can do much in the Pakhtun tribal regions without everyone else knowing exactly what is afoot almost as soon as it starts, and the Pakistanis sent messages to warn Wali Khan of the action they would be compelled to take against him, even before the tribal *laskhar* started on their way to the Indus from Tirah in Afridi country. But Wali Khan could not turn back now—pride drove him on, just as pride had driven him to Kabul in the first place. His *lashkar* reached the borders of N-W.F. Province administered territory, waving rifles and Pashtunistani flags. The Pakistanis were waiting for him with a small body of ground troops. They warned him again, but he took no notice. So they beat his *lashkar* up, good and proper, using also a couple of aircraft equipped with rocket-missiles. It must have been rather a shock to Wali Khan—because he is said to have been assured that if the Pakistanis had the inhumanity to use aircraft, he could count upon his friends' blasting the Pakistani aeroplanes out of the sky. There were, of course, casualties—which is what Pakhtuns expect in a 'war', after all—and what was in a sense almost more humiliating than defeat in the field, was the fact that the Pakistanis then sent a 'fighter' up over Wali Khan's Afridi village to destroy his fine fortress. This was done, with quite astonishing accuracy: Wali's fort was rocketed to destruction, and nothing else was touched.[1] That, briefly, was the situation, and we all pretended to believe that Shahzada Khan, for family reasons, took the part of his discomfited cousin, though we knew perfectly well that this was not so.

[1] I subsequently saw the air-photographs of the damage done. It was a remarkable piece of precision work. The inhabitants had been warned in advance, and not even the most rabid pro-Pashtunistani has suggested that any damage was done to human life or limb.

"I'm fond of Wali," Shahzada Khan told me later. "Do you know him? He is a good man—but headstrong, and sometimes stupid. He is proud, too proud."

I didn't know Wali. But I knew others of Shahzada's relatives. It is a family whose special importance must be ascribed to the British. They had given Wali's grandfather a title—Nawab—because he had rendered certain services to the government. Along with the Nawabi went allowances greater than those normally granted to maliks. Such support from the British might be expected to help the Nawab's prestige amongst the Afridis and, of course, it did—up to a point. But you can't invent leaders simply by putting money into their pockets. It would have been convenient for the British if you could: convenient for the Pakistanis, too.

"You are going to Kabul soon, Mir Badshah says. If you go, perhaps you will meet Wali Khan: and if you meet him, will you give him a message of friendship from me, because after all I love him— but don't allow him to think that we Afridis are pleased with him, even if we want him to come back to us."

I said: "If I meet him, I will give him your message, Shahzada Khan."

"They are using the wrong plates," Wadi Khan was whispering softly to Shna who stood behind his chair. "Look! *Not* the white ones—you should have used those with roses on them—like this." He pointed to the plate before him, and Shna nodded. The rosy plates, of course. And as Shna hurried off for the rosy plates, Wadi Khan stretched across and took my white plate away, substituting his own with the sprigs of pink and mauve roses. But he didn't say anything as he did it.

*   *   *

Our charpoys had all been carried out into the open space before the cottage—five or six of them. There had been a lot of movement before the lamps were taken away. Bundles of bed-clothes had appeared, shawl-like *chaddars* long enough to cover a man's body from head to feet, as if they were shrouds. Pakhtuns sleep with the head covered as a rule. I had a pillow on which 'Good Night' had been embroidered in multi-coloured silko. I don't know who was in the bed next to mine: either Alam Jan or his brother, probably. Mir Badshah had gone to his own tent.

The night passed anonymously in sleep.

In such circumstances waking-time is necessarily sun-up, or even a little before, the Kashmir mountains edged with a hurtful, shrieking gold. It could not have been more than five o'clock when I was shaken into the new day by one of Mir Badshah's men. He had big eyes, set in a face like that of a child. I think his name was Karam Ali Khan, and I had seen him the night before, heard him too as he sat somewhere on the outskirts of our group and played a guitar-like *sarinda* to himself. I had noted also, earlier, that he acted as Nek Bibi's nursemaid, and this possibly explained how it was that Nek Bibi's hair was never combed and why, for the length of my stay, I never saw her other than in her pink rayon pyjamas and silken shirt, and the bead necklace. I believe she slept near Karam Ali Khan in the kitchen tent, but I am not sure. Karam Ali was shaking me. He had a tray in his hand.

"Wake! Wake!"

He put the tray down on the rough ground and whisked away the crocheted cover. I saw a tea-pot, a sugar-basin, a cup, and a plate with six soft-boiled eggs on it, some of them broken in the fiddling process of picking off their shells. I drank the tea gratefully, but had no stomach for eggs yet.

"Eat!" ordered Karam Ali, who had squatted alongside to watch me.

I shook my head.

"Eat! Already you are thin. See how thin you are! Eat eggs! Don't shame me. Badshah sahib will be angry with me if you are not fatter by the time you leave us. Go on. Eat! Shall I bring you milk too?"

I had to eat the eggs, so as not to shame Karam Ali.

*   *   *

I have a great capacity for doing nothing, and I like to wander with no particular object, enjoying the purposeless movement of my legs and the rhythm it seems to give to my thoughts. I went walking alone that day. Mir Badshah had left, and we had all gathered round his jeep to bid him farewell and a return to health under the magic of the doctor's wand. The jeep had scurried away, carrying Mir Badshah, a driver and the three men who formed his honourable bodyguard. They had bristled with quite unnecessary fire-arms—the Kaghan valley is not Waziristan, yet the decencies had to be observed, naturally. But now I was walking under the sun, alone only for a few hundred yards, as it happened. Shna's friend, Rehmat Khan, came up and joined me.

"Where are you going, Rehmat Khan?"

He smiled but did not answer.

We walked together in silence for a bit. A mile or two up the road was the road-head. Ordinary wheeled traffic cannot go beyond, though the way is already open for jeeps. The valley was a great deal narrower. We were on the outskirts of a little township, Balakot. It is uninteresting, on the whole, though it contains the tombs of two Muslim martyrs of the nineteenth century. They were down-country men, from far away in the United Provinces that today lie with India: but at that time they were not called the United Provinces, and here in the far north the Sikhs were in possession. The softish Muslim tribes of Hazara and the Kaghan valley had been ruthlessly down-trodden by the Sikhs, and the two martyrs had come north to fight the oppressors in the name of Islam, and to die in battle.

"Do you want to see the tombs?" Rehmat Khan asked me.

"Yes. Very well."

"You can see them already," he said hopefully, pointing across the river. A bosky, walled enclosure from which two little domes stuck up, white and calm, stood on a slope above a line of shacks. Rehmat Khan was standing in uncertainty beside me:

"Or perhaps, if you prefer . . . You see, there's a girl here. If you would prefer. Of course she's not a girl any more, she is a woman, and she has started a business. . . ." He laughed like a conspirator.

"Does she do a good business?"

"Not very. She is getting old for business, but sometimes . . . a few of us."

Rehmat Khan, so Shna had said, had spent a year or more in the looser, steamy atmosphere of the Indian plains. He had learnt how other peoples comport themselves and rather enjoyed the knowledge. Pakhtuns in their home country are a very continent people. But

82

it did not seem to me an altogether suitable way for one of Mir Badshah's guests to spend his first morning, so I said: "That business does not go very well with martyrs' tombs, I think," knowing that I was quite wrong, that places of pilgrimage and ancient monuments go very well indeed with the business—at least, anyone who moves around cannot fail to notice that the business thrives in such an emotional climate.

Rehmat Khan may have been disappointed: I don't know. If he was, he hid it. We walked on, over a rickety suspension-bridge with a date-plaque on it—some date round about the turn of the century, I seem to remember—and up towards the tombs. As we approached them and passed an open-fronted lodging, I caught sight of the White Wyandottes and their brood of scrabbling children and, in a moment, of their man bowing politely to us.

The tombs themselves were charming in their little way, but not very remarkable. We peered into them and Rehmat Khan muttered a prayer, his hands held supplicatingly before him, and I gave the guardian a coin. Then we put on our shoes again and left.

Tea in a tea-shop, and chatter with the proprietor who was a friend of Rehmat's. A pleasant half-hour, one way and another. We came back down the slope towards the bridge, wooden booths on both sides of us, with their displays of cheap cotton-goods and the like. Rehmat left me for a moment. He stood, his back towards me, in one of the booths and I could hear the murmur of conversation, a voice bored, a voice urgent, but I paid no particular attention. His expression was pensive when he rejoined me on the track and we started off again. I glanced back at the booth and caught sight of a pouting, young-man's face behind merchandise. Rehmat saw, and his eyes half closed with a sudden sly amusement.

I laughed and said: "Is he in business too, then?"

There was a pause. Then he said: "Now what do you think that I should do? He is a very bad boy, of course, but he is beautiful and it happens that I like him. But he says no."

"I should forget about it, then."

"Don't you think that he is beautiful?"

"I think he is quite nice-looking, but... I suppose it is all a matter of taste. ..."

"Do you think I should *make* him say yes?"

"No. I don't think so."

"What would *you* do?"

"I told you. I'd leave him alone."

"But what would you do if you wanted him?"

I thought for a moment. "It's outside my range," I said, as this seemed the best thing to say in the circumstances. "But if you want me to advise you, I would say I believe it would be better—and more respectable, though not much, I admit—to try the lady who will shortly be too old for business. She would also be cheaper, I dare say."

"Ah yes, much cheaper. Moreover the boy's father objects."

"In that case you have another good reason for forgetting about it."

"How can I forget when he has said no, and shamed me?"

"If he says yes, you will shame yourself."

"My heart is big enough to support a little shame."

"Let us talk about something else."

Rehmat Khan ignored this. He said: "The boy is beautiful, greedy and proud."

I suddenly remembered a line from a Pashto verse, and quoted it, rather pleased with myself. "'Be not vain of your beauty, though handsome as a flower.'"

"That boy is vain."

"Let us now talk about something else."

"And what else is there to talk about, please tell me?"

"We will talk about . . . about birds and flowers."

"I do not care about birds and flowers when these ideas are in my head. They have been there for two weeks or three weeks now, and they are a great burden to me."

*   *   *

One of the Mahsuds, lying back on his charpoy, said that their tribe was descended from Sikunder—which is what they call Alexander the Great—but another said that it was not the Mahsuds who came from Sikunder, but the Afridis: an Afridi had told him this. And then someone else (Rehmat Khan, I think) said no, the Afridi people were Jewish, but bigger and more splendid than the Jewish merchants who used to live in Peshawar before partition. To confuse the issue still further I said that there had been a historian called Herodotus and that modern Afghan historians claimed that the Afridis were the people whom Herodotus had called the Apariti—and that they were evidently not Jewish. Nor could they have been Greek, in that case, because Sikunder had not come to Afghanistan till a hundred and fifty years after Herodotus had written about the Apariti. They said "Oh . . ." and then Alam Jan came up and we asked him.

"I believe that the Mahsuds are descended from Mahmoud of Ghazni," he said.

Nobody chose to disagree, least of all myself. It might even be true. It certainly is true that some time in the ninth century A.D. a Turki slave under the Samanids who at that period controlled large slices of Afghanistan and Persia, took advantage of his masters' waning power to establish his own little dynasty in Ghazni. He had the slave-name Alptigin, and his son who succeeded him had another equally nice slave-name, Sabuktigin, and the third in succession was the great Mahmoud of Ghazni whose exploits are still part of Pakhtun village conversation. Mahmoud came through the mountains of Waziristan and annexed the Peshawar valley, and from there he carried out a dozen or more important attacks on India between the years 1001 and 1026. He does not seem to have been called a Pakhtun at the time, but it is said that Pakhtuns joined his forces, and also that he deliberately encouraged Pakhtun settlers in the mountains of Waziristan to act as a 'buffer' between his own countryside about Ghazni and the Indian sub-continent. If these settlers were the forerunners of the present-day Mahsuds, that would give the Mahsuds a Turki origin.

Alam Jan agreed that this might be so. "It would make the Mahsuds an Afghan people anyhow," he said.

"What are Afghans, then?" I said. This is something that everyone is ready to disagree about. Alam Jan gave me the standard answer.

"The 'true' Afghans are the Ghilzai and the Abdali."

"But some books say that the Abdali Afghans are the Beni Israel, and that they claim to have originated in Syria, and that Bukhtunasar[1] carried them into captivity to Persia and Media: and that later they

[1] Nebuchadnezzar.

85

came to the mountains of Ghor, up in the highlands between Herat and Ghazni."

"Very well. Why not?"

"There's no 'why not' about it. I only meant that if the Abdalis are Syrian in origin—or Persian, and certainly the present-day Abdalis that I have met look, and talk, and behave much more Persian than what I think of as Pakhtun—then they are basically different from the Ghilzai. Yet people say that the Abdalis and the Ghilzai are the 'true' Afghans."

"They are all wrong," someone said. "Because the Ghilzais come from Noah. I have many Ghilzai friends and this is what they have told me."

"Are the Ghilzai the same tribe that produced the Khilji Kings that ruled in Delhi in the thirteenth century?" I asked, rather stupidly of course, because none of the Mahsuds here would be likely to be interested in the question, except perhaps Alam Jan. But my head was filled with garbled bits of knowledge, and I was probably trying to clear the ground for myself as I went on: "Many people think that the word Khilji and the word Ghilzai are really the same—and that these people were originally a Turki tribe called Khalaj, or Khallakh, or even Qarluq, who were up in the Lake Issik Kul area, away, far beyond the Pamirs even, in the seventh or eighth centuries after Christ. Then they came down towards India. But there is a man called Raverty who was writing about a hundred years ago and he thought differently."

"Raverty? Raverty? This is a new name. . . ."

Alam Jan said: "Yes. I have heard of Raverty."

"I don't know anything about the kings and the centuries," another said.

"Neither do I," I admitted, "and all I know about Raverty is that everyone else who has written since he did about the Afghans and Pakhtuns, is frightened of disagreeing with him. Mad, isn't it? But one of the other writers has said: 'If the Ghilzai be not the Khilji, then what has happened to the Khilji?'"

It was now Shna's turn to laugh. He said: "All these great men are wrong. And *I* can tell you what happened to the Ghilzai. But it was a very long time ago. A stranger came to a tribe in the mountains, saying that he was a prince of a far land, but he wasn't—and it was too late then, because a woman of the tribe (whose father thought it would be nice to be grandfather of more princes) was ready to have a baby. Instead of killing the woman and the baby and the false prince in the ordinary way, they decided to pretend that the stranger was a true prince after all, and that the marriage had been a true marriage. 'Son of a thief,'[1] you see?"

[1] Pashto—*ghal*: thief; *zoe*: son.

Chapter 7

HOWEVER misty the origins of the Ghilzai and the Abdali Afghans, and whether you follow your ears in accepting the Khilji Kings of Delhi as Ghilzais or (scared off by Raverty) you reject their lead, there is no doubt at all that the Abdali Afghans produced a king in the full sense of the word. His name was Ahmed Khan, and he became great because he carried the seeds of greatness in him and because of an accident that changed the course of history. The victim of this particular accident was a Turkoman called Nadir Shah.

Nadir Shah the Turkoman had seized the Persian throne in the early eighteenth century. He then marched on the Indian Empire of the Moghuls and in 1739 took and looted the very seat of their majesty—Delhi. Almost in his stride he took Kabul, which had been no more than a remote northern province of the Moghul empire. He had too much on his hands in Persia to remain eating the fruits of his victory over the Moghuls, so he left them to hold both Delhi and Kabul in disconsolate fief to him, and set off on his return to Persia. He never reached Persia because of the accident of which I have spoken: he was assassinated on the way, and this is where Ahmed Khan's real story begins.

Ahmed Khan, an Abdali Afghan of the Sadozai branch—a Pakhtun, that is to say—had become a general under Nadir Shah the Turkoman. With the unexpected death of his overlord, Ahmed Khan took Kabul for himself and proceeded to found his own dynasty. He changed his name, substituting the Persian honorific 'Shah' (for King) for the Pakhtun honorific 'Khan', and added a Persian appellation that seems to have pleased him: 'Dur-ı-Durran'—the 'pearl of pearls'. By 1773, when the great Ahmed Shah 'Durrani' died, his successors inherited an empire which had spread from the little original core of Kabul till it claimed not only the whole of Afghanistan as we know it, but also the allegiance of Sind, Baluchistan, the Indus valley, Kashmir, and the Punjab as far south as Lahore. The fact that some forty years later his successors had lost everything again, except the little core of Kabul, does not alter the importance of Ahmed Shah 'Durrani's' personal achievement, nor the place it was later to hold in the national memory of the Afghan peoples themselves.

By 1823, what remained of the Durrani dynasty could survey what remained of their empire by standing on the fortifications of Kabul. If they looked a little farther afield they could note other changes than those in their personal fortunes. For example, the Moghul Indian empire, tottering already in the previous century, had now finally collapsed, and the British were consolidating their power in the sub-continent. Delhi had fallen to the British in 1803. The Punjab and the Indus valley around the Derajat and Peshawar was in Sikh hands now—annexed while pretenders to the Durrani succession had been poisoning and blinding and killing each other up in Afghanistan. In 1818 a Durrani called Mahmoud, who had been Amir for a moment, died to make way for new blood.

The new blood flowed in the veins of a collateral branch of the Durrani Afghans—that of the Baraksai, rather than of the Sadozai: and in 1826 the first of the big Barakzais came to the throne. His name was Dost Muhammed. He was destined to play an important rôle in years to come, but he had to fight and lose a war first, accept exile, and regain his throne.

The British, working northwards from Delhi, had been watching the shift of power in Afghanistan with keen interest, but to be honest they were even more keenly interested in the manœuvrings of their own real rivals for supremacy in Central Asia—the Russians. The Russians were at this time moving south across Turkestan towards the Oxus river, though they were still a long way off. Dost Muhammed's attention, however, was focused on something closer to hand than either the British or the Russians. He kept looking at the Derajat and the Peshawar valley—peopled by Pakhtuns, fertile, until recently part of the Durrani empire. He wanted Peshawar, both for his profit and for his emotional satisfaction. When the British approached him with the suggestion that he and they make a joint stand against the Russian menace in the north, Dost Muhammed agreed—and named his price. British assistance in expelling the Sikhs and in recovering the Indus Valley for him. The British had other ideas, however, and said no. So Dost Muhammed at once turned to the Russians and asked them to help instead—in return for his aligning Kabul with the Russians against the British.

The result was the First Afghan War (1838–1840). The British marched in, deposed the Amir Dost Muhammed, occupied Kabul and now held not only the strategically-vital line Kabul-Kandshar but also the equally important approaches to the Hindu Kush, that great east-west mountain-wall that cuts Afghanistan in two. In terms of good sense, if not of Human Rights, the Hindu Kush was the obvious northern frontier of the British East India Company's 'Empire', but the British withdrew from Afghanistan in 1842 (suffering an appalling little defeat in the process, as their depleted troops struggled through the Pass of Jagdalak towards India again), and the deposed Dost Muhammed was on the throne in Kabul once more. It looked as if things were much as they had been before the war, but there was in fact a difference. For example, Dost Muhammed was now Amir with British approval. During his exile in India he had learnt to respect the British for the same reasons that they now respected him—determination and toughness of fibre. There were other differences to be noted quite soon, too: the British proceeded to annexe Sind, and Quetta and much of Baluchistan, and, on the collapse of Sikh power, the northern Punjab and the Indus Valley as well. All these territories, now under the Union Jack, had formed part of Ahmed Shah Durrani's short-lived empire.

Twenty years later Dost Muhammed was dead. There was chaos in Afghanistan again and another Amir arose who showed signs of flirting with the Russians. So the British marched into the country to fight the Second Afghan War (1878–1880) and win it. The pattern of the first war and its aftermath almost exactly repeated itself, with the Amir deposed, Kabul and the approaches to the Hindu Kush occupied, followed by British withdrawal for the second time and a new strong-man on the Kabul throne with British approval. This was the great Amir Abdur Rahman. He too respected the British and the undertakings he gave them—amongst which was a new one: British control of his foreign policy, in return for an annual subvention. Dost Muhammed in his time, and Abdur Rahman in his, were tough, despotic and unpopular but, together with Ahmed Shah the first

Durrani, they are remembered with pride, and rightly, as the founders of the Kingdom of Afghanistan.

For all his toughness and determination the Amir Abdur Rahman never managed to control the Pakhtun borderlands of his kingdom. This did not prevent him from claiming all the Pakhtun tribes as his subjects, however, and he objected vociferously when in 1893 the British placed their rose-tinted spectacles on their noses and drew the Durand Line, saying that it was to demarcate the respective spheres of British and Afghan influence in tribal affairs.

The Amir said that the Durand Line cut tribes in two, which it certainly did: that the British would never exercise effective control over those they now claimed for themselves, which was half true: he insisted that he himself had the power to manage them all, which was untrue. He was no coward, but he was forced under duress to accept the Durand Line. The Pakhtun tribes concerned had to accept it too, but it did not take them long to realize that the wretched thing, so loved or loathed (according to whether you were Viceroy of India or Amir of Afghanistan), was only a line on a paper map, as far as they were concerned. They could ignore it if they pleased, and they did, or use it for playing off one High Contracting Party against the other, which they did too.

It must not be imagined, incidentally, that the Pakhtun tribes had been quietly grazing their flocks and attending to their meagre harvests during all these years that the Abdali Afghans were gaining power in Afghanistan as a sort of by-product of Anglo-Russian rivalries. Very much the reverse. There had been constant tribal risings ever since the British had reached the north-west frontiers, constant punitive expeditions, accompanied by a rhythmic alternation in British frontier policy, the pendulum swinging: *tic*—Forward Policy, into the very heart of the tribal areas with the flags flying; *toc*—back again to something prudently called the Close-Border Policy, the flags a little limper perhaps, and a vigilantly ineffective policing of the administrative border along the foothills; then—*tic*—back again to the Forward Policy—*toc*—back again to the Close Border. . . . No wonder everyone got confused—except the Pakhtuns to whom muddle-headedness and movements of troops were meat and drink, and to whom death (their own or that of their enemies) had always seemed the natural companion of life.

The Amir Abdur Rahman died in 1901 and was succeeded by his

son Habibullah who, like his father, respected the British for their strength, and for the same reason respected his agreements with them. He could perfectly well have taken advantage of Britain's preoccupation with the Kaiser War in Europe, but he did not. So it seemed reasonable to him to demand of the British that his neutrality be rewarded by bringing up the question of Afghanistan's final and complete independence. He was assassinated in 1919.

His third son, Amanullah Khan, who then succeeded to the throne, was a different kind of man. He saw at once that the widespread anti-British disturbances that at that time threatened to paralyse administration in India, particularly in the Punjab and north-west border country, might be his opportunity. He appeared, rattling his sabre, near the Khyber Pass. It was a fine, schoolboy gesture, but it was based on a somewhat faulty appreciation of the facts. He seems to have expected that the Pakhtun tribes would rally to him as their leader and rise against the British, and no doubt Indian 'non-violent' nationalists had given him an exaggerated picture of what they were capable of achieving at that stage. The Pakhtun tribes did not rise—yet.[1] The Afghan armies were soundly smacked for their pains and the Third Afghan War was over within a matter of weeks—but not without one short-term and spectacular victory for Afghan arms. A Muhammedzai general, related collaterally to the Amir Amanullah Khan, swept over the Durand Line from Khost in the Southern Province of Afghanistan, took and occupied the British fort at Thal in Kurram. This man was General Nadir Khan, and he was destined to become King of Afghanistan in due course. Nadir Khan knew about the British, but for the moment Amanullah Khan was Amir and Amanullah must perhaps be forgiven for failing to understand because, although he had been rather ignominiously defeated, the Peace Treaty that was presented for his signature in due course suggested nothing of the kind. The principal effect of the Peace Treaty was in fact the granting of complete independence to Afghanistan, in external as in internal affairs. It was quite natural that King Amanullah should seem to himself, as to his peoples,

---

[1] They did so, one after the other, and without cohesion, very shortly, but the Third Afghan War was over by then, and the British were able to deal with each of the tribes in turn.

not only victor in a lightning war, but also great architect of Afghan independence, and of the new modernized state he dreamed about.

King Amanullah Khan set to work with a will.

Palaces, with strips of metalled roadway up to their splendid porticoes; central-heating plants, looking rather rusty and sad, now that they have lain for some thirty years and more awaiting assembly; consignments of bowler hats for the heads of tribal chieftains whose thumbmarks would be required to ratify the royal decisions in parliament; education for women and the rending of their veils of slavery—all these fine modernities! Amanullah worked with a will. A little too fast, perhaps. In 1924 the Pakhtun tribes of Khost in the Southern Province rose in rebellion and had to be appeased with concessions: the most daring of the innovations were cancelled. But directly that had quietened down, he pressed forward again, and by the end of 1927 he was ready to make a Royal Progress of Europe and the Middle East.

The Royal Progress started with a little hitch—nothing very much, but a symbol of something, perhaps. The British had provided a royal train to carry the King from the Afghan borders south of Kandahar, through Quetta to Karachi to take ship for the west. As the train passed through the long Khojak tunnel, His Majesty pulled the communication chain in the belief that he was flushing the royal lavatory-pan. The train stopped just where the engineers hated the idea of trains stopping—in the middle of a black, smoke-filled tunnel, on a dangerously steep incline. No harm came of this little incident, but it was embarrassing, and not something that should be talked about. The rest of the tour, however, was triumphant. The King and the Queen and their suite of courtiers returned in 1928 to Kabul with their heads whirling, and their trunks full of all sorts of exciting novelties to try out on their subjects. Their subjects were sullen, because it must be said that the Pakhtuns who constituted so important an element in the country and whose goodwill was essential to any Afghan ruler, were already sick of modernities before they had had a chance to know what they really portended. In their obstinacy they particularly disliked bowler hats and educated ladies. The situation was in fact dangerous. King Amanullah did not realize until too late that it was already too late. . . .

In the winter of 1928–1929 the Pakhtun tribes rose once more against the poor King. Wakened from his dream of a magical transformation scene in which the centuries would telescope themselves and Afghanistan would emerge as a model state, he was forced to flee. Strangely enough it was not a Pakhtun at all who actually seized the throne, but rather a common person, a small-time Tajik bandit whom people called Bachha-i-Saqao—son of the water-carrier. Bachha-i-Saqao assumed the crown and called himself Ghazi Habibullah. Heads got lopped off a good deal at this period, and quite a number of Afghans whom you may meet in Kabul today are fatherless because Bachha-i-Saqao blew their fathers from the cannon's mouth. The people may not have cared much for what Amanullah had been trying to do with such desperate good intention, but they cared still less for Bachha-i-Saqao, and it was remarkable that he managed to hold on to the throne for nine months.

By the autumn of 1929, Nadir Khan, the general who had so distinguished himself against the British in the Afghan War of 1919, was on his way back from Europe where he and his brothers had been living because Amanullah had feared their influence at home. Nadir Khan raised the Wazirs and the Mahsuds of the British side of the Durand Line and marched at their head on Kabul. Kabul fell to him, Bachha-i-Saqao was put to flight (and subsequently to death in a necessarily barbaric public execution) and, in default of money with which to pay his Pakhtun hordes, Nadir Khan was compelled to let them loot the city instead.

The Wazirs and the Mahsuds looted Kabul with enthusiasm, and returned to their mountains with a splendid new conviction—that king-making for others was even more profitable than teasing the British. They still saw no reason to consider accepting a king over themselves, naturally.

King Nadir Shah—the Pakhtun honorific 'Khan' had been changed to the Persian honorific 'Shah' for 'King'—was on the throne in Kabul. Together with his brothers, amongst whom he distributed the important state appointments, he ruled for four years with the sort of ruthless wisdom that was still necessary in Afghanistan, and was then assassinated. He was succeeded by his son, King Zahir Shah, who still rules today.

After World War II, when it suddenly became evident that the British really did intend to relinquish dominion over their Indian

Empire instead of being content to talk about it, the Royal Afghan Government laid formal claim to be inheritors of certain territories that had formed part of the Durrani Afghan Empire a hundred and fifty years before. The claim included, of course, Pakhtun country and the Vale of Peshawar, but the British said no.

Chapter 8

A PRIM little row of chairs had been set up, fronting a plot that could have been intended for a parade ground, though I never saw a parade. We had fed early that evening. It was quite dark, and up in the mountains the green phosphorescence of nightfall had gone. The sky was black and swimming, but in the encampment itself torches moved. I asked Alam Jan what the chairs were for and he nodded towards Wadi Khan, the subedar-major. Wadi Khan swallowed once or twice, glanced towards me and back to Alam Jan and then said—apparently to me, but not looking in my direction: "I think you will like to see the *jawanān* dance. I have told them."

Was Wadi Khan so shy? This was the first sentence he had addressed to me since I had arrived in the camp.

The word *jawān* means 'young man' and, in the plural *jawanān*, it is loosely used to cover the rank and file of any service unit: 'the boys', as you might say in English, and in Pashto as in English the term has no particular reference to youngness.

"Wadi Khan asked me if you would like the dancing," Alam Jan whispered, "and I said that he must ask you himself." He was smiling, like a young father proud of his middle-aged son's progress. "But I suppose in the end he didn't ask you. He just arranged it. Do you like dancing?"

I had been given a handbook about the North-West Frontier Province and its peoples by someone in the publicity department. It was a useful booklet, practical and informative, and I had read in it, under the heading 'Dances', that '. . . the Pathans look upon dancing with a mild contempt, yet . . .' (it continued, half-proud, half-apologetic), 'the Khattak dance, amongst others, has gained world-wide fame'.

It seemed to me that the handbook had entirely missed the point. The point, oddly enough, is closely linked with the question of hair.

A note on dancing

Amongst the Pakhtuns only those tribes dance who traditionally wear the *tsanray*. The *tsanray* is the bobbed-hair style, cut clean up to about the level of the ear-lobes but thick and shining above that, parted in the middle and kept in place as a rule with a couple of biggish wooden combs. There are variations, of course, but the tribal Pakhtun alternative to wearing the *tsanray* is to shave the head clean. You begin to see tribal Pakhtuns these days wearing their hair cut in the European manner, but that is a different thing. The point is that only those tribes who traditionally wear the *tsanray* dance. The shaven-heads don't dance, but they much enjoy it as a spectacle, making certain inferior elements in their society dance for them, such people as their barbers, for instance—or their *dams* and *lakhtais*, whose side-professions are sometimes equivocal. It is hard to determine which is chicken and which egg. Do the shaven-heads refuse to dance because they consider it improper? Or do they not dance because their *dams* and *lakhtais*, being vaguely improper themselves, are given to dancing? Certainly for the shaven-heads dancing is inextricably mixed up with what men are inclined to do and not talk about.

It happens that none of the major tribes I am calling Pathan for the purposes of my narrative wear the *tsanray*.[1] Thus the writer of the handbook would be right in saying that Pathans are mildly contemptuous of dancing, if he accepted my terminology: but I imagine he uses Pathan to cover all Pakhtuns and, if so, then he is altogether mistaken. The *tsanray*-wearers, such as the Mahsuds, the Wazirs, the Suleiman Khel Ghilzais and others, are probably the toughest Pakhtuns that exist, and the shaven-heads are not silly enough to brand them as contemptible for their dancing, whatever they might feel about themselves if they chose to dance.

Anyway, there it is. Mahsuds wear the *tsanray* and they dance. It is a ritual in which even the audience must participate, with all the senses keen. This is something quite unsuited to a formal stage with

[1] I don't know whether to call the Khattak tribe Pathan or Pakhtun. They are mountain people for the most part: but their territory is encircled by the administered districts and they have consequently been penetrated and 'tamed'. Some of their tribal sections wear the *tsanray*, and dance. They have for years been recruited into the regular army—proof in itself that they have been satisfactorily 'tamed', and their dancing must have been seen in many quarters of the globe.

proscenium and backcloth: there has to be the closeness, the tang of sweat, the sound, the feel of earth reverberating, dust tingling in the back of the nostrils, feet bare, and the calms when the mind closes. 'By the snorting chargers, And those who strike fire with their hoofs, And those who make incursions in the morning, And raise up the dust therein, And cleave through a host therein!' It is a dance for battle, as the hundredth chapter of the Qoran from which I have quoted is for battle. The Pakhtuns dance it in the mountains before the attack and the sound is carried across the valleys in the still, dark air, horrible and exalting. They dance it in peace-time too, for the elation it brings—but why, oh why that wretched row of chairs?

I wanted to have the chairs taken away, but Wadi Khan had placed them there to please us and there was nothing I could do about it.

No one is specially dressed. They all wear their ordinary workaday clothes, ballooning trousers closing in round the ankles, a long shirt, and those that have one wind a coloured scarf round their waists or round their necks. Their heads and feet are bare. You can see clumps of sandals and unwound turbans lying about.

It starts in a smallish circle, with the dhol-player in the centre. The dhol is a two-faced drum, slung on a cord round the shoulders. Some tribes, such as the Khattak, include one or two surnai-players as well, shrill reedy surnais that skirl like the Scottish pipes. But Mahsuds dance to the dhol alone.

Men come through the fluttering darkness to join the circle, a few at a time. Others have lagged behind. For some minutes the slow round-movement is no more than preparation for what is coming, much as a Flamenco singer tries out his voice, clearing his mind and his throat before he launches into his song. It takes a little time to get going. The dancers move back and forth over the perimeter of a dusty imagined circle, forward a pace, back two, forward again and a half-pace to the right, anti-clockwise along the circumference. After a while, though there is no seen signal for it, their arms rise limply on the forward pace, the hands dropping loose on the wrists as they sketch a languid little gesture in the air. Soon a double hand-clap is added, and the tempo of the dhol increases. More men have joined. A double step forward, four back, two forward, still un-disciplined, the edges still blurred, though there is a feeling of some communal elation that may be stirring underneath. It is not quite

yet that the head comes into play but, in time, and almost impercept-
ibly at first, you will see that the head droops forward on the advancing
step, that the *tsanray* hangs in a long, slack fringe hiding the face and,
as the tide turns again, it flicks in a quick, sudden, circular motion,
stands out momentarily, a wheel of silk, and then flops back neatly
against the head.

Alam Jan had joined them: a man had come and dragged him in.
They tried to make me join too, and I would have gone if I had not
been afraid of acquitting myself too clumsily—as if anyone cared,
except me sitting there watching on that silly seat.

It is much faster now, and there might be forty dancers, or fifty—it is
difficult to know how many though there seem to be more dancers
then men watching: and if you were a night-bird above them the
shape would be an expanding contracting kinetic circle, chevron-
edged, a cog with as many sharp teeth as there may be dancers. A
discipline has imposed itself from somewhere, from the dhol perhaps,
the sort of natural discipline that harnesses the water at a river bend.
The tempo quickens, the chevron movements are now marked by a
sudden twist of each body, right-left-right, each man spinning on
his own axis, spin, stop, spin, stop, spin, the head following the vertical
of the body a fraction of a second behind time so that the semblance
of even greater speed is given to it. There is dust everywhere, dust,
and flares flickering, and eyes that alternate between a blaze and a
filmy trance, generating their own heat and their own elation.

I was alone now, except for Nek Bibi whose eyes shone and whose
hand gripped my knee. She was so small and young that she didn't
count as a woman, and no one took any notice of her.

A spin and a sudden squat on to the hunkers with the pose held for
a second, then up again to another spin, the *tsanrays* spinning like wheels,
and always the same unhurried turning of the larger circle. The
dhol-player has reached the limit of his speed, whirling in the middle
of it, and then without warning it dissolves, as if the current that
animates each man, the centrifugal force that holds him rigidly in
space, had been switched off.

When the dhol starts again it is for a different movement. Groups
of four or five dancers detach themselves and perform one of the many
variations—backward, flowing motions, flippety and elegant, corn-
stalks under the breeze, not men at all. It is strange and moving and
you forget that these are peasants as violent as any you can find in the

world. They must have faces and separate identities, I suppose, but they seem to have neither—till suddenly I recognized Shna, because he winked with deliberate vulgarity to make me laugh.

It stopped as it had began, formlessly. They had danced for more than an hour. Wadi Khan had pushed someone towards me and I had an impression of food and tea-pots. Then we all squatted round and made rather unsatisfactory conversation.

*   *   *

Time passed under a sun that came up golden and had worked itself into the white heat of passion by midday. Yet there was a consolation: Peshawar, a hundred and twenty miles away in the plains would be infinitely worse. In actual fact the heat did not greatly trouble us, there in the Kaghan valley down-river from Balakot. The men broke off from their road-making at ten or so, and we slept unrepentantly through the worst of the day, arranging our lives around the hours of dawn, and again around the hours of dusk and the night that followed it. There were soft-boiled eggs at sun-up, the teeth crunching dutifully on triangles of overlooked egg-shell, there were visitors from Waziristan, conversation, strolls with no purpose except as an accompaniment to the passage of hours, there was time off to tease Nek Bibi and as long again to placate her. There were Wadi Khan, and Rap Khan, and Shna and Rehmat Khan and many others, and quite often the mullah with the berry-beads of his rosary. I had taken to wearing a pair of Moorish *sarwal*, which are baggy trousers fastening below the knee, and a shirt. It seemed to suit the company better than English clothes. I was a lot with Alam Jan and Shahzada Khan the Afridi, and grew to like them very much indeed. Major Mir Badshah had not come back, nor had we any news of him. I gathered that he was being treated by a doctor in Abbottabad. Within a few days now Alam Jan would have to return to a new term at the Military Academy.

It was time for me to move on too. A message had come through from Peshawar to say that my application for an Afghan visa had been granted. I was surprised at this, but pleased. Afghan-Pakistan relations were not at their happiest, and my known association with Pakistan was an unhelpful factor. It was weeks since I had filled in and presented my visa application form at the Royal Afghan Consulate in Karachi, and it had begun to seem as if they planned to turn it down, either with a categoric 'no' or, more probably, by giving no reply at all.

I told Alam Jan that my visa had been granted but he, with no experience yet of the suspicions that attend the crossing of frontiers, appeared to think this perfectly normal.

"We don't need visas, or whatever they are," he commented, meaning the Mahsuds, of course. "We just walk over the border."

Of course. Mahsuds just walk over the border. Actually they have no common boundary with Afghanistan themselves—to go into Afghanistan for them involves passing through Wazir country, but it comes to the same thing. They, and the important Pakhtun tribes whose boundaries run with those of Afghanistan, go and come as they please. There is nothing to stop them, there are Pakhtuns on both sides of the frontier, and Pakhtunwali with its food, protection and shelter. It isn't that the governments of Pakistan and Afghanistan prefer it this way, but because there are really no means of preventing it, short of establishing control posts that would be laughable nonsense.

"Yes, it's convenient for you, Alam Jan. In fact the Durand Line is a great and wonderful blessing for the Pakhtuns who live this side of it."

"I've never been in Afghanistan," he said.

There was no reason for him to go. Mir Badshah's family fortunes have been linked for years with the British, and are now linked with Pakistan.

"Neither have I," I said. "This will be my first visit."

"*Insha' Allah.*"

"Yes. *Insha' Allah.*"

Shna and his friend Rehmat Khan came to help me pack my bags. I had scarcely opened up anything, so it could have been quickly done —and it would have been quickly done if they had not wanted to see what clothes remained hidden in my suit-case. When it came to the point it was more an unpacking than a packing. I had two sorts of clothes with me: on the one hand, rough, hard-wearing things for travel, and, on the other, necessary but silly-looking as Shna spread them out for the examination, a dinner-suit with its black etceteras— socks, patent-leather shoes, bow tie, a gaberdine suit (which had failed to fascinate Fateh in Peshawar but would, I still hoped, appear summertime cocktail-party smart in Kabul), and finally a dark grey formal suit of which Shna was now struggling into the coat. Bobbed hair did not go well with London tailoring, but I didn't say so because Shna rather liked the idea and asked for my shaving-mirror so that he could see properly. I hadn't got one so he had to borrow a little round tin that Rehmat Khan kept his *naswar*[1] for chewing in: it had a piece of mirror in the lid.

"Hm-m..." he commented, inclining his head to one side. "And now those pretty shoes, please—but how do you take the wooden pieces out?"

I said: "No. Not the shoes, I think." Shna's feet were wide and splayed with years of life in the mountains. "But you can have this, if you like. For dancing. I give it to you as a present." I held out an old silk square.

Shna said nothing for a moment. Then: "Blue, green, red."

"Is it from your country?" Rehmat Khan demanded, greed glinting in his eyes.

I said yes, it was.

Shna knotted it round his neck, loosely, so that a corner of it covered his shoulder. "How much money did it cost?"

I made a quick inaccurate calculation from sterling to rupees and said: "Twenty rupees."

"Ah-h..."

"Now, take the coat off, and we must pack everything up again. And perhaps Rehmat Khan would like *this*." I had emptied an imitation-leather wallet. It had air-mail wings embossed goldily on top. He seemed rather pleased.

"Shall I come with you to Kabul?" Rehmat Khan asked, opening and closing the wallet.

"No. I don't think so."

"Yes. It will be nice to come. I speak Persian."

"He doesn't," Shna said. "But he has a cousin-brother in Kabul."

I laughed and said: "And I expect he's got another cousin-brother who's in the khassadars,[2] and perhaps an uncle who's a malik getting an allowance from the Pakistanis, and a ..."

"... another cousin-brother who's an outlaw," put in Shna, digging Rehmat in the ribs delightedly.

[1] A mixture resembling tobacco.

[2] Irregular levies, operating in the tribal regions under the political authority.

"That's convenient," I said. "And after all he's in the Mahsud battalion himself."

"Yes, I'm a soldier," Rehmat agreed. "So you see that all the family is working one way or another."

"All ways at once, it seems to me. Very nice for the family."

"Yes. Very nice. And of course the cousin-brother in Kabul is hoping, too."

"What is he hoping for?" I asked. "For an allowance from the Afghans?" This would complete the traditional spreading of tribal eggs amongst the various baskets available.

"Well, I don't know. Perhaps he won't get a proper allowance from the Afghans. But they will probably give him a Pashtunistan flag to put on his watch-tower when he comes back to his village."

I had forgotten for the moment about Pashtunistan and the Pashtunistan flags. But however little I knew, now that the subject had cropped up again, I could at least understand the principle on which a Pakhtun accepts anyone's money in advance in order to do (or not to do) something that he will reserve the right to make his own decisions about.

"Of course," I said. "That's a new business for Pakhtuns, isn't it? Is it paying?"

"Not very," Rehmat admitted. "But it's better than nothing, till you can get an allowance out of them. Well, we'll see. And my cousin-brother who is an outlaw is complaining about business, too. Before, it was all right: in the days of the British. With all those troops in Waziristan, a man had at least a chance to steal a rifle, or something, and then there was work too, collecting wood and so on for the contractors who supplied the troops. Oh yes, I know all about that. And then shooting at British officers, and sometimes kidnapping them, you know. But now, with the Pakistanis—after all, they *are* Muslims. It is not quite right, you see, to shoot Muslims, unless they are your enemies. It's a pity the British have gone, in some ways, even if there's this new business of the Pashtunistan flags."

"What *is* Pashtunistan?" I asked them.

"Don't you know?" Rehmat Khan started to laugh. "It's what my cousin-brother is expecting to get flag-money from! He's a married man, and his wife is expecting a baby."

"I don't think it's right," Shna said. "Why doesn't your cousin-brother ask the Pakistanis for a Pakistan flag instead? It would be rude, I think, to have a Pashtunistan flag. It would certainly be much better to ask the Political Agents to give some money for not taking money from the Afghan Government for having a Pashtunistan flag. Don't you think so, Peter sahib?"

"I find it very complicated," I said. "I wish you would tell me about Pashtunistan, though."

"Oh me, aren't you going to Kabul yourself? Ask them in Kabul about it! I really can't tell you. I'm just an ordinary Mahsud and how can I know all these things? But we are having many new schools now in our villages, and I suppose the children will be learning all manner of new things."

"Then you think we should not take these flags?" Rehmat demanded. "You think the Pakistanis would mind?"

"I think it would be impolite—and remember also about the Faqir of Ipi and the flags too."

I remembered about the Faqir of Ipi very well—though not about any flags in connection with him. He had been a fanatic—fanatically anti-British, fanatically Muslim—and had waged a constant, and rather successful guerrilla war against the British for years before partition. He had made his headquarters in a series of caves near the Durand Line. He suffered from asthma.

"But I thought the poor old thing was finished by now," I commented.

"Well yes, I suppose so—but he did try with the flags. He offered all sorts of people, mostly Wazirs like himself, but some Mahsuds too, I am told, these flags, and said he would pay two hundred rupees each month to the people who let them fly in the wind over their towers. But when the end of the first month come, he said that the money had not yet arrived, and he was unable to pay."

"What a pity!" I said.

Shna was examining his scarf again. "Did you say that the scarf cost twenty rupees, Peter sahib, or thirty?"

"I said twenty."

"And the little case with the golden bird on it? How much was that?"

"That was free," I admitted. "From the company who sold me tickets for the aeroplane to come to Karachi."

Shna laughed at Rehmat Khan when he heard this, and Rehmat quoted a Pashto proverb, reprovingly:

"'Even if it be no more than an onion, give it with grace.' Peter sahib has given it to me with grace and you will perhaps have noticed that the colours of your scarf have become faded a little."

"You have closed and locked the suit-case, and I now see that the pretty black shoes have somehow been left under the bed, Shna," I said, reproving in my turn.

"I will certainly come with you to Kabul," Rehmat said, spitting on one of the shoes and polishing it with his sleeve. "And you will never have reason to complain about me. What pay did you say that you would give me?"

"As I am unable to pay you, I will give you permission to loot the city instead."

"Do you think that the Amir Amanullah will return and let the Mahsuds loot Kabul, if we help him to be king again?" Rehmat asked thoughtfully.

Chapter 9

I REMEMBER very clearly from my childhood that my mother wore a particular expression when she had tasks to do that she didn't care about. As children we had called this a 'distasteful face', and I think I must have worn such an expression during the two or three days I had to spend in Peshawar before setting off for Kabul.

Not that Peshawar could ever be really distasteful to me—very much the reverse—but I struck it this time during a period of heat-wave. A straight Fahrenheit reading of well above 115 degrees in the shade is something to shutter your eyes and your house against. I went about in a sort of trance. Everyone else was in much the same condition. so it is understandable that nothing really got done at all.

I was staying in the club on this visit. I did so for reasons of nostalgia, I suspect, and was allotted a little kennel of a room for my pains.

"Can't you give me a proper quarter?" I asked the clerk.

"All those are taken."

"But the place looks empty, empty . . . !"

"The proper quarters are full. Perhaps it is that no one comes out once he gets in."

So I had to be content with a little kennel-like room for members in transit. It had a skylight, impossible to curtain, through which the sun struck white on the white walls, and there was a bed, and an enormous fireplace spread across one corner. There was a split-cane door-screen, hanging in the entrance in such a way that the only means of getting by, so narrow was the room, was to push the screen forwards and up, to walk under its upheld length (which meant walking two-thirds of the way down the room, past the bed) and then let the screen fall back into position behind you. Then you could come back into the middle of the room again yourself. There was a padlock on the door, fashioned in two separate parts: when you turned the key the works of the padlock fell to the ground, and a horseshoe-shaped section remained hooked in the ring. There was a feeling of madness about the room.

I lay sweating there on the afternoon of my arrival from Balakot, and a table-fan roared and whirred and blew the white-hot sunlight on to my body. I got a towel and wetted it and spread it across my face, and was delighted to find how pleasant this cool contrast could be. It was as if my face were the real me, and my body some other person to be pitied and forgotten. But the pleasure palled with evaporation, and after a while I went to the bathroom and lay flat in a big bath-tub, with the shower playing on me. This was more lastingly agreeable than anything I had been able to devise in my room. A servant found me in the bath after a while, and said that I had a visitor.

The visitor was Fateh. I returned to my room to find him standing in front of the table-fan with his shirt-tails held up to his chin, cooling his stomach (the shirt is, of course, always worn outside the *partug*). He said he wasn't working that day—perhaps it was a Sunday. He had heard that I was back again and had thought I would like him to sit under the fan and talk to me. But now he saw that there wasn't a proper ceiling-*punkah*, only a table-fan that roared and rattled like a taxi. I told him to find a servant and order some tea for both of us while I put some clothes on.

Tea came—but in heat of that order, tea tastes of nothing but heat itself, and our conversation drooped. Fateh said that he had had no news of Sadiq, brother of the murdered Gul Khan.

"Please don't stop trying," I said.

"How long are you staying?"

"Two or three days. I have a few things to do, but I want to go as quick as I can. I'm going to Kabul. But I shall be back again."

"Ah-h . . . Kabul." He looked pensive. Then he said: "Do you remember Fulana Khan?" and I asked if he meant a man we had both known rather well years before, and he replied that this was in fact the man.

"I saw him yesterday," Fateh said. "He is in Peshawar, busy trying to arrange something."

"What is he arranging?"

Fulana Khan had seldom come to Peshawar in the past. He lived a two-day journey away, in tribal territory. Fateh picked a currant·

out of a piece of cake and ate it deliberately. Then he looked up into my face—he was sitting on the floor, because he does not like chairs: I was on the bed—and he seemed to be trying to judge what my reactions might be if he told me more. Perhaps he decided that they would not be favourable. Anyway he looked down at the cake again, and started to eat it.

"What is he arranging then?" I asked once more.

"I don't really know exactly. He didn't say, exactly, but—you see, I think he is unable to arrange it. He made me promise to ask you if . . . But never mind."

I was not at all sure whether this manœuvring meant that Fateh wished me to compel him to tell me, or that he genuinely did not want to pass on Fulana Khan's message. He sat moodily for a few seconds and I left the initiative to him. Finally he pushed back his *khulla* and *loongi*—it is proper for the head to remain respectfully covered in the ordinary way—and scratched his shaven scalp, saying suddenly to the white walls: "You do not know any hospital nurse here in Peshawar, I suppose?"

Hospital nurse? I must have known hospital nurses here in the past, but now, on my first visit for so many years . . . No, I certainly did not know one. I told Fateh so.

"Then it is a pity." He looked nervously up at me again. "I do not quite know what Fulana Khan wants from a hospital nurse. Perhaps it is something bad. But he made me promise and I have now carried out my promise."

"You mean you promised to ask me if I knew a nurse, and now that I have answered 'no', your duty has been completed?"

"*My* duty has been completed, but Fulana Khan's trouble is only starting, I think."

"You had better tell Fulana to come and see me," I said.

*　　　　*　　　　*

My mind remains rather a blank on the subject of those two or three days. Heat, of course: appalling heat, tarred roads melting, horses with their heads hung to their knees, dogs with dry tongues, men glazed and distraught. I know that I collected my Afghan visa from an Afghan official who was kind, but gasping for air, as I was: and I remember a map of Pashtunistan hanging above his desk and that I lacked the energy to ask him about it. I borrowed a copy of the works of the poet Khushal Khan, Khattak, in Pashto, with an introduction and some *vers libre* renderings into English: this was from the University library, and I carried the book away in the knowledge that later, when I returned to something nearer normal, the dehydrated pleasure of my find would open up like a Japanese flower in a tooth-glass. It is useless to try to think rationally in such a climate. I believe that when, the day before I left, Fulana Khan came round to see me, I was not even shocked by what he had to ask of me, though I subsequently felt that I ought to have been.

Briefly, Fulana Khan—who is a tribal-area Pakhtun I do not intend to identify;[1] even the name I have chosen means no more than So-and-So Khan—had fallen in love with a girl in the next village. He had seen her working, or fetching water, and he had yearned for her. Finally he had slept with her, because she seems to have returned his love, and now she was going to have a baby. Fulana Khan was in great distress. No doubt the poor girl was too. He thought that if I knew a hospital nurse, I could find out from her how to produce an abortion. Amongst a people by instinct and social custom so continent, 'affairs' of this kind are rare (except amongst those whom contact with city life has changed). Illegitimacy is as nearly unknown as rape. Practically the only extra-marital relations are homosexual, and even there the rules of decorum must be observed. Fulana Khan was not concerned with the ethical aspects of abortion, and presumably he saw no reason why I should be either: but he was very much concerned with the outcome of his bastard baby's birth.

"They will have to kill us both—and, of course, the baby," he said. "Some tribes kill only the woman, and cut off the man's foot, perhaps. But with us—well, we kill them all. So you see . . ."

"I see. You thought that if the baby were not even born . . ."

"Yes."

"I don't know about these things," I told him. I was on the point of adding that even if I had known about them I would not have told him, but I am glad I resisted the self-righteous urge to say this. Instead I asked: "When will the baby be born?"

"In about six months—but they will kill her first."

"So she is growing big already. She is not married, is she?"

---

[1] I need not have worried. Fulana Khan is dead now.

"Not married. She can't hide the bigness much longer. What shall we do?"

"Why do you ask me, Fulana Khan?"

"I have to ask somebody. I hoped you might know someone who would know. We thought that *Ferangis*[1] knew such things."

"Did you tell Fateh Khan all this?"

"No. But perhaps he has guessed. I don't know what to do. I am very troubled."

"Troubled for yourself?"

"Myself? Oh yes, I suppose so—but it would be easy for me. I could go away—Karachi, Lahore . . . If I went to Karachi, could you perhaps help me to . . ." And then he suddenly stopped. "But that girl," he went on.

"Can you take her away from the village?"

He hung his head for a moment and then swung round with a sigh that came from deep inside him. "Do you know, Peter sahib, it took only one little hour to sleep with her: only one little hour, less perhaps—and that was difficult enough, and dangerous enough. But we were mad, you see. To get her away from the village would take two days. You know what it is like in our valleys. Everybody would recognize me, everyone knows that I am unmarried. None of my friends would help me. How could she come away with me? I don't know what to do now."

"If you stay in your village, they will know soon—and they will kill the girl in any case."

"Yes. They will kill her even if they never know it was me."

What could I say to him? I said: "I can't help you, even with advice, but I think that you should try to save . . ."

He interrupted me with his hand and was silent for a short moment. Finally without emotion, he said: "Yes, I think I will try to . . ." But he didn't finish the sentence either, and I didn't ask him what he would try to do.

*　　　　　*　　　　　*

At best Peshawar to Kabul is some twelve hours too long. I have not myself experienced the worst, but I suppose it would be not to

[1] Foreigners.

arrive at all. Whatever the case, the journey is merciless and a morti-
fication of the flesh.

If there were no pretence at a road at all and if you were to set out
with a camel-caravan in the pious expectation of reaching the goal
more than a week later, *Insha' Allah*, the mind would adjust itself more
contentedly to the truth. A caravan is an agreeable thing in itself,
unhurried, rhythmic. I'm uncertain if I care about camels personally,
yet how gentle is the placing of their woolly Bactrian feet, how round
and spreading the feet themselves, like two-toed boxing-gloves!
How silent the dust as it splutters up under them! I like the sway of
saddle-bags, and the men and women and the long swing of their
garments. The bigger children walk with the caravan, the smaller
are carried, or else they ride high on camel-back along with the
chickens, and with the lambs in the lambing season, swinging and
swaying and watching the heavens as they wheel overhead. It is
locally believed probable that blue eyes result from watching the
heavens in this way. The mountains and the deep defiles pass by at
leisure. Dogs like heavy bristling wolves lope alongside with their
lips curled back and their hackles up, growling in their throats when
they meet strangers. The voices of the men are softer and quieter
than you would expect. The women are often beautiful and always
unveiled, but if they look at strangers at all, they harden their expression
so that the stranger shall know that his charms have left them unmoved. Everything that can possibly be needed is there, from
cooking-pots to tents of coarse, black goat-hair, and a lunatic but
entirely efficient system of poles and cordage that supports them.
Water is a problem, but there are springs here and there: and at intervals there will be a crazy tea-shop, hung like a shrine with offerings—
votive tea-pots, or trays, brass. People talk as they stride along, or
remain silent, sometimes listening, or even answering, and sometimes
just letting the sounds pass through their heads unheeded. If you
were travelling with a caravan I think you would approach the journey
with a proper feeling for the truth. But a motor-car . . . A car is
the wrong kind of magic hereabouts, the kind that does not quite
work.

I travelled by car, and rather a grand one at that. It was an elegant
station-wagon belonging to the French Embassy in Kabul. It had
come to the Peshawar rail-head with some guest, or possibly some
French official who was travelling to Karachi, and it was returning to

Kabul filled with flags and tricolour pennants for the Embassy's Fourteenth of July celebrations. They had been kind enough to say that I might travel in it. No: this is not quite correct: I should say, rather, that when they learnt later that I had done so at the invitation of their driver (a Pathan I already knew) they smiled with French good manners and said how pleased they were that I had taken advantage of the empty seat.

The driver drove with brilliance, but no virtuosity could make of those twelve mechanic hours an experience that was other than hateful —a sullen hate, not the keen, glittering hate that everyone enjoys.

Yet there are compensations—such as the sudden emergence of the Hindu Kush, sprawled like a snow-leopard all over the north: or looking southwards, when you have passed Dakka and look back across a plain strewn with boulders and discover that the horizon has been blocked by a wall of mountain seen against the sun, so that only the skyline has shape, and below it hangs an opaque veil, without definition. It is the Sufed Koh—the White Peaks beyond which the Afridis live their hawk-like lives. Sometimes the driver would draw up at a tea-shop on the outskirts of a hamlet, and we would get out, stretching ourselves, at each stop more silent. Green tea, bread shaped like snow-shoes and as big, with a diaper-patterning of little holes in it. Sometimes there were some rather horrible pieces of meat and a raw onion.

Twelve hours is too long, too dull, too much. There may be occasional bursts of thirty-mile-an-hour speed, but not often. Ten miles an hour was more usual and it is too slow for a car—even three miles an hour on foot would seem better progress. You can learn to contemplate your navel for twelve hours at a stretch, I dare say, but not the landscape. Your capacity to take pleasure in the fleeting compensations of a journey such as this depends upon your capacity to remain unflustered and withdrawn into your own navel during the long voids. It would be much easier on a camel.

Nevertheless the driver drove beautifully, motionless behind his wheel, his eyes focused to receive only those impressions that concerned his driving. We talked less and less. Little fortified townships, and Jalalabad (a big one), a gorge deep and endless with the Kabul River tearing down its length and banking its waters at the bends like the curves on a national highway. Sarobi with a wide, cultivated valley. Some miles beyond Sarobi we stopped, as many others had before us, outside a row of shacks. They were all tea-shops, and all these people and all these trucks were drawing breath for the Lataband Pass that was just ahead. When we reached the Lataband there was nothing alarming about it, except its duration. Quite near its approaches there was a sentry-box of twigs and straw, perched on the edge of a precipice. A man was standing there and he waved as we passed by. He represented the saint whose tomb could be seen way down in an adjacent valley. He didn't expect payment from wayfarers making for Kabul, because it would not be reasonable to ask it in advance of a safe journey. On the way back a toll, yes—provided you got over safely. In fact there is no difficulty, except through the snows of winter, so the saint makes quite a good living out of the Lataband— being dead himself these many generations.

The mountains that enclose the pass are the colour of Irish tweed, yellowish-green and a brown like snuff, ten-thousand-foot mounds of it with the track snaking its way through for mile on heavy mile. There is nothing to see but these immense tumuli and distance and the Hindu Kush still sprawling across the north. But when you get through and start on the descent, the landscape changes and you find yourself amongst harsh, broken hill-tops, in a belt of forbidding country that tries to hold you back from Kabul. And then, suddenly, the landscape opens out, and when this happens you can forget every-thing that has gone before and thank God for such loveliness as climax to such a journey. A high, wide plateau, corn, and the city of Kabul sheltering under its little hills, though still a half-hour distant.

"Nice," the driver said.

Part 2

KABUL

■

Chapter 10

KABUL is divided into two parts—indigenous and foreign. Afghans can live where they please, I suppose: but their foreigners are required to live in barrage-balloons. They must float, gas-filled, in an element in no way their own, with nothing to do but observe, and even their observation is limited by the distance from the earth at which they are moored so securely. Not all the foreigners are Ambassadors, though it seems at first as if this might be the case, with so many distinguished-looking diplomatists sitting about in balloon-baskets. Some are Chargés d'Affaires, some Counsellors, a great many more are Secretaries one two and three, or Attachés with their bewildering range of subjects, or archivists and clerks, and the wives and children of all these. For so long as they are posted to Kabul they must remain suspended at the same unvarying altitude, some hundreds of feet more than the five thousand odd above sea-level at which Kabul suns its summer flanks (or snow-blankets them in winter). This altitude, as anyone who has lived in Srinagar or Nairobi or Parachinar perfectly well knows, is the optimum for the development of a mild (and not disagreeable) form of madness. Those that do not like it could in the last extremes cut their cables, or even their own throats, but they don't. Some even grow to love their aerial lives, bobbing about within reach of each other but of nothing else, and smacked at by the pale blue winds of heaven. The Afghans must laugh themselves silly to think of the lives they make their foreigners lead.

It seems a peculiar existence to begin with, as you sit each day in the isolation of your balloon-basket, but the sun comes up in the normal manner (though over Pakistan), and you can watch it swimming comfortably in its huge curved orbit and learn to accept the idea that the world gets on very well without you. By evening you can observe a sunset hundreds of miles distant (over Persia), and soon you will know that here in Kabul Persia is good, and Pakistan tabu. The Hindu Kush still lies relaxed across the northern horizon, pink in the glow of sundown. Nearer to hand a garland of lights has been lit on the fortified spine of Bimaru. There is a little break in this Bimaru ridge, to let the Kabul river through. In the gathering dusk you can still see gardens and trees and palaces, though they are almost hidden behind their outer walls. There is dust in the air.

As night falls Kabul is very beautiful. As with most beautiful things you may sometimes long to touch it or smell it, but this is denied to you. You must do the best you can with the organs of sight and sound. On my first day in Kabul the only truly Afghan sound I heard was singing, down in the distant fields. They were men's voices, and they repeated over and over again the opening phrase of the Walton Symphony—over and over again and a little inaccurately. I didn't hear it again in Kabul and had no means of identifying the singers. My guess now is that they were Aka Khel Ghilzai tribesmen—but this is no more than a deduction based on a subsequent experience. It was very pleasant, and seemed to relate me to the Afghan earth with much more certainty than any balloon-cable.

Yes, a good deal of dreamy imagination is needed for Kabul, and I shall ask you to imagine that the foreign barrage-balloons are in fact nothing of the kind. They are, for the purposes of my narrative, buildings of bricks and mortar, more or less splendid, housing Ambassadors of flesh, blood and letters of credence.

The British Embassy is the biggest and most splendid of all. The American Embassy may be the busiest-looking, and have the largest staff and the most notices about not honking motor-horns, but if an Englishman wants to say that he's got the best something, then he can say it of his Embassy in Kabul. It is so fine and aloof that as your car comes curtseying over the transverse corrugations of the highway leading from the city five miles distant, it gives the impression of an Institution. Strangely enough, as you draw nearer, still curtseying so brusquely that your discs threaten to slip, the British Embassy gets no bigger. In this it affronts the laws of nature. It is in fact quite small for its size—like certain male movie-stars: or perhaps like a production number at the Théâtre des Folies-Bergère. It is probably best seen from half-way back in the dress circle. But it has a very big entrance-porch, as solid as 3-D, under which the driver of the French

Embassy station-wagon had driven me before I realized what he was doing and could stop him. We accelerated out again.

"I'm staying with the First Secretary," I explained as we gathered speed.

I am told that Lord Curzon was responsible for all this splendour. He had said that since at long last the British were to have a permanent mission in Kabul, they should ensure that it would remain the most magnificently housed. This was in the nineteen-twenties, after the Third Afghan War.

The First Secretary at the time of my visit was Bernard Ledwidge, a very old friend, and his house was evidently round the bend of a little wood the other side of Chancery, a hundred yards ahead. His house had been sited so that its front should survey the back of the Ambassador's house, at an oblique angle. Beyond Bernard, round yet another bend of a little wood, was another house, much the same as his but smaller, and sited to survey Bernard's back view. It was the Commercial Attaché's. In such ways as this the architect had responded to the Order of Precedence.

Bernard's house had the air of a home built for the retirement of some modestly-successful banker. The period would be about 1910, architecturally, and the banker would be someone less grand than the biggest, of course. The house had such desirable features as gables, a rough-cast surface, bow-windows, a Georgian-type porch (quite small, naturally), and roofing of something resembling, but smarter than, corrugated-iron sheets. It also had a veranda at first floor level facing north-east, which would be nice for summer, and a glass-house appendage to the dining-room on the ground floor facing south-west —intended, I dare say, for out-of-season grapes and winter tea-parties. It housed the central-heating furnace, inactive at present. Some might think that the house would better suit a western city suburb than Central Asia, but there was no doubt about the gardens. They were remarkable, wide as parkland, well-treed, landscaped with the skill that seems granted to the British whenever they have space and money for it. It was free, open, deceptively natural, yet disciplined. Demoiselle cranes walked together in it.

All this I took note of later. At the moment I was in a state of exhaustion. The driver rattled on the front door and I sat waiting. A servant came out: a Pakhtun butler, and I knew him. Was I destined to know most of the servants in the houses I visited in Kabul? Later it seemed so, and in due course I learnt the explanation. Bernard came out and found his butler embracing me, but it did not strike him as peculiar because he knows Pakhtuns as well as I do.

Who remembers the early Buster Keaton? I do, and I thank God for it. I remember a two-reel comic, perhaps it was even a full-length feature. A father had been jailed, and it was his son's duty to carry bread to him in his miserable cell. Buster Keaton did so in this lovely picture, an enormous loaf in the French tradition, long rather than wide, but a good solid loaf for all that.

"I've brought my dear father bread," the caption said suddenly. In those days we accepted the alternation between image and written word without effort.

He had indeed brought bread, and he was permitted to squeeze it through the bars of the cell. But somehow—from nervousness or because of some fault in the baking, possibly—the loaf split open, and a two-foot file, a gimlet, a chisel and a scalpel or something like it came clattering in silence to the ground. I remember the effect it had on me.

For all the years that I have known Bernard Ledwidge he has had exactly the same effect—his dead-pan face, wide-eyed, bland, the same impression of a magnificent golden loaf, a loaf filled with every sharp and brilliant implement of mind and spirit, and a slow, steady voice through the chinks of which these objects gleam. What could be nicer and more stimulating than Bernard, and his wife Anne —tallish, dark, with a lovely figure?

"Well?" Bernard said. "What do you think of it?"

*   *   *

They showed me my room, and my bathroom, and how to light the hot-water system, and Francis (their four-year-old son), explaining that Francis had said I might use the celluloid duck, if I cared to. I was introduced to Nanny, who was charming, and then the butler made me go into the kitchen to say 'hullo' to the cook and to be embraced by him too. Protocol required a simple handshake with the under-butler whom I had never met before. I had last seen the cook in Peshawar, playing squash-rackets with a young gunner officer who fancied himself, and beating the poor young man in two straight sets.

"*The owls . . . and the* midges*!*"

The entire household had a welcoming feel to it. I had a bath, slept for an hour or two, and was ready for all comers.

All comers on a Wednesday evening in Kabul congregate in the Club Français—a nice little clubhouse in a side road somewhere or other in what is called Shahr-i-Nau—the New City of Kabul. Here, and almost nowhere else, do non-diplomatic foreigners meet the Diplomatic Corps, drink with them and take their money at Canasta. I have only the haziest recollection of what went on, I suppose because my senses were still dulled by the journey. I have an image of three handsome but incompetent barmaids, amateurs with looks superior to their bar-technique, of bottles and glasses and long, long waits, of notices in French, of a fretwork ceiling, of heat and smoke. My keenest recollection is of the wife of the French Ambassador, delightful beyond words; a Mongolian princess, elegant, witty and highly intelligent. It was she who said how pleased she was that I had travelled in their Embassy's station-wagon. The driver had told her, and had added that I had been a model passenger. She had a way of laughing behind her eyes that was charming.

But I was tired and, after an hour or so, I wanted to go home. In due course we went. Bernard and Anne had a gold-embossed dinner engagement, so they deposited me at the house, where I dined alone and then went upstairs. My bedroom was just beyond the nursery suite, and as I passed the open door of the day-nursery, I saw Nanny sitting in a dressing-gown and bedroom-slippers. She was reading Peter Cheyney, I think. I stopped to chat for a moment.

"Those owls," she said. "I don't get a wink of sleep."

"Screech . . .?"

"Screech . . .?" She hesitated for a moment and then said: "No. Not screech . . . Big ones, with ears. And then the *heat* . . ."

The windows were tightly shut—both the glazing and the fly-screens.

"Perhaps if you were to open the . . ."

She took no notice. "And the *midges*!" she went on. "They squeeze in through the wire gauze if you're not careful, so I close everything up."

After a pause she gave me the news. "Francis threw up this evening, poor little mite. It must have been the excitement." But she didn't explain what had excited him.

*   *   *

Kabul

It was specifically to see Bernard and Anne that I had come, but it was also interesting to take a quick, tourist look at Kabul that I had never before visited. I intended to limit my stay to a week, or ten days at the most. It would have been nice to see something of the country, too, but with my Pakistani background and my personal interest in the Pakhtuns—who are as much a thorn in the side of the Afghan Government as ever they were in the sides of the British—it would have been naïve to hope for special facilities. So I had asked for none, beyond a straightforward visit-visa to cover a ten-day holiday. Bernard would be working much of the day: Anne would be busy with her household and her ladies' bridge, and Red Cross sewing-sessions and semi-official gatherings of diplomatists' wives and who-knew-what. I thought that I would profit by a week of motionless leisure to write up my Pakistan notes.

For a day or two I did just that, in an atmosphere of insulated calm. But I didn't work very hard, and I gave myself plenty of time to wander off in the park-like grounds of the Embassy. Sometimes Francis would come with me, dragging a long articulated wooden train behind him. I disliked the train and in the end I had to tell him so. It had to be picked up so often. Almost anything proved an obstacle to that train—even rough grass. Though of wood, it did not float for some reason, and twice it had to be scrabbled for in the long, wide ornamental water that stretches back from the Ambassador's house to where the ground drops away. When I told Nanny about the train's not floating, she gave me rather a pursed-up look and explained that in spite of the fact that the Embassy grounds seemed just a lovely park for our enjoyment, there were territorial frontiers to be memorized. Thus the lawn with the walnuts and the clusters of mulberry-trees outside the Ledwidge drawing-room was the Ledwidges': theirs also the rose-garden seen from the dining-room, and some parts of the wood dividing them from Chancery. The Commercial Attaché had other clearly-defined domains. The Military Attaché had others again, and the other officers of the Embassy, yet others. The tennis-courts were common property, she said. But the whole length of that vista stretching back from the Ambassador's house—'the big house'—right to the vegetable garden concealed by trees, distance and a dip in the land, the whole of it was the Ambassador's. If I wished to visit the Military Attaché and his family, I should either creep through the vegetable garden or, if I were in a hurry, I could scuttle, head bowed, across the Ambassador's personal sunk rose-garden in the axis of his vista. I could make use of a little stone wall as a screen.

"But that water . . ." she finished up. "No."

Then she thought for a moment and suggested that if, after all, the Ambassador's own little boy were with me, as well as Francis, she supposed it would be all right for us to play in the ornamental water —but why did I not go to the swimming-pool if we wanted to float things? The swimming-pool was tacitly understood to be open to all living within the Embassy grounds.

It is a very fine pool, round and deep, and the water is a bright metallic blue. I had already visited it, as it happened, but had come away at once, not knowing the rules, because I had caught sight of a tall, remarkably handsome woman standing in it, reading a book. I mentioned this to Nanny.

"Ah," she said. "That was the Ambassador's wife. Poor soul, she feels the heat. Did you manage to sleep at all last night? Wasn't the heat awful?"

I had managed to sleep wonderfully, but did not say so. Kabul was hot by day—after all, it was high summer—and hottish by night, but people attended dinner-parties in formal European clothes without suffocation, and a thin blanket was needed on the bed.

*   *   *

And so my Kabul visit started, in blissful near-idleness, hot but not too hot, iced-beer in the shadow of trees, whisky at sundown (or quite comfortably before, since dusk was already dinner-time), good food, Bernard and Anne and their many friends who came to the house, and a lovely sensation of aloofness from the world. I had not yet taken a step beyond the Embassy grounds since my arrival. Probably I was still at the stage where, following a brief period of acclimatization, I still felt no chafing from the balloon-cables. I began to sort out the regular visitors. Within three days or four, invitation cards for me started to include themselves amongst the flutter of pasteboard that winged its way to the house like gold-crested birds. On the fifth day, with me already a household fixture, Bernard and Anne gave a cocktail party on a larger scale than the earlier entertainments.

"I've asked a number of Afghans," Bernard told me.

I was very pleased. It seemed a pity to come to Afghanistan and to remain in complete isolation, however enjoyable the conditions, but this was evidently what happened to foreigners, and it would have been pointless to battle against it. I spent much of that evening with Bernard's Afghan guests, and found them most friendly. I liked them and they seemed to like me, which was agreeable. One was Ahmed Ali Kohzad, Director of the Kabul Museum. Another was Ataollah Naser-Zia, a member of the Afghan Foreign Service. A third was Ahmed Jan.

In treating my Kabul visit as, quite simply, a diversion unconnected with my intention to write about Pakhtuns, I had of course been influenced to some extent by a wish to avoid embarrassing Bernard, my host. I could not help being the product of my past, which had linked me so closely not only with Pakhtuns but also with Pakistan—nor, by simply wishing it so, could I regard with complete neutrality the bitterness that had arisen between Afghanistan and Pakistan on the question of the Pakhtuns and the lands they inhabit. So when Ahmed Jan asked me about myself (which he did with friendliness and some humour), I told him frankly that I was writer of a kind, with a keen interest in Pakhtuns—and an uncompromisingly Pakistani background. It may be that he knew this already: anyway he didn't turn a hair and when I went on to explain about the book I hoped to write, he smiled and said:

"And what about Afghanistan?"

I had to say that I knew almost nothing about Afghanistan, and none of it from personal experience.

"It will be difficult for you to write about Pakhtuns without at least a nodding acquaintance with the Afghan point of view. If you're interested, why don't you go round to the Press Department, and see them?"

And Ataollah Naser-Zia said: "Yes. On Monday, if you like. I'll tell them to expect you."

A good many people stayed on to dinner. Neither hosts nor guests had thought this out in advance, but the decision was received with perfect equanimity by the kitchen staff, and only by the lateness of the meal could you have guessed that a dinner-party for about fifteen had not been planned from the beginning. Anne is splendidly unmoved by such things. She just waves a wand, and there you are.

There was bridge after dinner. At one of the three tables the game was of so low an order that I felt I might take a hand.

"I didn't know you played," my partner commented.

"I scarcely knew myself," I admitted, but as the evening wore on I grew less and less surprised at myself. I grew bold, in fact, bidding a little slam as if it were small change thrown to a beggar. My partner came round to look over my shoulder, having laid her cards on the table, as dummy.

"Ah," she said, with a sigh, as if she had discovered the secret to the universe. "I see now. You hold your cards left-handed, so you have no means of knowing quite what you have got."

"I hold them left-handed in order to baffle our opponents," I told her. And because I happened to hold everything worth having, even if my left-handedness with cards denied me the detailed knowledge that most players consider essential to the game, I made my little slam.

*   *   *

In this way it was that, a week after my arrival, just about the time I had meant to start making plans for a return to Pakistan, I decided to stay on.

"Stay on for as long as you like," Bernard said, and I think he meant it. I hope he meant it, because I stayed on and on and on, enjoying every minute of it, even (if in a different, retrospective sort of way) the set-backs and periods of near-lunatic frustration that lay just round the corner but had not yet started to wiggle their antennae.

My life bifurcated. One half of it continued to unspin itself gently in the parklands of the Embassy, the other in and out of government offices, getting a little tangled in the process, meeting officials—or perhaps not meeting them, when circumstances prevented them from keeping an appointment. My interest being Pakhtuns, and the principle Afghan interest being Pashtunistan, conversations were apt to centre on this new 'state'. They gave me a map of it, and a good deal of literature in English and in Pashto to illustrate it. When I had had time to read it all, they suggested a discussion. I didn't really want a discussion because it was almost at once obvious to me that they started from one major premise, and I started from another.

"It's difficult for an Englishman to understand how deeply the Pakhtuns feel about their new state," they told me. "British contacts with the Pakhtuns always had a background of officialdom—

which meant that you only met those Pakhtuns whose personal advantage was linked with lip-service to Britain."

I nodded. I couldn't deny that both statements were fairly true.

"The truth is that the Pashtunistanis are determined to be free— determined to establish their own independent state. After all they *are* a nation."

It was rather awkward for me to say what I thought about the Pakhtuns as a 'nation', since acceptance of this ideal seemed to be the cornerstone of the whole edifice. I believe I said that I had seen no evidence in the administered districts of the N-W.F.P. of a desire to secede from Pakistan. "Of course," I added, "I have yet to go to the real tribal areas, but I'm bound to say that the people of the N-W.F.P. proper not only seem very well off under Pakistan, but to recognize the fact. Pakistan has made remarkable strides in terms of N-W.F.P. development since partition."

He smiled and said: "Do you think so? But it doesn't surprise me the you have heard and seen nothing. It is a Rule of Fear——" (the capital letters rolled out on his tongue). "They are afraid to speak, and the leaders who could speak for them are all behind bars. But it's coming, all the same. It's come, in fact. Pashtunistan Regional Assemblies already exist in the Tirah and in Waziristan."

I said: "Don't you think that most tribal Pakhtuns consider themselves 'free' anyway? But you've got several 'Pashtunistani' leaders with you here in Kabul, I gather" (I tried to soften the effect of the inverted commas). "Could I perhaps meet some of them?"

"Anyone you please. Who, in particular?"

"Wali Khan, Kuki Khel Afridi, for example."

This was the cousin of Shahzada Khan, the Afridi with whom I had recently spent those days near Balakot in the Kaghan valley.

"Yes, certainly."

"And there are a couple of Chitrali princelings with you too, I believe. I've seen their photographs in your Pashtunistan pamphlets. By the way," I went on, coming now to a point that seemed to me of fundamental interest in trying to understand the concept of Pashtunistan, "can you explain to me why the Chitralis are included in the Pashtunistan map? Chitralis aren't Pakhtuns, and don't even pretend that they are."

"But of course Chitral comes into it! It's all part of the one geographical unit. Don't you see?"

I didn't see, and was faced with the prospect of being either rude or silly. So I remained silent as he continued:

"But of course it is. Look at the map again . . ."

I looked at the map as he showed it to me again. Alas it is not always given to us to recognize someone else's truth when it blazes up before our eyes. I knew that the Chitral valley and its river flowed into Afghanistan by way of what becomes known as the Kunar valley to the north-east of Jalalabad, but that would seem to link it with Afghanistan rather than with the Pashtunistan map. I was as confused as ever. It was perhaps at this stage that I decided to avoid argument on the subject, if I could.

"You can meet anyone you please," he said patiently. "I'll arrange it at once."

For some days I waited for news that meetings had been arranged, but nothing happened. Perhaps all the leaders were out of town.

After a while, feeling that I ought to justify so much waiting around, I asked to be allowed to see Shamsuddin Khan Majruh, the Director of Tribes, and I did meet him. He was a Pakhtun himself. Most of the other government officials had graduated from Pakhtunwali to a culture more Persian than Pakhtun. I at once took to Majruh, and to his assistant Salimi, because they were closer to the sort of Pakhtuns I knew and was fond of. So warm and friendly were they, in fact, that it seemed as if we had known each other before, and I asked a favour I had hesitated to ask up to date.

A year earlier, in Europe, I had met a captain of the Afghan army who had been sent by the Ministry of War to England for special study. We had become good friends. He was a tribal Pakhtun—a Suleiman Khel—a member of one of the most powerful tribes in Afghanistan, the Ghilzai. He had returned to Afghanistan meanwhile, but I had no clue as to where I could find him. I had written to the address he had given me, long before—before there had been any question of my visiting Pakistan or Afghanistan at all. But I had received no answer. Now that I had come to Kabul myself, I had wanted to see him. But I had done nothing about it because I felt instinctively that, in Kabul, association with an Englishman, and a 'writer' at that, might be harmful to him. The Afghans believe, against all the evidence, that Britain still controls the policy of Pakistan. Pakistan, for the Afghans, is a phenomenon worse than unwelcome.

Hence an Englishman is apt to be less than welcome himself. This is what I had thought.

Yet, today, in an atmosphere of pleasant good-fellowship with Majruh, I decided to ask to see the man in question—Captain Sher Ali. The Protocol Department of the Afghan Government maintains a list of those Afghans who may be invited to foreign households, and Sher Ali's name was not on it.

"Sher Ali?" The Director of Tribes proceeded to identify him by tribe and father's name. "Is he a friend of yours? Of course you can see him. He's working in one of the departments of the War Ministry at present, and living just outside the city. I'll get in touch with him and tell him you're here. Or . . . yes, that would be better. I'll get him round to my office. Tomorrow? Would that do? Ring me up at ten tomorrow."

I thanked him with genuine pleasure.

"Where did you say you were staying?" he asked, and I told him for the second time.

"H-m . . . The British Embassy." And then he smiled and said: "It's the easiest thing in the world."

*   *   *

The next day I telephoned from Bernard's house to the Directorate of Tribes.

Telephoning in Kabul is a strange performance. It is not enough to know the number you want and how to dial it. You have to have skill and patience of a very high order. The various Embassies have a man specially trained for this. After some minutes of anxiety the operator said he had got the thing under control.

"Is that Peter Mayne?" It was the Director of Tribes' voice. "Hold on. I've got Sher Ali here beside me."

And so it was. Sher Ali seemed as pleased to hear my voice as I was to hear his. He said: "Where are you staying? The British Embassy . . . ? Hm-m!" There was a brief pause, and then his voice came through again. "All right. Wait there. I'm coming round right away. Will you tell the guard at the gate not to shoot me?" I could hear him laughing.

I went across to Chancery to see Bernard.

"An Afghan friend of mine is coming round," I said. "I suppose

128

there's no objection, is there? I thought, if you didn't mind, I'd take a couple of chairs in the garden, and he and I could chat. I haven't seen him for a long time."

"Coming here . . . to the Embassy?" Bernard seemed surprised. "Who is he? Coming *here* . . .?"

I told him, but the name rang no bell, obviously.

I took chairs and a table into the garden, established them under a tree and waited. I waited a long time. The Embassy is perhaps five miles out from the city, and probably Sher Ali had no transport: but, equally, perhaps something had gone wrong. Bernard's surprise had disturbed me. I started thinking that Sher Ali had been prevented from coming after all, and I wondered if this had the makings of trouble for him. Then I told myself that he had spoken in the very presence of the Director of Tribes, so surely it was all right.

I had worried needlessly. Half an hour later Sher Ali turned up, striding across the lawn in a suit too small for him.

"Look!" he shouted, still yards away. "Look! I couldn't come to your Embassy in uniform, so I had to find someone who could lend me a suit. There was only one man in our department wearing civilian clothes, and he was too small—but it had to do, because otherwise I would have had to go all the way home to change. But it doesn't matter—here I am."

He was full of plans and questions. How long was I staying, would I like to come and stay with him and his family, did I remember a particular girl he had known in Europe—or that other girl, yes, the one he had been rather stupid about? He laughed and then, changing his expression, told me that he had been very ill (perhaps that was why he had not answered my letter). Did I know that on his return to Kabul, which had meant travelling across Pakistan in transit from Karachi, the Pakistanis had been very troublesome about a visa, and he had been the victim of malice when it came to passing his baggage out from Peshawar across the Afghan border?

"Contraband?" I asked, smiling.

"Certainly not! But things are very bad between us and Pakistan. Specially over the establishment of Pashtunistan. It shows everywhere, not least amongst the subordinates—the police constables and the little customs officials."

It was difficult enough to discuss Pashtunistan and Afghan-Pakistan relations with government officials, impossible with friends. So I laughed and said:

"Never mind now. You're here, anyway."

There were plenty of things to talk of, and the morning passed contentedly till nearing lunch-time when he said he must leave.

"Shall I come again at the same time tomorrow?" he asked.

"Aren't you working then?"

"Yes. But I can take a day's casual leave, I think."

I didn't mean to be unfriendly when I said: "Do you think they will mind your coming here . . . to the Embassy?"

"No,"

"It might look better for us to meet outside, all the same."

"The people who matter know I've come to see you here, Peter, and why I've come. They know it's all right. The British don't mind my coming, do they?" He looked round the landscaped grounds appreciatively. "I've never been here before. It's like England."

*   *   *

In the deep countryside of England, as in the deep countryside no matter where, I have no doubt, the villagers lucky enough to have a railway station congregate to see the express go by. The great monster comes roaring past and everyone reels back, mouths open, clinging to each other in excitement. It all happens too fast, of course, and details are missed. You are left with no more than the feel of horror, and a heightening of your awareness.

There is no railway line to Kabul, no brief roaring contact with a distant world—except aeroplanes, and spectators can't get close enough to them as they land or take off to participate in the drama of it. In Kabul, mail-lorries have to stand in for locomotives.

The British Embassy mail-lorry sets out for Peshawar once a fortnight, and in some ways it has a more intimate importance than ever a train could claim. Goodwill surrounds it, and a tingle of envy. All the officials, all the wives and the household staffs and dogs and the children meet outside Chancery (where the ritual of sealing the diplomatic bag is already taking place), and walk around the dear old truck as if it were a train that for some wonderful but unexplained reason had stopped here. They peep into it, as into someone else's *wagon-lit.* The official whose turn it is to take charge of the diplomatic bag stands self-consciously aware of his honour as Queen's Messenger. One or two of the many Pathan orderlies attached to the Embassy—most of them are recruited from Pakistan—have been detailed as escort. Their fellows envy them. For weeks now these escorts have been sleeping in the solitude of a single bed—just one in a sad row of 'celibates'. Tomorrow, *Insha' Allah*, they will be back in their Pathan villages, doing their duty by their wives. Three days later, exhausted and self-satisfied, they will be returning to Kabul in the same truck, and the nerve-racking solitude of 'celibacy' will start again for them. The Queen's Messengers are generally chosen from 'celibates' amongst the British staff too. Newcomers perhaps hope that Peshawar may provide some distraction—but those who have been there more than once or twice already know that it is a forlorn little hope.

It is charming, the departure of the solid old war-horse of a mail-lorry. It has been doing it for years, pounding at ten to fifteen miles an hour over the rocks of Afghanistan. It does not expect to make Peshawar in a day, so it stops the night at Jalalabad, and sets off again before dawn for Pakistan and the rail-head.

Goodwill is perhaps touched with anguish as the lorry pulls away from Chancery. People wave to it with the dumb flutter of handkerchiefs. It trundles off, overcrowded, overladen, doggedly British and determined. The Union Jack waves to it from the Ambassador's porch, the dogs bark. Then those who are left behind turn back in silence to their homes. Only the children, still too young to 'realize', are glad that the lorry has gone and they may now return to the rabbits they have hidden in a disused central-heating furnace.

It was nearing dusk, and as we passed through the hall on the way to a whisky and soda, Anne picked up a little pile of envelopes from the table. One was for me. It was an elaborate invitation—in verse—to a fancy-dress dance at the Lals, the Indian Military Attaché and his wife. I looked across to where Anne sat laughing as she read an identical invitation addressed to her and Bernard.

I said: "I'm afraid I shan't be here for it."

"Of course you'll still be here," Anne said. "Don't talk nonsense."

Of course I would still be here, but every now and then, as the days swam past, it was polite to make these little gestures of going soon.

■

Chapter 11

My life trifurcated. Two lives are manageable, but three are difficult to co-ordinate. There was the life of the British Embassy enclave, with its country-house comforts and the Ledwidges dispensing them so generously. There was the distracting business of Pashtunistan which, on the face of it, made no sense for me even now that I had read and re-read Afghan Government hand-outs on the subject. I began to wish that I had never broached the subject, because it seemed to stand between me and the government officials I was getting to know, making it hard for us to meet on a normal human plane: and it was even a dark little cloud over the third life that was opening up for me—thanks to Sher Ali.

Sher Ali comes of a leading tribal family, and his close relatives hold high appointments in the armed forces. Their loyalty to government is unquestioned, yet once or twice I paused to wonder if it were wise for him to be seen so much in the company of a foreigner. He merely laughed at me and continued to propose this outing or that, and to introduce me to his friends. His friends were, naturally enough, Pakhtuns like himself, and most of them army officers. The Pakhtun atmosphere has been so much part of my past life that it seems to fit itself comfortably round my shoulders, and I was very happy. I felt myself to be amongst friends of long standing. Being with them was easy and effortless, but as often as Pashtunistan cropped up I would find myself cut off, an agnostic surrounded by fanatical 'believers'. Occasionally I was compelled to make some comment, and I would say: "If the Pakhtuns want Pashtunistan, there is no doubt that they will have it": or perhaps: "I think it may be a question of 'leadership'. Directly a real Pashtunistani leader springs up, the rest will follow." All this was non-committally vague, and yet as true as it needed to be. After a while even the infrequent references to Pashtunistan ceased, and we were content to leave such controversies alone.

We would take tea and sticky cakes in some small restaurant in the city, or walk beside the river, or in gardens. Sher Ali would want sometimes to talk about London, and the others would ask questions, never having been there. One or two, who had been to Turkey for military study,[1] would tell me about Turkey that I have never visited. There had been no further talk about my leaving the Embassy and going to stay with Sher Ali and his family. I think we both realized, probably with regret on both sides, that he had been over-precipitate with his invitation. The formal entertainment of visitors is one thing —it is part of Pakhtunwali, and justified by the code, enjoined by it even, no matter who the visitor may be. But friendship has little to do with formality, and I could see that his relatives could not be expected to look upon me in the same light as did Sher Ali himself. Nevertheless I would have liked to experience something of the real Afghanistan—the Pakhtun Afghanistan, I mean. Tea-shops are so anonymous.

"I'd like to make a tour somewhere or other—outside Kabul," I said to Sher Ali one day.

"Where do you want to go? Kandahar? Or up to the north— Herat, for example?"

"I don't think so. I'd like to go to your part of the world. To the Southern Province."

He made no comment. As a matter of fact I knew that foreigners were excluded from the Southern Province, as they were from the Kunar valley in the Eastern Province up beyond Jalalabad, and anyone who troubles to look at the map will see that those two areas are the homeland of the important Pakhtun clans. Strangers are not encouraged to travel about amongst them. I must add that strangers are not encouraged in the tribal areas of Pakistan either. I suppose I felt that I was not a stranger with Pakhtuns.

But I said no more to Sher Ali.

On my next visit to a government office I tentatively suggested that a visit to the Southern Province would help me to understand the temper of their tribes better than any official publication.

"The roads are rather bad," the officer replied. "What about going to Kataghan and Badakhshan? Up in the north. We've established big Pakhtun settlements there, you know."

I did know this, as it happened. The Pakhtun colonies planted

[1] There is a big Turkish Military Mission in Afghanistan, and has been for years.

amongst the quite distinct Uzbeg tribes of the north, beyond the Hindu Kush, were said to have been rather successful. But a coloniz- ation project, interesting as it may be from an administrative point of view, is not the same thing as a people with their roots in the centuries.

"Or Maimana and Herat? Herat is very beautiful," he suggested.

"It's the Southern Province Pakhtuns I want to see, you know."

"There would be language difficulties . . ." We were speaking in English. Actually I don't think the officer spoke Pashto. "And, after all, what is there to see? Just people, and villages, and one or two bigger towns. It's wild country and—you haven't got a car, have you?"

"I can speak Pashto, and I could hire a car, perhaps."

"Hm-m . . . Well, I don't know. But why particularly the Southern Province? Where exactly do you want to go? Gardez?"

Gardez is a medieval city, capital of the province. It is the seat of the provincial governor. It was thereabouts that the Pakhtun tribes rose against King Amanullah's 'modernizing' programme in 1924. Of course there would be nothing to see, nothing to see with the eyes, that is to say, except mud fortresses, mud villages, mountains, and tracks that passed for highways. And obviously there would be little to perceive with the other senses either, unless the visitor were granted quite exceptional facilities for moving around. Was it reasonable to expect Afghan officials to believe me when I claimed to like Pakhtuns for themselves—Afghan officials who spend their lives fearing Pakh- tuns for themselves? I knew I was asking for something unlikely to be granted, even if they trusted me. And why should they trust me? So it was rather a surprise when the officer said contemplatively:

"But after all, why not . . .? You'd need a permit from the internal security people."

The next time I saw Sher Ali I told him that it looked as if I might be allowed to go south, and that I proposed to apply to the security people for permission. He looked surprised, and then pleased, and offered to take me there himself. So we went together. We were ushered into a room lined with sofas, and someone made space for us on one of them. A very senior officer—an obvious Pakhtun, and a General, as it proved to be—was holding court. A man stood before the General's desk, saying his piece, while the General played with a ball-point pencil. After a moment the General nodded, scribbled something on a block and the man bowed. As soon as the man had gone, I was asked to state my business. I did so as best I might and the General listened politely. Everyone else listened too, which embarrassed me a little. It was bad enough to be making so unusual a request on such flimsy, personal grounds, but to do so in Pashto before a crowded room, and to have been heard at once, while others who had perhaps been waiting for hours must wait still longer, made it worse. The General put a question or two to Sher Ali (whom, it was obvious, he knew well), and the answers appeared to satisfy him.

"Gardez? When do you want to go?" the General asked me.

"As soon as I can arrange transport, sir," I said.

"Very well. Take your passport to the office just behind this building." He scribbled something and gave it to an orderly. "Go with this man, please. They will fix it up immediately."

I thanked him, bowed, and left the room with Sher Ali.

Sher Ali had to get back to his work, and now that everything was settled there was no need for him to stay with me, so he left me with the orderly. I followed the man. As it happened the passport office was closed when we got to it. This did not worry me, however, because it was the principle that mattered, and the principle had been established. I was, in fact, jubilant.

Later in the day when I saw Sher Ali again I said:

"I suppose you couldn't come with me to Gardez?"

"I've got my work here, you know."

"Yes, but couldn't you take a few days casual leave? Would you like to come?"

He thought quickly and said: "I'd like to come very much. I'll see what can be arranged."

I saw the officer who had referred me to the security people and told him what had happened.

"When will you be going, then?" he asked.

"Just as soon as I've fixed up about a car. Should I come back to you for any further formalities?"

"To us? Not necessary at all. If the General has given you permission, that's all that matters. Have a nice trip."

I bustled about the town, searching for a car for hire. I failed miserably. Some people quoted their rates in detail, and then admitted that they had no car available. Others regretted that they could not spare a car for the number of days I had stipulated. Another referred me to the mail service, suggesting that the driver of the mail-truck might, for a consideration, accept me as a passenger: but, although I found the mail-truck, the driver was not to be found, and was never expected till a few minutes before the truck was scheduled to leave

"When does it leave, then?"

"On Mondays and Wednesdays—or is it Tuesdays and Thursdays . . .? I'm not sure. But you can ask the driver. He'll know."

"But the driver is not . . ."

"He will be coming," they said, consolingly.

A man lounging near-by said: "Why don't you go in one of the trucks that carry wood? Why not do that?"

"Thank you. Can you tell me where to find them?"

He told me and I found one, and the driver agreed to take me.

"When will you be going?" I asked him.

"As soon as the return load for Gardez is arranged for."

"And when . . .?"

"Ah, that . . ."

*　　　　　*　　　　　*

Back in the Embassy I told Bernard of my plans.

He said: "Fine. But I still think you ought to get a written permit from the Afghan Foreign Office, as well as an endorsement on your passport from the internal security people, oughtn't you?"

"I've been assured that all I need is the endorsement."

"I'll ring up the F.O. and make sure."

He did so. The officer concerned said that it might be best to have a formal F.O. permit too, and that if I were to make a written application to them, they would issue it and this, combined with the passport endorsement, would put everything tidily in order.

"You'll have to do it in Persian," Bernard said.

Someone did it for me in Persian, and in English also, and I borrowed Bernard's car and delivered it to the Foreign Office.

"I'll send the permit to the British Embassy for you at once," the officer said. "You'll have it in the morning. Where are you going first?"

"Gardez first. And round about, if they let me."

"Would you like to go right up to the Pashtunistan border?"

"To the . . .?" But I recovered myself and said: "Very much."

"Don't get shot by the Pakistanis," he said laughingly.

"Shall I wave a Pakistan flag at them?"

"A Pashtunistan flag would be more appropriate, I think."

"I don't think the Pakistanis would agree."

"No? How silly of them."

*   *   *

The formalities were not as easy to get through as I had hoped.

A couple of days had passed before I managed to present myself at the passport office at a moment when not only was it open, but also the officer in charge of it was at his desk. They could not have been nicer and more friendly and conversational, but each time I left them some part of my waking mind recalled that I still lacked my endorsement. I had by now received the Foreign Office permit, however. Sher Ali continued to encourage me.

"Be patient. You'll get your endorsement. The General said so—don't you remember? And, apart from that, I've got something to tell you." He cleared his throat and said: "I invite you to dinner on Wednesday. I've asked a number of Pashtunistanis. Wali Khan Afridi will be there too, if he's back from the country."

This was excellent news. I very much wanted to meet the Pashtunistan leaders, and there had been no further indications from the various government offices that they were arranging it for me. I thanked Sher Ali suitably. To meet these people, informally, with him, was more to my taste. I thought I knew what they would tell me about Pashtunistan—it was all in the booklets, after all—but what interested me a great deal more than the theory of it, was the personalities of the men who had been chosen to put the theory into practice. I wondered if Sher Ali's party had official sanction from the authorities. I asked him.

"Oh, yes," he said. "They know, and approve. By the way, dinner can't be in our house, I'm afraid. So I'm arranging it in the Military Club."

"That will be just as good."

I had been to the Military Club with him and various of his friends who were members. Foreigners don't go in the ordinary way, though I expect that the Military Attachés of the different foreign missions make a formal appearance from time to time. It is a good building, in a garden, and well run. But while I was remembering all this, I

K

suddenly remembered too that Wednesday was the night of the Lals'
fancy-dress dance.

"What time is your dinner-party, Sher Ali?"

"Any time you like. What about half-past seven?"

"Excellent. I've already been invited to a dance—a fancy-dress
dance—that night. I shall have to go on there afterwards. I suppose
you couldn't come too. It's at the Indian Military Attaché's. I'm
sure he'd be happy to see you. The Lals are very nice, as you probably
know."

"No, I couldn't come," he said, and I left it at that.

You become used, in time, to the idea of an expanded metal curtain
through which you can see, but not stretch your hand. Even the
Indian Embassy, so friendly towards Afghanistan. . . . I said nothing,
however.

Chapter 12

IT was like preparations for a costume ball on board ship, an elaborate cruising liner, shall we say, with a passenger-list covering all sorts of nationalities. Some of the passengers, ready for anything, would have brought a costume with them as elaborate as the occasion demanded. Others would interchange national dress with a shipboard acquaintance. Others would be content with the traditional joke-dresses, wives as nursemaids, husbands as immense fat babies in napkins.

The Ledwidge household was preparing for it. Anne had been busy all day, sewing things on to a dress and making a complicated sort of a crown. Bernard was unmoved, because he had an authentic New York Yankees' baseball outfit. I had nothing but the Moorish *sarwal* which I proposed to wear with a shirt and cummerbund and a knobbly crocheted skull-cap of red wool, as I had while at Balakot with the Mahsuds.

"What is it?" Anne asked.

"Just something for a summer street-corner," I said. "You'll apologize for me to the Lals, won't you—and say that I'll be coming as soon as Sher Ali's dinner is over?"

"Yes. Of course. And meanwhile you'd better give yourself a lining of whisky. You won't get anything to drink at your Afghan dinner."

"Thank you," I said, tipping some more into my glass.

*　　　　*　　　　*

I don't quite know what I had expected—perhaps half a dozen guests at the most, and amongst them, say, Wali Khan and the Chitral boys (whom I would probably recognize when I saw them. I had been to Chitral a number of times in the past and these two young men would surely prove to have grown out of a nursery of Chitrali children

139

that used to be seen about the palace). There would be, I supposed, at least one member of one of the government departments and a Pakhtun officer friend or two.

Sher Ali was waiting for me at the entrance to the Military Club and took me upstairs.

"Good heavens! It's an enormous party!"

It wasn't really enormous, I dare say, but it was a great deal larger and more formal than I had hoped it would be. A long room, with windows on to the night: a succession of Chesterfield sofas end to end, two rows facing each other, like a Pullman-car. Tables down the corridor between the sofas. Paper flowers. Every seat in the Pullman was occupied by a silent guest. Capital-C Conversation, I thought to myself with a sinking heart.

Capital-C Conversation amongst Pakhtuns is conducted not with the bright, electric smiles of a western drawing-room, but with a primming of the lips a great deal more dignified. It is something that I have never managed to learn.

"Some of them are already your friends," Sher Ali said. I don't know if there was a sinking in his voice, or whether I now imagine it. "Look!" he went on encouragingly: "There's Salimi. And 'Sial'."

Salimi was the young assistant in the Directorate of Tribes, and indeed I had begun to think of him as a friend by now. He had been consistently kind. Mira Jan 'Sial' was a Mohmand tribesman—a Pakhtun from the Durand Line border where it abuts on the Eastern Province of Afghanistan. I had met him several times and liked him, though I did not know him well. He edited a Pashto-language magazine—*The Pashtunistan Monthly*—and had given me a copy to read.

". . . and here's Malik Wali Khan. You don't know him yet, but you know his family."

I turned and found myself beside a very tall, very fair Pakhtun whom I recognized from publicity photographs—the Kuki Khel Afridi, Wali Khan. I was delighted, not only because I particularly wanted to meet him, but also because I felt an immediate sympathy for him. He had a slightly quizzical smile and—on the purely physical plane—hands as large as legs of mutton. Sher Ali introduced me to him and to the many others, but steered me back finally to a sofa with Wali Khan on one side, and Salimi and 'Sial' on the other. No one, except Sher Ali and me, seemed to talk English, so conversation was in Pashto. The Chitrali princelings had been unable to come, it appeared.

I can't pretend that it was very satisfactory. General conversation between a score or more distributed down a Pullman-car was obviously out of the question. It meant raising the voice even to be heard by the man on the opposite side of the double row of sofas. It was like a Press conference in which I was to play the part of the sole journalist, and I had no talent for the rôle at all. Yet at the time, since I was the 'guest', I could not hope to talk quietly with, for example, Wali Khan. The conversation had to be shared with the whole company. In-evitably they embarked upon Pashtunistan—which was reasonable enough since they thought so strongly about it and imagined that I did also—even if they suspected that I held an opposite view. But Pakhtuns much prefer personalities to political abstractions, and I do too, so with a little manœuvring it was possible to steer things round to 'people', to this group of people as individuals, or to me. They were very friendly and I decided that there was no reason why it should not after all prove an agreeable evening. They asked me about myself and why I had come and I replied candidly, and we laughed a good deal. I began to enjoy it.

"You were a 'political'?" 'Sial' asked me, to the amusement of the others.

'Political' has been adopted into the Pashto language. Everyone knows the term—properly it refers quite simply to any officer of the old Government of India Political Department that had provided the Frontier administration. It suffers two little changes in reaching Pashto: the accent is carried to the final syllable—Politicál—and it is given a special nuance: sly, wily.

"No," I said, firmly. "Not even in Pashto. Why? Have you any doubts about me and what I have come to Kabul for?"

He laughed outright and then, with a sudden switch to seriousness, said: "Please don't think that—even as a joke."

Someone commented: "Peter sahib is very direct," and laughed too.

Thereupon, unexpectedly, from the far end of the Pullman, a voice said in English: "Table-talk!"

We all looked round. Away at the end of the opposite row, where I had not really noticed him except for a fleeting moment of a hand-shake on arrival, was a thinnish, unremarkable, bearded, middle-aged man with button eyes. In the second that we all looked towards him, and while the echo of his first comment was still shivering aroun d us he said it again: "Table-talk!"

It was well done. In just such a way must the Fairy Carabosse have struck a chill into the christening-party we have all read about. He did not move, he did not even raise his voice—the trained voice of the public speaker—but directly he saw that he had the ears of his audience, he embarked on what he had to say. He said it in English. His English was excellent. No one, of course, could understand a word except me, to whom it was addressed, and our host Sher Ali, to whom it must have been an embarrassment.

"Table-talk!" he said. "If I mistake not, you propose to write a book about the Pakhtuns. A general sort of book. It is to be about their standards of living, their speech, what they eat and drink and think and do. You have told us that you have lived for some time amongst Pakhtuns. You have spoken as if you thought you knew something about us. You have declined to speak about Pashtunistan. You have said that you will visit Waziristan—and then Baluchistan."

He paused. I should have broken the thread at this point, but I didn't.

"Yes? Am I right?" he asked. "May I tell you that you, who know so little, will learn nothing more about Pashtunistan by your visits to Waziristan and Baluchistan. All the leaders are in Pakistani prisons. Eleven thousand of them."

He paused again, to let this sink in. Still I said nothing, Wali Khan whispered to me: "It is Muhammed Ayub Khan, Achakzai."

I knew then who he was. The Achakzais are a tribe of Pathans inhabiting Baluchistan, a nice, well-behaved, peripheral-Pakhtun tribe. This man had been vice-president of an anti-government political body called the Anjuman-i-Watan, and he had 'escaped' when things got too hot for him, about three years before. He had taken refuge in Afghanistan. He had encouraged a biggish block of the Achakzais to migrate to Afghanistan with him too—and like sheep they had done so, because they are rather different from the Pakhtuns of the N-W.F.P. They are biddable and inclined to follow a bell-wether. Muhammed Ayub Khan was a 'leader' of a sort. The emigrant Achakzais had settled down, rather disconsolately, just inside the Afghan border, at a place called Toba.

"Shall I go to Toba to visit the Achakzais and to ask them about Pashtunistan, then?" I asked him.

"What good to go to Toba? And how can you go there? The Pakistanis would not let you. How will you go anywhere? How to Waziristan—and from Waziristan, how to Baluchistan? Tell me that?"

This did not seem very relevant, but I said: "I will go to Waziristan from Peshawar by bus or by truck, *Insha'Allah*: and in the same way from Waziristan to Baluchistan."

"You can't."

"You mean the Pakistanis won't let me go?"

"There is no road."

There are, of course, roads. I said: "I shall have to go by whatever means present themselves."

"Of course it is theoretically possible to go on foot, or by camel."

"And, in the purely practicable sense, by road or by air . . ."

"There is no road, and there is no air-service."

"There are roads and the Pakistanis have aeroplanes—and moreover they can fly them." It was not very polite, perhaps, with poor Wali Khan sitting beside me, and his fortress in Tirah in ruins, and what was worse was that I had said this in Pashto. I was tired of the ding-dong schoolboy exchange—I'm not, you are, you are, I'm not. 'Sial' broke in, saying quietly:

"There are, of course, roads."

And I said: "None of this seems to matter much. I shall manage to get where I want to go, *Insha'Allah*, though I am grateful to you for your prophecies, Muhammed Ayub Khan."

Cassandra-Carabosse . . .! This was no sort of conversation for a dinner-party. I looked at Wali Khan, but he was looking down at his hands. I had a nasty feeling that Muhammed Ayub Khan's tirade had been planned in advance: and then I knew that though he may have planned it, it could not have been part of a general plan. Pakhtuns don't treat their guests in this way. Capital-C Cassandra-Carabosse was at it again.

"You will see nothing, you will learn nothing, you know nothing. If you wish to hear about Pashtunistan, ask us about it, here and today! But what *really* is your mission?"

It was a rhetorical question, but I was annoyed by now and quite ready to be rude. It is not difficult to disturb the pattern of a politician's speech if you are ready to heckle and—what is much more important—if the bulk of the audience is inclined to side with you. I decided to be a little impertinent:

"Mission? Mission? Why do you use such a ridiculous word, Muhammed Ayub Khan? Your English is perfect. Why do you say 'mission' as if to suggest that I consider my journey important? Why? Do you think I am a spy? Why?——" And as soon as he started to answer I interrupted with a repetition of my "Why? Why?" and began laughing.

He cleared his throat and this time I let him speak.

"You say that you are writing a book for the Americans. Why should the American Government engage you to interpret Pashtunistan? You—an inhabitant of England?"

I turned to Wali Khan and said in Pashto: "Do you follow what he is saying?"

"No."

"Someone must have told him that I am employed by the American Government—or do you think that Ayub can have thought of that for himself?"

"Never mind . . ."

"What do you know about the problem? What *can* you know?" Muhammed Ayub Khan was demanding.

"Not much, Muhammed Ayub Khan, I admit." I stuck obstinately to Pashto because I wanted the others to understand as well. "I am someone who has to make a living, just as you are someone who has to make a living. I try to do it by writing. You are a professional politician. I am not paid by the American Government—they aren't fools—and I'm not paid by the British Government either, or by the Pakistanis or anyone else—though I hope to earn some money from a publisher in due course. I have come back to the 'Frontier' because I love Pakhtuns and wanted to see them again: and because, God forgive me, I think I can write something about them that will be true in the way I see it, and sympathetic and publishable."

"I *see* . . ." he murmured, nodding his head, and contriving to give the sibilant a certain sinister significance, but 'Sial' snapped the spell by putting in:

"It is true. He does love the Pakhtuns. I know this."

I said: "Yes, I do—though I don't know why." And in the back of my mind, as perhaps in the front of Muhammed Ayub Khan's, was the thought that Muhammed Ayub Khan and I did not love each other.

Sher Ali who, I suspect, was deeply embarrassed, broke things up by the announcement that dinner was ready, and we all rose.

"Come," Muhammed Ayub said with careful good manners as we walked down the room. "You are our guest tonight, and we are happy to have you here."

We washed our hands. Muhammed Ayub could not, apparently, resist the temptation to ask me why I was washing mine.

"It's usual, I think."

"You do not eat with your fingers. *I* do not use a knife and fork."

"Nevertheless I was taught to wash my hands before meals."

Everyone used a knife and fork except Muhammed Ayub who ostentatiously ate with his fingers—the true-blue Pakhtun.

How tiresome professional fanatics can be.

*   *   *

Dinner was a relief because Muhammed Ayub Khan remained silent. The rest of us talked—table-talk, shapeless. I think we were mostly concerned to get through with it. Wali Khan made a few observations about Pashtunistan, however.

"If Pakistan will not give in to the wishes of the Pakhtun nation," he announced, rather as if he were repeating something committed to memory, "and if neither the British nor the Americans will help the Pakhtuns to gain their rights, we Pakhtuns will have to look for help elsewhere...."

"You mean . . . over *there*?" I waved my arm towards an approximate north. "Other peoples have said that, and some have even tried it, I believe!"

One of the others quoted a Pashto proverb: "A good enemy is better than a bad friend."

"Yes."

"There are no less than eight hundred British army officers serving in the Pakistan armed forces," somebody else announced.

I didn't know exactly how many specialist British officers were fulfilling short-term contracts with the Pakistan army—and I didn't think I wanted to make a farcical counter-attack with the suggestion that Turkey runs Afghanistan through her Military Mission to Kabul. So I said:

"Rather less than eight hundred British officers, I think. About fifty, perhaps."

"Eight hundred senior British officers," the speaker repeated with conviction.

". . . . The British still control Pakistan: it is a well-known fact."

So I said: "And on the other side of the Durand Line the Pakistanis complain, with some truth on their side, that the British have ignored them and treated them like step-children within the Commonwealth."

"The British . . ." someone remarked contemplatively.

"Which do you prefer, Peter sahib? Pashtunistanis or Pakistanis?"

"I think my favourites are the Pakhtuns," I said, and they laughed pleasantly.

"Then which do you prefer—Afghans or Pakistanis?"

I hedged and said: "I don't know anything about Afghanistan. But, *Insha'Allah*, I shall be going to the Southern Province within a few days, and I'll tell you all about it when I come back."

Muhammed Ayub Khan, who had been sitting in po-faced silence, chipped in quickly: "What? You are going to the Southern Province? They have given you permission?"

"Yes. Why not?"

"Then I trust you will find it interesting."

I caught Sher Ali's eye. He cannot have enjoyed his dinner-party very much, I'm afraid. Nor had I. Nor had anyone, probably. I glanced down at my watch and started to make some sort of move.

That was all, except that Muhammed Ayub Khan—uncertain, I suspect, whether the others had fully appreciated the force and brilliance with which he had delivered his pre-dinner English oration, stood up and gave them a Pashto version at top speed: "We do not know what his mission may be . . . we know nothing about him except that he was a Pakistani and is British . . . but he is our guest tonight. As our guest, we must thank him for giving us the pleasure of his company."

He made a slight inclination towards me and said, in English:

"On behalf of the company here present, may I thank you for having honoured us by coming tonight?"

I bowed and said graciously: "You may."

At the bottom of the steps, under the porch where Bernard's car stood waiting with its Corps Diplomatique plate, I said good-bye to

Wali Khan, and 'Sial' and Salimi and the others.   And then, finally, to Sher Ali.

"I'm sorry," he said, standing beside the open door of the car. "This was to have been a pleasant, friendly dinner, but . . ."

"Never mind: I don't . . ." I said.   "So long as you and the others don't think of me as . . . as he does."

*   *   *

My Moorish *sarwal* and the cummerbund and the red wool skull-cap were all rolled up together in the car.   I made the driver stop on the way to the Indian Military Attaché's house and I got out to change my clothes.   As I took off my coat and trousers and tie and socks and threw them into the back of the car, the driver turned away with pantomime modesty, screening his eyes with his hand: but the head-lamps of a car passing by were less modest than Bernard's driver (though more modest than me)—the head-lamps dipped, concentrating their beam on my flapping shirt-tails and bare legs.

"'I take refuge in the Lord of the Dawn,'" murmured Bernard's driver, horrified.

I got into the car again and we started off, careering over the bumps to a party which by now would be in full swing.

*   ·   *   *

I must say at once that the Lals' party was almost certainly nothing like my recollection of it.   They must be held responsible for the choice of their guests, of course: but even here, in an informal party, they were not completely free.   Diplomatists must invite some whom they could otherwise have omitted.   Must I class myself amongst the 'some'?   I hope not, because both the Lals are charming people, and I would like to think they remembered me with the affection I hold for them.

Let me say, then, that the Lals were responsible for inviting their guests, but not for their guests' actions.   They cannot be held respons-ible for me.

I reached the party when it was already in full swing.   I had a full stomach certainly—Sher Ali's dinner had been admirable—but there were sour little vapours floating about inside my head.   I had told

Sher Ali that I didn't mind, but in fact I had minded profoundly. I wanted to put the whole thing out of my head as quickly as possible, and I overdid it. That wasn't the Lals' fault. As a matter of fact it was largely someone else's.

It is disagreeable to be so late for a party that you find it hard to catch up with the mood of the other guests. The party was going very well. The gardens had been transformed into a ball-room. There was a moon, and lights had been hidden in the trees, and the guests were dancing on an improvised floor laid over what was probably a tennis-court. It was not difficult to recognize Mrs. Lal in her dress of a *gopi*—a milkmaid of the Ramayana: it is not difficult to recognize her anywhere, because she has good looks and a distinction typically Hindu. She detached herself from her partner and came over to welcome me. Her husband detached himself from his partner too. He is a big man, well-built, and that night he was dressed in the formal half-nakedness of the Lord Krishna who loved milkmaids. They looked fine together, this couple, but they were in the middle of their dances, and so they said: "Better late than never. The bar's over there. We'll see you in a moment."

Behind the bar was Mahboob Khan, smiling. He has been smiling as long as I have known him, wherever he might be, even in prison where I had visited him some years previously. That had been in Delhi: he was 'in' for murder (with a hockey-stick and a big, flat stone, if I remember correctly Pathans are disarmed when they go to live in what they call 'down-country'). Two of the others who were with him in prison were also friends of mine, and I had taken them cigarettes and some sweets called *rossagulla*—no bread, no gleaming files. Taking food to prisoners is a very proper thing to do in Islam. We were glad to see each other here, I think. He told me that he had been released after a modest little five-year term—'because of good behaviour'—and the thought of it caused him to explode with laughter.

Anyway, that was the situation. Me, sour and unhappy, with my nerve-ends twitching, anxious to forget the reason and to join the other guests in what was obviously a highly successful evening: Mahboob anxious to mark the reunion with some token of friendship—and a good way of doing this was to ensure that I was given whiskies of a size corresponding to his pleasure and my need. While I put down the first two, he gave me a list of the Pathans I would know from villages around Peshawar who were now employed in the various Embassies in Kabul.

"That's what many of us are doing now," he said. "Looking after Europeans and Americans, here in Kabul, because there isn't much easy work left for us in Peshawar."

"There are new factories, and all sorts of new jobs to do . . ."

"Yes, yes," he admitted, waving them aside, "but I mean nice, easy work, like at the Club in the old days. I've been here ever since I came out of prison. My master brought me this evening to help with the drinks. Look! That's my master—the tall one. And my memsahib is that one—the very pretty one. You see her? Americans, they are."

The dance was finishing and I left the bar to speak to the Lals for a moment: I wanted to apologize for, and explain, my lateness. I knew a good many of the guests, of course, and they introduced me to others, and shortly after I found myself with a couple who were disposed to talk about the economic progress of Afghanistan, and what should be done about education of the Pakhtun tribes. They were intelligent, serious people: but I did not feel either, myself. Yet I held my own through a mounting miasma of whisky fumes, and wondered, in parenthesis, if I was being altogether wise.

"Paranoiacs," they said, talking about the Pakhtuns.

That's exactly what I say, of course: but now, on thinking it over as well as I can, I wonder whether I said it before, or only after . . .

"Of course," I agreed, tapping my glass. "Paranoiacs."

I wonder if I can remember how it goes. The prominent and particular . . .? No. Not quite that. 'The prominent and *distinguishing* symptom of paranoia is the delusion which is gradually organized out of a mass of original but erroneous beliefs or convictions till it forms an integral part of the ordinary mental processes. . . .' Rather good, I think. Who said it? Or wrote it? Systematization. That's what happened. It could be persecutory, or it could be delusions of grandeur and ambition. No persecution for the Pakhtuns, however—at least, nobody has got away with it yet in their dealings with the Pakhtuns. So with the Pakhtuns it must be the second possibility.

"Paranoiacs, of course," I repeated. "Delusions of grandeur and ambition."

"Yes," they agreed, rather startled, and the conversation began to flag because they were losing confidence in me. Not so me in myself: I was gaining it rapidly, but by the time I had returned to them from the bar with the drink that Mahboob had forced into my hands, they were flinching and making a getaway. I allowed them to go, and tried someone else—an Afghan girl, very attractive: not Afghan at all, as a matter of fact, but that nice, sweet Thelma who said that she would have to sit down because her slippers hurt. Bernard was there too, thumping about in his New York Yankees' suit.

"What are you dressed as, Peter?" Thelma asked.

"A Moor pushing a hand-cart, I think."

Someone else was beside us, saying that he was disguised as Lawrence of Arabia disguised as an Arab.

"Thelma's wearing her servant's sister's wedding-dress," he said. "But it seems that her servant's sister's feet are a different shape."

"Her feet are just fine so long as I can keep the weight off them," Thelma said.

"May we join you, Thelma?"

A girl had come up to our table with her dance-partner. It was the pretty American that Mahboob had said was his 'memsahib'. I don't remember what she was wearing except that it was dangerously strapless and *décolleté*. Thelma introduced me and said that I should catch the barman's eye—which I did without difficulty—and there we were again, all very jolly. There were goings and comings, I dare say, and Thelma pleased me by saying she had heard of my triumphant little little-slam—standing on my head, or something: she hadn't exactly understood, but knew there had been an unorthodox angle to it.

"Upside down," I explained.

"Ah-h...."

"Culbertson can't, they say."

The girl in the strapless *décolleté* laughed and then winced sharply. It was over soon enough. Yet, as the conversation flowed liltingly on, she did not look altogether happy and after a while she got up, excusing herself. I expect that good manners would have prevented my asking what the matter was, but I was spared any such tussle with my social conscience because Thelma knew and told us.

"Poor kid," she said. "It's the Scotch tape. She keeps it all up with Scotch tape instead of shoulder-straps, and if she moves in a certain way, or coughs, or laughs, it catches on a piece of skin. You'd never guess, would you?"

I had been looking quite carefully and had seen no sign of it—but of course Scotch tape is wonderfully transparent, invisible, almost, if you aren't looking for it.

Another dance, and a little later a grand parade of costumes with everyone feeling slightly self-conscious and only the bravest miming the sort of actions they supposed would go with the characters they represented. Mahboob was tiresomely attentive. Really, these Pakhtuns! As hosts they become slave-drivers, and the bar-supplies seemed inexhaustible, and away on the terrace were mountains of food. Indian food at the level of the Lals' kitchen is something to be goggled at but, alas, I was full of meat already and could not do justice to it.

"Then you must have another drink, in any case," Lal said encouragingly. And there was Mahboob, ready with it.

"Thanks," I said, and I may have hiccuped. Anyway I did notice that Lal was giving me a quick, peculiar look—friendly, but peculiar, and I knew that I must pull myself together for the sake of England. Probably I stood about, considering how to do this, though not very successfully, and, soon after, Bernard came up to me and said we must be going. I suspect that he and Anne returned to the party when they had deposited me at home. I remember thinking as I lay in bed: 'I must listen for the sound of the car starting up again.' But I heard nothing. A few more moments of thinking were left to me, however, and it occurred to me that I should write to the Lals to apologize, that I ought to get out of bed and do so at once, as an act of contrition—and then I decided that, even if I managed to write this note, I would never find the Lals' house at this hour of night in order to deliver it, even on foot—let alone on hands and knees (as an act of contrition)—alone, friendless, with no one to guide me —that as an alternative I could never master the Kabul telephone and, finally, a wall of bed-clothes came up before my eyes and I could no longer see what it was that I had to apologize for.

Thus comforted I turned to my bedside-table and switched off the carafe of barley-water, and through the drip-drip-drip heard a voice in my ear saying: '*What is your mission . . . ?*'

I found the strength to strike one more blow for sanity and clean living:

"Do you mind getting out of my bed, Fairy Carabosse?" I said loudly. "Nobody invited you to the Wake. I shall count up to ten, and if..."

I looked out of the corner of my eye when I reached five and found that I was alone.

Chapter 13

THE human spirit is remarkably resilient. The next morning, which ought to have been a misery to me, was in fact nothing of the kind. A single piece of good news emptied my sky of clouds and queasiness—a message came through asking me to deposit my passport with the officer concerned at the Ministry of the Interior, and saying that I could thereupon have the endorsement I needed for the Southern Province. So I hurried to the Ministry and presented my passport and they said I could collect it on Saturday. It was Thursday, for the moment. It would have been nice to get my permit then and there, but it required an important signature, and the personage was not in his office at the time, and he did not sign papers after the lunch interval, or something of the kind. The next day, Friday, was of course the weekly public holiday. Anyway, Saturday had a nice positive sound.

I went back to the house and told Anne about it.

"I think the best thing to do would be for me to move to the Kabul Hotel for a couple of nights," I said. "I shall probably have an early start on Saturday. It will make things easier to be in the city."

"But you won't get the signature you need till after the offices open on Saturday," she reminded me.

Perhaps, after all, it wouldn't be an early start on Saturday. I might even have to delay my start till Sunday. But in any case I decided to move to the Kabul Hotel, leaving the bulk of my luggage at the Embassy.

While I was still within reach of a telephone expert I rang up Sher Ali.

"What about tomorrow. Friday. Are you free?" I asked him.

He said: "Yes. We'll go to Paghman. I'll call at the hotel at about ten in the morning."

L

The Kabul Hotel was possibly a bit better than I had imagined from the—let's be honest—saddish impression it makes on anyone passing by. The rooms in the main building proved to be all taken, but they gave me a room in the annexe, over the street: for two nights, they said. I said nothing about a possible third night, and hoped for the best.

They took me to my room, and I was surprised to find how good a room it was: quite big, reasonably well furnished, an adequate bed and sheets that looked clean. A big Afghan carpet covered the floor right up to the wainscoting. There was a bathroom down a little passage-way. For the price I was to pay I was entitled to morning tea, breakfast and one of the two principal meals—luncheon or dinner. I went to inspect the dining-room but I wasn't hungry that day—not hungry enough, I mean, to be easily tempted. So I returned to my room, intending to do some work.

I felt that I ought to get down to this question of Pashtunistan. I had met a number of Pakhtuns of the tribes living in Afghanistan by now, and it was clear that if they at all represented a cross-section of Pakhtun opinion hereabouts, this new independent state meant something important and real. The men I had been meeting were, of course, in terms of education, a good deal more advanced than could be their brothers in the provinces, but I suspected that there was less of a gulf between them than existed between their equivalents in Pakistan. I read all my pamphlets and examined the Pashtunistan map carefully, and I still failed to understand its real meaning. Back in Pakistan the subject had cropped up from time to time, and although it was certainly tiresome for the Pakistanis to have 'Pashtunistanis' ranting over the Kabul Radio and demanding their rights of self-determination, and although some Pakistanis got hot under the collar and ranted back just as rudely, I had had the impression that Pashtunistan, so far as the tribes in question were concerned, was really not much more than a side-issue. Yet, ultimately, anything that can poison relations between two neighbouring countries is potentially serious, and it was clear that in Afghanistan Pashtunistan was real.

It was rather hot, and now that I came to think of it I did not feel my best, but the pamphlets were spread out on my table in front of me, and my note-book was open. Progress was slow. Whatever my point of departure I seemed to come up against the same basic barrier to comprehension. I tried once again, right from the beginning.

154

Who are the Pakhtuns?

'Pashtunistan, the land of the Pakhtuns' [I read], 'is the country lying between the Afghan border and the river Indus, which is the natural and historical border of the Indian sub-continent.'

It seemed to beg the question, perhaps, but never mind. The Afghan border? Did they mean the Durand Line? The Afghan House of Representatives was later quoted in the pamphlet as recognizing neither the 'imaginary Durand Line nor any similar line'—and yet what other border could be intended? Possibly the Pashtunistanis objected to it less fiercely. I read on:

'It extends from Chitral in the north to Baluchistan in the south and is separated from Kashmir by 350 miles of frontier. Pashtunistan covers an area of more than 190,000 square miles and has a population of over seven millions.'

I glanced again at the Pashtunistan map. Yes, there it was, approximately covering two complete provinces of Pakistan—the North-West Frontier with its tribal regions (but excluding Chitral), and Baluchistan with its States. I also glanced again at my own sketch map showing the territories the Pakhtuns inhabit. I had made this comparison several times during the past week or two but, being anxious to avoid having to discuss it with Afghans, I had chosen not to draw attention to the fact that 'Pashtunistan' and the lands actually inhabited by Pakhtuns have quite different shapes. My sketch of the Pakhtun areas had an immense tumour stretching over parts of Afghanistan (see sketch map opposite). Polite people avoid their friends' tumours in conversation: in the privacy of my room I felt that I might at least think about them, and I found myself back again at that awful question of so long ago—who are the Pakhtuns?

Who indeed? I hadn't the energy to re-check all my references that afternoon, so I shut my ears to doubt and, skipping a bit, read on:

'. . . The Afghan Rulers of India before the time of Ahmed Shah referred to their own land, Afghanistan, as 'Pakhtun-Khwa', the territory lying between the rivers Oxus and Indus . . . '

'Khwa', in Pashto, means approximately 'side', in the sense of 'direction'. Thus 'Pakhtun-Khwa' might reasonably be translated 'the Pakhtun country'. That was all right in a general sort of way. Great blocks of Afghanistan could still be called, in the same sense, 'Pakhtun-Khwa'. The odd thing—the thing against which my mind had been shying—was that these important Pakhtun blocks in present-day Afghanistan were to be denied the glory of Pashtunistan nationality, so far as one could understand. All those Southern Province tribes—Sher Ali's Suleiman Khel included, incidentally—all the Eastern Province tribes, all these people who supported the concept of Pashtunistan for the Pakhtuns so fervently, were content to stand back and let their Pakhtun brothers beyond the Durand Line take the prize for themselves. They demanded no share. I wondered why. This was a question I had lacked the courage to ask of my Afghan friends for fear of turning up a stone that would prove to have something embarrassing under it. Of course I ought to have asked Mahummed Ayub Khan the night before. He had had no hesitation in embarrassing me, so there was no reason why I should have felt squeamish with him.

So, on the one hand it looked as if the Pakhtun tribes in Afghanistan were to be excluded from what was claimed as the birthright of the Pakhtun peoples and, on the other, as if certain other peoples whom nobody had ever even pretended were Pakhtuns, were to be given a share—such peoples as the Chitralis, the various Baluch tribes, and the Brahui, and the people of Mekran and Kelat. I felt a little bewildered by this. Moreover, as I read doggedly on, I was now required to accept without a tremor the statement that:

> '. . . in addition, Pashtunistan has the advantage of access to the sea in Baluchistan which is obviously a factor of great importance in the future trade of the country.'

Yes, yes, of course: it is nice to have an outlet to the sea. This would explain why Kelat and Mekran were to share in the new state, although they were not Pakhtuns themselves. Mekran would bring her seaboard to the marriage as dowry. But I did stop to wonder why, when it was all so easy, the city of Karachi (which those Pakistanis thought of as their capital) had not been included too—it would only have needed a little loop southwards in drawing the south-eastern borders of the Pashtunistan map. Karachi had a fine, modern port, all ready to serve the interior. However, one must be generous, so the Pakistanis might keep their Karachi, and Pashtunistan would perhaps develop a new port on the Mekran coast, and perhaps Afghanistan—

a land-locked country—would be allowed special facilities that the Pakistanis were said to be denying them in Karachi.

Sometimes you must follow instinct rather than the shining logic of things, but it was difficult, that afternoon in a Kabul Hotel bedroom. It wasn't so much the heat, though Kabul City is hot in July if your room faces the sun and there are no shutters, and if the curtains are lacy webs not quite wide enough for the windows they decorate. Perhaps, after all, my personal clouds and queasiness had not completely dissipated themselves. I decided, weakly, to stop taxing my brain, and I put myself to bed for the afternoon instead. When, later, I got up and went to the bathroom for a shower, I found that a lot of men had arrived and were camping out in a big vestibule of a room next to mine—a room with no door, because it was really an ante-room to some cubicles beyond it. The newcomers were Afghans with steel trunks and rolls of bedding. A servant was squatting with them and chatting, and he asked me if I would like tea and I said I would and then rather forgot about it. For some while I sat in my window and watched the Kabul world go by. It was very unlike what I had been used to in Peshawar. Kabul was more silent, more soft—more Persian, I supposed, without knowing Persia. The men were for the most part thinner and more lightly-built than the Pakhtuns, though there were Pakhtuns amongst them here as well. The non-Pakhtun majority in this city had an obviously Central-Asian cast of face, the flatness about the eyes and a certain impassivity, with a slope to a smallish chin. Many wore loose robes of Bokhara silk in narrow stripes of colour—a rich red, a yellow, greens, sometimes black. Some wore tightish turbans, but the commonest headdress by far was a Karakul cap. Karakul is 'persian lamb' with its close curls. Grey was fairly usual and very chic, and black probably the cheapest, to judge by its relative frequency. There was also a middle-toned brown that I liked, but the chic-est was a brown approaching gold, to be seen on the heads of a few only.

Since I had decided not to try to work on my notes that day, it was quite pleasant sitting in my first-floor window, watching without effort. Later on I went out and wandered round the neighbourhood. The Kabul river was close by. It seemed to be popular to stroll on a little suspension bridge—no more than a foot-bridge, conveniently midway between two traffic bridges—there to contemplate the water, though there was little water to contemplate at this season. The river was for the moment mostly stationary mud, with a moving, almost liquid snake of it in the middle. I stood watching for some time myself, sharing its agreeably-soothing swing, as in a cradle or a hammock, as men crossed back and forth. Then I continued to the far side of the river and walked up and down the furriers' shops, examining Karakul skins and caps. I checked prices, vaguely thinking 'I fancy myself in such a cap', but I was shocked to discover the price of the 'gold' skins. Language was a problem. Perhaps I misunderstood. No one, or scarcely anyone, spoke English, and very few Pashto—which surprised me because I had been led to suppose that Pashto was being encouraged as the official language of the country. Persian—a Kabuli version of it—was really the current coin.

Tea-pots. A whole street of them. The Japanese seemed to have captured the market with copies of the traditional Russian and Chinese designs. Just as festoons of cheap rayon brocades and muslins in a department-store can often be exciting and beautiful, so these cheap tea-pots seemed beautiful in their hundreds—though less so if you picked one out and examined it. One little shop contained nothing but old, cracked and riveted tea-pots for which the owner wanted prices of such fantasy that I questioned him more closely. I had been accustomed in Pakhtun towns and villages to the snob-concept of 'Russian' tea-services, in much the same way as people in the west are accustomed to the idea of Crown Derby or Sèvres. I knew, for example, that from the eighteenth century one of the most famous Russian makers of china for the central-Asian markets had been a man called Gardner, of English extraction. Most respectable homes had at least one Gardner tea-set, probably of pigeon's-blood red with a flowered medallion on the stomach of each tea-pot, and a similar but smaller medallion on the side of each cup. If you turned the various pieces up, you would find the maker's name—GARDNER—and the Imperial Russian double-headed eagle stamped there—the name itself in Persian script. There were some Gardner pieces amongst the crocks in this shop too.

"That's the price," the man said, politely enough and without emotion. "Americans like them very much and would pay more than I have asked you."

"But it's lost its lid!" I complained.

I decided not to think any more about buying. It was clearly an off-day—a day for not-doing things. I would simply cosset my queasiness and walk beside the Kabul river and so back to the hotel. I walked on through the soft, grey dust.

When I reached my room I found a tray-load of tea-things awaiting me. I suppose it had been there for an hour or more. Never mind. I went to the bathroom to wash my hands before dinner, passing again through the vestibule where the room-less passengers had spread out their bedding now. I tried out a few words of Pashto on them and they replied in Persian, so we got no further than gestures of greeting and farewell, hand on heart and lips politely sealing a half-smile.

"Are you taking the full pension or only the half pension?" the waiter asked when I reached the dining-room.

"The half pension."

"Ah yes," he said. "I remember now. But, sir, you were here at lunch, weren't you?"

"I didn't have the lunch, after all."

"No, he didn't have the lunch," another waiter told the first, and the first said: "I'm sorry, sir. I understand now. Will you sit here?"

There was no menu-card that I could see. But on the other hand I could see what was being served at the next table and somehow— well, a day's starvation is never a bad thing, after all. An off day for starvation. I got up and was almost at the door when the waiter returned with a laden plate.

"Aren't you taking the dinner, then, sir?"

I said: "Never mind. I'll start eating tomorrow, perhaps."

Back in the room again, the servant came to collect the tea-tray and ask for the money. Afternoon tea was an extra, possibly. So I paid him and he left the room and only then did I think about the piece of nice-looking, plain Madeira cake that had come with the tea. I went to the door and called after him. He turned and I saw from his mumbling jaws that his mouth was already stuffed with cake —my cake. O well, never mind.

Chapter 14

FRIDAY brought Sher Ali just before ten. I was delighted to see him. Yesterday had been an unsatisfactory day. He was in fine spirits, and so was I by now, after a long night's rest. I was eating a belated breakfast, rustled up from the tea-shop that gave on to the street immediately below my windows. There was difficulty in bringing the hotel breakfast over to the annexe, it seemed. Sher Ali sat on the window-ledge, talking and sipping a cup of tea. We'd go to Paghman, he said. Many trucks and public buses would be carrying people there, because it was the Friday holiday. We'd spend the day at Paghman, and then, tomorrow Saturday, I would have my permit—before lunch, he supposed—and meanwhile we'd just check about the departure of some truck for Gardez, and that would be that.

"Are you coming with me to Gardez?" I asked hopefully, and he replied in a vague voice that he would like to and that perhaps it would be possible.

"How long will you spend in the Southern Province, Peter?"

"That depends on what I am able to do. I'm not a journalist, and I don't want to be taken round the local hospital or shown a saw-mill or anything. But if they let me move about, I'd like to visit the villages. I'd love to go to your village, for instance. And I'd like to go to Matun, and towards Lakka Tigga."

It was from Matun that General Nadir Khan, who was later to become King Nadir Shah of Afghanistan, had led his men to the attack and capture of the British fort at Thal, in 1919. I have always liked this story and admired the general who with such slender means achieved his victory. People say that if he had pushed on immediately towards Kohat, the Pakhtun tribes would have risen in his support and he might well have reached the river Indus. But I have heard it said that he himself knew his limitations: the limitations imposed by his tiny resources. Courage is not always enough, though he had plenty of that too.

"That would be interesting . . ." Sher Ali was saying, but his face was turned away and he seemed to be signalling to someone in the street. He swung back towards me: "I want to say something to a friend. Will you excuse me for a minute?"—and he got up and started towards the door.

"Why not call him up here?"

He called the man up. Another man whom Sher Ali did not seem to know came up with his friend too. While Sher Ali discussed whatever it was with his friend, I had conversation with the other. He was a Pakhtun.

"We're going to Paghman when we've finished our tea," I said.

"Very good. I will come with you."

There is a polite Pakhtun convention that a friend of a friend's friend is automatically acceptable as a companion. So I said: "Very well."

The man said his name was Gul Muhammed Khan, and he was from the Eastern Province, near the Durand Line.

Meanwhile Sher Ali's friend was leaving. We all went downstairs together and the party split up on the door-step. Sher Ali and Gul Muhammed Khan and I now formed a trio.

"We'll find a truck," they said.

It wasn't difficult. There were several trucks waiting for passengers. The thing was to choose the one you supposed would get filled up first, and consequently leave first. This called for judgment. There was an air of uncertainty, so passengers already installed in one truck would suddenly decide that another truck might be nearer the point of departure, and they would abandon their seats and scurry across to the new one. Then, perhaps, they would fail to get seats in the new one and have to run back to the first where their original seats had meanwhile been occupied by another party. This, in its turn, would give others the quite false impression that it must be this particular truck that would get away first, and a maddish onslaught would develop. Yet, in the end, one of the trucks would pull away, full beyond bearing, and with luck your party would be in it.

I had never before seen so many people willingly cram themselves into so small a space. The Amir Abdur Rahman of Afghanistan, back in the nineteenth century, had of course been accustomed to throwing his prisoners into a well where the bottom-most layer would already have died, and the layer above would be dying and the newcomers would in due course sink slowly towards death as those beneath them disintegrated and made more room, and others were put in on top. But in that case it was the Amir himself and not his prisoners who were being wilful. Here, in this truck, with its camel-tassels swinging, and the little amulets and *tawiz* flapping against the windscreen, we were all jammed in for our pleasure, not for our disintegration. I was lucky to have a corner seat, which meant that I had air, and could look out.

We had left the city behind. It was suddenly full country: a wide, cultivated valley flanked by hills, with here and there a village and well-treed gardens.

"Whose is that house?" I asked Gul Muhammed Khan, who was beside me.

"I don't know. Probably the Prime Minister's."

It was a fine house. There was another fine house a little farther along.

"And that one . . .?"

"That? It must be the Prime Minister's, I suppose."

"But you said . . ."

"Oh, yes I forgot. Then it must be the War Minister's . . . or someone's." He turned to me and laughed.

" . . . and that one?" It was like an impertinent game, but Gul Muhammed Khan had lost interest in it. He said:

"I really don't know about any of these big houses. I don't live in Kabul. I'm Pakhtun. But I suppose it's one of the King's houses, or one of the houses of one of the uncles of the King. They're the ones who have the big houses."

I glanced across Gul Muhammed Khan to where Sher Ali was sitting, hoping that he had not heard. But to my relief he was talking to his neighbour.

We climbed stertorously up the valley. It was already a good deal cooler. When we reached an area under full and elaborate cultivation, with here and there large modern houses of a certain vulgar magnificence, I knew enough not to ask to whom they belonged.

"Is this Paghman?" I asked instead.

"Very nearly."

There were the beginnings of movement in the truck, a wriggling like that of eels spawning, or of prisoners declining to disintegrate. The road had narrowed, and improved, and soon we were riding over

162

tarmac, a relief after the miles of bouncing that had gone before. There were trees, and terraced gardens, and when the driver switched off his engine the sound of water suddenly filled my ears. Paghman and its gardens.

We got out and stood for a minute to let the blood seep back into our legs.

"We'll have tea—and some cherries," Sher Ali said.

A servant from a little châlet that was evidently a tea-shop was running up with a couple of chairs, and another appeared in the doorway carrying an old carpet.

"We shall need three chairs," Sher Ali told him. But as a matter of fact Gul Muhammed Khan was no longer with us. I hadn't seen him go. Not that it mattered.

A party of Europeans, a girl amongst them, walked by chattering together. My eye had been caught by the girl, not only because she was rather pretty, but also because, now that I came to think of it, she was the only woman in sight.

If there were no mothers, there were nevertheless plenty of fathers, and numberless small children, bobbing along like little dinghies behind the parent boat, sometimes in line, linked hand in hand, more often swinging out in a curve, slightly out of control. Then they would swing in again, bumping against things sometimes, but without complaint.

Two men came up and joined us—Pakhtuns again. Whether Sher Ali knew them or not, I am uncertain, though they seemed to know who he was. We abandoned the rickety café chairs and lay on the carpet with the cherries and tea-pots. After a while Sher Ali reversed his cup on to its saucer.

"Have you finished your tea?" he asked me, and proposed a walk.

He had not gone far, however, when his attention was distracted by someone and he went off with this man, leaving me with the two others. These two were spending a couple of days at Paghman, they said. They had carpets and pillows with them.

We wandered off together, carrying the bundles, with the cool green of Chinar trees floating over our heads. By autumn they would be gold and brown and red, like maples. The Paghman gardens are an enchantment. There are water-courses, grass lawns hang in terraces, and everywhere, in a manner reposefully haphazard, are chinars, and mulberries, walnuts, apricots, cherries. Farther up, as the little valley rises and narrows, are more formal gardens which—as I saw later in the day—attract the bigger crowds with their fountains and trim pathways and flowers. But it was this unordered part that I found so charming. Here and there would be small houses, a little crumbly with inattention, modern and yet with a Moghul feeling to them. The Moghul emperors had held Kabul for generations, starting with the Emperor Babur who loved Kabul more dearly than any other city, perhaps, and was buried there. Paghman could never compete with the splendours of the Mohgul gardens of Kashmir—Nishat, Shalimar—but in its way it has much to offer.

One of the two men was spreading his carpet under a chinar. When he opened it up a big sausage of a cushion was revealed—black satinette with a patterning of cabbage-roses. He made me a formal bow, motioning me to rest my elbow on a cabbage-rose, and to stretch myself at length. So I took my shoes off and did so. The party of Europeans with the girl came past, talking languidly, and the other Pakhtun of our trio stopped in the middle of laying out the second carpet and looked at her covertly. Then he looked at me, made a shy little cough and said he wished to talk about girls. So I said, why not? Fornication and the weather are easy things for strangers to discuss, after all.

"Here in Kabul?" he asked, in answer to a question I had put to him. "Oh, difficult . . . very difficult. Sometimes, if you are lucky. And if there is a field of corn. But only when the crop has grown tall, of course."

"It is more modest indoors, I would have said. And more comfortable, too."

"And *where*, indoors?' he demanded.

"Oh surely . . .!"

"Well, *you* tell me where! In your house, or my house, or the girl's house? I have been told that in Europe it is easy, but here . . ."

"About the girls," I asked him—and I noticed that his eyes were secretly following the party of Europeans as they disappeared amongst the trees—"first of all you don't see so many women in the streets of Kabul, and secondly they all wear *burqas*. How can you decide *which*?"

There are very strictly-applied rules about veiling for women in the cities of Afghanistan. The ill-fated King Amanullah's attempts to move too fast towards the emancipation of women has actually put things back for years to come. The women are compelled to wear the *burqa*, though under the hem of it you can sometimes see that the wearer is dressed in modern western clothes, short skirt, nylons, high-heeled shoes. It looks rather silly, as a matter of fact, or at least I find it so.

He looked at me in astonishment. "How? But you can see their eyes, of course!"

"I don't think eyes are enough," I said.

"I can tell from the eyes at once, I can," he said, and his friend nodded. Obviously they could not understand why I should not be satisfied with eyes seen through a crocheted slot.

"But what can you see through that slot?" I asked them.

"I can see her eyes and what they are saying."

"Oh yes, of course you can see if her eyes are saying 'yes', but what can you know about the rest of her?"

"We know everything at once from the eyes."

And I remembered how a French girl had told me something years before. She had married an Afghan, a man of respectable family who lived in Kabul, and had, of course, to submit to the normal conventions. He had therefore required his wife to wear the *burqa* when she went to the bazaars to do her shopping.

"I do not mind the *burqa*," the girl had told me, "though it is ugly and inconvenient and, in summer, so hot that one suffocates. I wear it as a rule, when I go out in the streets of Kabul. But sometimes . . ."

Sometimes she did not put it on: and because no one in the bazaars was likely to recognize her as the wife of a particular Afghan, it didn't really much matter, even to her husband. The men in the bazaars were in fact most decorous, she had told me, never staring at her or embarrassing her in any way.

"But when I pass through a crowd of men wearing my *burqa* . . .!" she exclaimed, laughing at the recollection of it: "*Yai, yai,* my poor *fesses!* They pinch me, the men, black and blue!"

The *burqa* can be a fetish—a symbol far more compelling than the reality it hides. I have already noted that some people claim to find the *burqa* beautiful in itself—and everyone knows that tight-lacing, and perhaps button-boots, are beauty in the specialist-eye of the beholder: but that French girl, so pretty, so much more pinchable, you would have said, when you could see what you were pinching. . . .

"There are some women in the city of Kabul, hidden away," one of the two men went on, "but they are expensive—because someone has to be paid not to take them away to prison. It is the visitors who have to pay the woman enough so that some can be spared from her earnings for the people who would otherwise take her to prison."

"And some women have husbands who are unable to keep them satisfied." the other said. "All that is very dangerous because it is easy to get killed that way."

"By the husband or other relatives, you see."

"Of course," I admitted, and was going to ask some more questions when Sher Ali appeared, carrying a frying-pan. Gul Muhammed Khan was with him too, and another man who looked as if he might be a servant of some kind. The 'servant' carried a brazier of burning charcoal.

The air was full of peace. No politics, no animosities, just the slow-moving rhythm of summer, with friends who demand nothing and the trees above us. I lay contentedly on my carpet, bolstered by the cabbage-roses, watching the meal come slowly forward to readiness—spitted meat, and rissoles of mutton spiced with onions, cooked in clarified butter—of which the frying-pan was half-full. Someone unwrapped some pieces of bread from a cloth: they were smaller and finer than the great bread snow-shoes of the wayside villages. They were about the size of a good Dover sole, and the same shape, slashed across the width and baked to a light gold. Then cherries. We lay back under the chinars, talking quietly, till two more men came up, greeted Sher Ali and begged us to take tea with them. They even protested with vehement good manners that we had shamed them by not coming straight to them for our midday meal.

I suppose it was already tea-time, or nearly. I had lost track of the hour. I suddenly realized that this was my first contact with something truly Afghan: it had proved familiar and easy to slip into. It was not so very different, after all, from the life of Marrakesh and the countryside about it, except that here it was more formal.

"They are theological students," Sher Ali told me.

We left someone to stand guard over the carpets and cushions and followed our hosts. Their hostel was near-by. It might have contained a dozen little rooms, on two floors. I saw only the staircase and the little room that our hosts shared with four others, their bunks set in tiers of two, round three sides of the four walls. The fourth wall contained a big window, open on to the branches of a walnut tree, thirty feet above the ground. We seemed to be suspended in leafy greenness. They served us a sweet tea, on the surface of which butter floated. One of the students produced some hard pink sweets from a box. In between begging us to eat more, to drink more tea, they spoke of themselves and their life here—four years of Qoranic study, Shariat, Islamic law, following twelve years of general education.

"Then we do two years studying civil law, and finally—as a rule—a couple of years in Cairo or somewhere else in the Middle East."

I was no longer surprised that they looked too old to be students. They were well-mannered, and charming hosts, and even if no more than a few tens of them graduate each year and are finally dispersed about the country to administer justice, it is a move that is perhaps already paying dividends. They were Pakhtuns. A fanatic Pakhtun mullah can be a disastrous disturber of government planning. A cadre of tamed Islamic jurists, taken from amongst these students, would be a useful, stabilizing element in the life of the country.

*   *   *

Like flighting birds people were making for home. We searched for, but could not find, the truck that had brought us—but it had no importance. There were others. The one we finally chose was very satisfactory because Sher Ali and I managed to get seats alongside the driver, the driver being a man of a related Pakhtun tribe. There was no room for our knees, so we sat diagonally on the little bench. While we were waiting to start, Mira Jan 'Sial' came by with a group of friends and stopped to talk to us. It had only been two days before that we had last seen each other, at Sher Ali's dinner-party, but the change in my routine from Embassy to city had somehow disturbed all sense of duration. It seemed that we had not met for an age.

"What do you think of my magazine?" 'Sial' asked me.

To be honest I had not had time to read more than a little of it. The particular issue concerned itself principally with the 'economics' of Pashtunistan: I had read enough to know that. I can struggle with the vernacular script much as a schoolchild struggles with his first adult newspaper. But it takes time and concentration. So I said:

"I'll let you know in a month from now."

"A month? But you said that you would be leaving Afghanistan . . ."

"Yes, I'm afraid so. I'll have to write to you, then."

He turned and made a joke at my expense with his friends. I felt very warmly towards them all.

In spite of the amulet attached to the windscreen to preserve us from misfortune, we had a blow-out on the way back to Kabul, and we had no spare wheel. Having no spare wheel, there was naturally no great need for tools to deal with such an emergency. So we spent a long while, hoping that some other traveller would be able to help. A succession of trucks making for Kabul passed us, but beyond stopping to console us they could not help much, having no tools either. We all got out and wandered about, or sat on the roadside. A father arranged himself like a great fleshy mattress against a bank, disposing his children about his thighs and knees, where they sat, tired and patient.

The driver said: "I hope you aren't angry with me."

"Why should I be?"

"Because of the waiting."

I said: "It's God's will. Of course I am not angry with you. It's very pleasant here with you."

"Yes, isn't it?" he commented.

It began to grow dark after a while.

A passenger gave me a piece of bread which I felt obliged to eat out of politeness though I didn't want it. Sher Ali still had some cherries. Gul Muhammed Khan, whom we had supposed must be somewhere in the back of the truck, was not there at all.

"Did you enjoy it?" Sher Ali asked me.

"Yes," I said. It was true.

The air was hot and still. A little dragon like a big iguana scuttled across the road and was chased by some of us, but nobody could catch it. The rest of us waited, peacefully, endlessly. Over above Kabul, miles away, the lights on Bimaru lit themselves like candles.

Chapter 15

I was at the passport office early the next morning, according to plan, and from time to time I asked how things were going with my endorsement.

"Very soon now," they said.

Shortly after eleven they started to say something else—that the high personage who had to sign the endorsement had not yet arrived. Then, a little later still, they said they now heard he would not perhaps be coming to the office before lunch because of some important state business.

"He does not sign papers *after* the lunch interval, I think you said?"

"Well, sir," they replied politely, "he doesn't as a rule, but we think that in this case . . ."

After lunch I learnt that the personage would not after all be returning to his office—though 'returning' did not seem quite the right word to use.

"We will send your passport to the hotel, with the endorsement signed and everything in order," they said. "Please don't worry at all. It will be signed and sent to you."

"Should I cancel my plan for leaving today, do you think?"

"We wish you to please yourself exactly," they assured me.

I said thank you, adding that I would wait at the hotel. But on the way back I telephoned to the Foreign Ministry.

"Oh yes. I'm sorry about the delay," they said. Then, just as I was about to ring off, they said: "By the way, your passport says that you are a 'merchant'."

It was said quite lightly, as if it had no importance.

"Yes, of course. I *used* to be a merchant, years ago."

"And now?"

"I suppose I have become a writer."

"I think you said you were a merchant and that you were coming to Afghanistan for a private visit."

"Well?"

"Well . . ."

"Well, what?"

"Oh nothing, really."

"But I explained all that, surely. And it was an Afghan Government official—was it you yourself, or your colleague?—who suggested that I stay on so as to learn something about Afghanistan. Don't you remember?"

"Oh yes, I think it was. Anyway, it doesn't matter. You are going to have your permit all right. I'm only sorry about the delay."

"Thank you very much. When do you think I'll get it?"

"Just as soon as the endorsement is signed."

"Thank you very much," I said again, without a trace—I hope—of irritation. After all, what could it matter—an hour, a day, even a week more?

I telephoned to Sher Ali and got that connection too. Saturday was evidently an auspicious day for telephones. Permits were, possibly, different.

"What a nuisance," Sher Ali's voice said. "But it's all right. These things always take some time—and it's not usual to go to the Southern Province."

I walked back to the hotel and on the way ran into Muhammed Ayub Khan talking to a group of tribesmen who looked much like men from Waziristan. Muhammed Ayub Khan himself seemed to be in excellent spirits.

"We had a most interesting discussion at dinner the other night, didn't we?" he remarked.

"Yes, very."

"I was with the Governor of the Southern Province yesterday," he went on. "The Governor was in Kabul on a brief visit, as you may have heard. I took the opportunity of putting in a word with him about you."

"That was kind."

"Only too glad to be of service," he said, comfortably. "When were you planning to leave for Gardez?"

"This morning."

"But . . ." He laughed politely. "Oh, I see. You are joking."

Then he indicated the group of tribesmen, saying: "These men are

Pashtunistanis from Waziristan, you know. Perhaps you would like to hear from their own lips all about it."

"I don't think so, Muhammed Ayub Khan, thank you. Not just at the moment."

"But I gathered you were anxious to meet Pashtunistanis."

"I shall be going to Waziristan, you know."

"Do you think the Pakistanis will let you?"

"I imagine they will."

"Oh well, but it seems a pity not to take the opportunity of meeting Wazirs when it presents itself, I should have thought."

*   *   *

Back in the hotel bedroom I was suddenly conscious of afternoon flies and heat, of the ugliness of Kabul, of dust—and of despair. All these things came crowding in through the three shutterless windows. I suddenly knew that I would never get to Gardez, let alone to·Matun or to the villages of the Southern Province. I was not surprised at the knowledge. I had been a great deal more surprised at learning that permission was being granted. I don't think I even troubled to consider exactly what had gone wrong. It was obvious, of course, that they were suspicious of me, and this was not surprising, either, since they were suspicious of each other. But I felt deflated, and overburdened by the things that were coming in at the windows, the heat, the dust, the flies, the suspicion . . .

I lay on the bed with a folded magazine—'Sial's' exposition of the economic potential of Pashtunistan—and struck at the flies with it, but I failed to inflict even surface-wounds. I thought of green park-lands and of the Embassy swimming-pool: of the poor, distraught-looking inhabitants of the Kabul Hotel, and of riveted tea-pots. I thought of three weeks and more, a month, of Afghan time that had led me to my creaking hotel bed.

Something had certainly gone wrong with my stars in their courses. I lay wondering what to do about it. Should I, for example, buy myself an amulet—a little *tawiz* in a leather pouch to suspend round my neck? Or knuckle-dusters? Or a bromide? The more I wondered what to do, the less my thoughts responded. In fact they started to circle in my head on their own account. After a while they were going quite fast and seemed to be laughing—though I was not.

"Whirling mice," I told myself. Whirling mice, a-spin on their own axes because of some little disorder.

You don't see much when you are whirling. Dervishes know this, too, but whereas they end in ecstasy, I do not. I can therefore record only a few imprecise images, none of them in the least ecstatic. Plates of food in the hotel dining-room, for instance—a succession of days and plates, accompanied by a frieze of lodgers' eyes, stencilled eyes of a dozen or more long-term inmates—and plates of food rejected already at a previous meal. The eyes would watch for the moment when I laid down my despairing fork and would then turn themselves up into their sockets with a long-drawn ah-h-h-h...! as if at last I was becoming one with themselves. Amongst all these poor sunk-socketed starvelings I seem to see one well-nourished person —a scientist's control?—munching, munching—delicious vitamin tablets, Vita-this, Bio-that, Bévitine, Bénerva Forte, and a Gaylord Hauser canister of Brewer's Yeast. I am still aware today of a big room, curtained in mud-colour, and of the whine of insects trapped inside with the inmates.

It was a peculiar experience, but the British, even at their most peculiar, must never admit defeat....

I braved the hotel telephone, several times I did it as the days slunk by, each time astonished to find the cylinders dropping into their automatic slots—click ... brr-brr .. brr-brr ... brr-brr ...

"Ah, it's you, Mr. Mayne. Listen, will you try again on Tuesday? I gather that the Governor of the Southern Province is temporarily out of Gardez. He will naturally wish to be there to greet you ... Ah yes, Mayne. Will you ring up again on Wednesday, shall we say? Or Thursday might be better. Perhaps the breach in the road will have been mended ... or Friday? How silly: of course, the office will be closed on Friday. I was forgetting. Then Saturday, perhaps. Try again on Saturday, Peter, will you ...?"

I would sit at my window, recovering from the *angst* of telephones, and watch the city of Kabul disintegrating in the dust. I thought of getting in touch with Sher Ali—not for his help: I was past helping, but for his company—and then decided against it I stared at the Karakul-skin caps. It had been the beautiful golden-brown that I had fancied for myself so long ago, but today they looked very different. A jaundiced, sickly gold. My personal vision had settled itself on the poor things.

I sat for hours, waiting for I don't know what. Once the hotel reception clerk came over and knocked at my door. He said:

"You know, sir, we only promised you the room for two nights, and it's already . . . We need your room, sir. It was reserved in advance for a gentleman. I'm very sorry."

For an unholy moment deliverance drew near—deliverance not of my own seeking but the very best kind, forced upon me by circumstances beyond my control as certainly and honourably as if my second had thrown in the sponge. The clerk stood watching hope surge up inside me and promptly slapped it back again:

" . . . but never mind. I think we can manage. Above all we don't want to inconvenience you, sir. If I put the Persian gentleman and his wife and babies into No. 8, and . . . Yes, and that lady in No. 12, and I'll make those two old gentlemen share No. 11. Yes, I can manage." He smiled with triumph. "So you see, sir, there's no need for you to go, after all!"

My stomach had dropped out again, but I went walking by the bed of the Kabul river where the dusty, treeless boulevards line it. I had intended, perhaps, to take up position for a while on the little foot suspension bridge, but when I got there I found it closed to the public. It seemed that the day before too heavy a group of citizens had squeezed themselves into its hammock, and had stood soothingly a-swing as they watched something nasty float down the sludge. As this object passed beneath them, they had evidently all turned in their excitement to lean across the downstream handrail, and the hammock —unprepared for this—had tipped them into the mud below. In the tumble one of their number had snapped off at the neck, I was told. There was a big crowd leaning over from the safety of the embankment now, looking at the place where this had happened the day before.

Even other people's misfortunes, however, failed to lessen my own. I sloped back to the hotel. An untidy old woman was sitting on the kerb, with a burden of wood laid beside her. I ought, I suppose to have offered to carry her load home for her, like wayfarers in a fairy-tale, but I compromised with a coin. She looked up and I found myself staring into eyes that I knew, even through a crocheted-cotton grille.

Carabosse . . . !

Of course I was mistaken, and yet . . .

That afternoon I embarked upon a rationalization. I said that time was marching on, that I still had a long way to go before I had finished my Pakhtun journey, that I had autumn obligations in Europe. I said that for my family's sake it would be a pity to go quite dotty in a far-off land (what would they tell people?). I packed my bag in a trance, paid my bill, tried to telephone Bernard at the British Embassy to announce my return, and failed. But I had gathered momentum by now—too much to be halted by little cylinders giggling automatically into the wrong slots far off in the Telephone Exchange. Gone all vestige of British phlegm. I hailed a tonga. The driver reined in his pony.

"Where?"

"The British Embassy."

"Eh?"

"I'll show you where it is."

It was just after five. My watch had kept its head, even if I had not, and whatever the day of the week I realized that after all the Embassy would have closed down till tomorrow—and that the telephone expert would have gone home. In the back of my mind I knew that I must provide something for my momentun to feed on, so that it could carry me along with it. I must ask the Pakistanis to signal to their North-West Frontier Government in Peshawar so that, weeks late, my ruptured tour-programme could be resumed.

"No! Stop!" I said to the tonga-driver. "Go to the Pakistan Embassy."

"Eh? . . ."

"Yes. Go on. Go to the Pakistan Embassy."

I left the tonga in the road and walked across to the gates. A very old beggar with only one leg poking out under his rags stood near the sentry-box. He had a long, yellow-stained beard, but I dared nor look into his eyes for fear that . . . nonsense, of course, though you can stick another beard on, I suppose, and strap your second leg up like Long John Silver in a movie.

"'I take refuge in the Lord of the Dawn,'" I murmured, not looking, then made a sign to ward off things and walked, head high, into the Pakistan Embassy.

✱ ✱ ✱

Bernard and Anne did not seem in the least surprised to see me an hour later. They were sitting under a mulberry-tree, with the mulberries dropping and exploding all round them in little spurts of a red too vivid. Francis was there too, with his articulated wooden train. For my part I merely said that I wasn't going to the Southern Province after all. Whether this undecorated statement satisfied them or whether it did not, they asked no questions.

"I must ring up the Afghan Foreign Office and tell them, I think," I added.

"It's too late today. Ring them in the morning."

"Yes. And then I must look round for some truck going back to Peshawar."

"Don't hurry."

"You know that Bernard's Chargé d'Affaires now?" Anne asked, in a wonderfully calming voice. "The Ambassador left yesterday. And the new one doesn't come for some time. Nanny's very pleased and wants us to move into the 'big house' immediately—but, of course, we shan't at all. She's busy picking apricots. There's an enormous and very spectacular tree in the 'big house' garden."

"And a very spectacular pot of caviar has come round from the Soviet Embassy. If it were marmalade there would be two pounds of it, at least. Whom shall we invite to eat it with us?"

This was the sort of soothing, domestic conversation that I felt inclined for. I had no need to search for the answer to Bernard's question. I knew it by instinct.

"You may be quite certain that if they've sent you caviar, they must have sent pots to all the other foreign diplomatists as well, so it wouldn't seem a special kindness to ask anyone in to share yours. It would be coals to Newcastle."

Anne thought for a moment: "We could eat it tonight, perhaps. With a squeeze of lemon."

"And spoons," Bernard suggested.

"Just the three of us—a quiet, restful dinner at home."

"And me?" Francis asked.

"You shall have some of the Ambassador's lovely apricots in the nursery, darling."

"They're ours now. Nanny says so."

"Yes, dear."

*   *   *

I went to Sher Ali to thank him for all his kindness and to say good-bye. Neither asked the other why he had kept away for days, nor did I explain how it was that I came now only to say that I was leaving that same afternoon. We both knew, I suppose, that a barrier had grown up between us—a barrier that concerned neither of us, yet for him real, and for me an opaque intangible.

"I have done almost nothing," he said blankly. "So little . . "

"So much. I would like to come back one day, but I fear it is unlikely. If ever I do, it will be for longer—with no book to worry over. No barriers."

He nodded.

It is miserable when something troubles a friendship and cannot be put right.

With the brittle fatuity of leave-taking I said: "Perhaps next time we meet it will be in Europe again."

"Who knows, Peter?"

          *   *   *

I was in a truck this time, and others waved their dumb handker-chiefs, and eighteen hours later the sun was coming up over the Peshawar Vale like a giant into battle. There was a menace in the air, but I was too weary to accept the challenge. We had halted briefly at the far end of the Lataband to give the saint a thanks-offering, and again at Jalalabad for a meal and mosquitoes, less briefly at the Frontier customs-post. They had opened the barrier for us at Torkham to let us through into Pakistan and to offer us their fine metalled roads. The Khyber Pass had been in deep shadow still, as quiet as the blessed smooth-running of wheels on tarmac. The watch-towers of the Afridis and Shinwaris watched us as we slipped by, down into the open, golden valley. I was given a room at the Peshawar Club—the same blinding-white little cubicle that I had had last time. I left the sun un-challenged in his heavens and went to bed till dusk.

Part 3

PATHAN—PAKHTUN

Chapter 16

WHEN I went out that evening into the Peshawar streets, I had not walked more than a hundred yards before I had been told three times that a thousand people had died of heat-stroke in the province since the beginning of the month. Tragically, and quite without precedent, it was true. The next morning, at the Provincial Government Secretariat, I was told that it would be some days before I could go up to the Kurram Valley, because the Political Agent happened to be on tour.

I had already had to revise my programme, as a matter of fact. I had spent so long in Kabul that I had necessarily to cut one or two visits originally planned in the Pakistan frontier areas. Chitral, for example. Chitral had nothing to do with Pakhtuns, of course, or even with Pathans (despite the Pashtunistan map), but it was country I liked and I had hoped to put in a week or so there. Dir and Swat and Malakand —these had been on my original list too, but if something had to be left out now, then these three areas, Pathan rather than Pakhtun according to my impertinent definition, were the obvious omissions. But now I learnt that I must in any case hold up my departure for the Kurram Agency, and I delightedly slipped Swat back into the list again.

"I think I'll spend a few days in Swat, then," I told the officer at the secretariat. "And possibly Dir as well."

The secretariat was almost empty. On my way in I had passed a few orderlies collapsed on benches. Through reed-screened windows over which a gardener would presumably squirt water from a syringe when he remembered to do so, I had noticed one or two electric-lit officials and had known them to be sacrifices on the altar of High Summer, their task to send the files up and down the Nathia Gali mountainside. The theory from the days of the British had been that a move to the mountains was necessary during the hot weather to enable senior officers to continue working themselves to a standstill.

Down in Peshawar, too, work was at a standstill, here in the silence, with the bowl of heaven reversed to hold the steam in. The offerings seemed to be cooking nicely. Down here the most one could do was to die, and in doing so give a last convulsive twitch to this file, a tweak to that. The torpid mail-bags must go through.

"Hm-m . . ." said the official I was talking to. "We must first write to the Political Agent of Dir, Swat and Malakand. Will you kindly give me the proposed date of your visit?"

"If I take the morning bus, I can be in Swat by tomorrow afternoon," I said.

"Tomorrow is the . . ." He was looking for his calendar under the piles of paper that fluttered in the roaring of his fan. ". . . is the . . . but even if I write today, my letter will not reach the Political Agent sahib tomorrow."

"Perhaps we had better telephone to him, then."

"I see that your programme said you would be going to Waziristan —in June," he murmured to himself, as he re-read his copy of a letter the Chief Secretary had sent round to all the agencies so long before. "It is the end of July now."

He sat back again in his seat, observing first the fan above him and then the effect of its awful turbulence. The papers on his desk fluttered like birds—doves trapped under paper-weights. He spoke his thoughts. "People say that August is the worst month of the year in Peshawar. But I sometimes say that July—the end of July—is the worst time."

"I, too, believe that now is the worst time, and that is why I want to go to the coolness of Swat tomorrow, rather than await my death in Peshawar."

"Many have died. It is unheard of, terrible." Then, after a pause, he said: "You have read in the papers, perhaps?"

"Yes. It is terrible." I paused too, for a decent interval. "Could we not telephone to the Political Agent?"

"First we must get the Chief Secretary's permission for you to go to Swat. Swat is not on your programme now, you see."

We seemed to be losing ground, rather than gaining it. I said: "Let us pretend, shall we, that I am carrying out a delayed original programme? Shall *I* telephone to the Political Agent?"

"We ought to write . . . but I suppose . . ."

I reached over his desk towards the telephone but he snatched it away as if it were his virginity: "No, no! Not with mine! Don't you understand? There are rules about such things! Only in cases of extreme need could I let you use mine, except for local work of course. You must use a public one."

"I shall go back to the club and do it from there, then," I said.

Back in the club I telephoned to Malakand in the hills a hundred miles to the north. The Political Agent was not available, but a clerk answered the call. He was helpful and kind and said he would pass on my message to the P.A. and call me back. He wanted to know exactly when I would be arriving and by what means of transport. I told him my bus timings.

"I plan to spend a few days in Saidu Sharif," I said. It is the capital of Swat State.

Both Swat and Dir are semi-independent states under Pakistan, just as, before partition, they had been under the old Government of India. The rulers, a Wali and a Nawab respectively, are both complete autocrats. If I were forced into a corner I might admit that their subject-peoples were Pathan, but I would decline, even on the rack, to admit that they were truly Pakhtun. The Wali of Swat, Jehan Zeb, is a good friend of many years' standing.

"Is the Wali sahib expecting you?" the P.A.'s clerk asked me.

"No. But I think he will be quite happy to see me."

"Ah."

"I could stop the night in Malakand on the way through, if the P.A. sahib wanted to see me."

"Please stop and see the P.A. sahib."

"I am coming by bus, as I explained, and that creates a problem. If I get out of my bus in order to meet the P.A., the bus will go on without me. In this way I shall miss the connecting bus which is to take me from Butkhel to Saidu Sharif, and I will have to stop the night in Malakand. Is there accommodation available in Malakand?"

Malakand is no more than a little settlement with the Political Agent's house and his offices and courts, and a small fort.

"The Rest House is full, sir. I know this because . . ."

"Never mind why. But since there seems to be nowhere for me to stay, I don't want to stop to see the P.A. sahib. I am sure he will understand."

"Oh, sir, I don't think he *will* understand."

I rang off. I was rather irritable. Everyone was in the same condition at present.

*   *   *

"They say that Abdul Qadir Khan is waiting for you," a club servant said.

"I thought he was in Abbottabad. I saw him there. Has he come back to Peshawar, then?"

"Yes."

"If you see him, please tell him that I'm at the club—and that I leave tomorrow, *Insha'Allah.*"

"Tomorrow? For where?"

"For Swat."

"I will be unable to tell him because I am busy this evening, and working now. And he will be unable to come to the club to see you, Peter sahib, because he is sick, in hospital."

"Sick? But you people don't go to hospital to be sick as a rule. What's the matter with him?"

"He has been shot—and a police found him near his village and he was brought to the hospital here."

"Do you know what happened?"

"I don't know. Abdul Qadir Khan is not my friend."

"He is not my friend, either."

"Then why does he ask for you? You must go to him, of course, since he is dying and he asks for you."

"Dying . . .?"

I went to the hospital at once. I ran into a house-surgeon.

"Yes," he said. "It must be that man who was admitted last week. He's getting on very well indeed. He'll be out soon. You'll find him in the ward at the end of that corridor."

I was relieved, and thanked him. Then I went into the ward. There was a group of villagers in their rough country clothes round a bed and, propped on a pillow, his eyes closed, was Abdul Qadir Khan. As I came up to him he opened his eyes.'

"Ah-h, Peter sahib. So you have come in time," he said. "You remember what I told you and what you told me?" He broke off for a moment, and his jaw clenched as if in a sudden spasm of pain. Then he relaxed again. "They have killed me. You said I should

go back to the village. You remember? Never mind. It was written."

Mektūb—it was written, fated.

"But the house-surgeon," I began. "I've just seen him. He says
that . . ."

"What can he know? He is kind and good, but he knows nothing."
The villagers at his bedside nodded, nodded.

"Listen, Abdul Qadir Khan," I said. "All you have to do is to
lie there quietly and let them dress your wounds, and within a week,
Insha'Allah, you will be out again. They told me so. It's not
serious."

He smiled a little. "Dying is not serious, it is true, Peter sahib. I
am glad that you have come and that you are in time. You know
who has killed me, of course?"

They all started talking at once now, excitedly, ecstatically, and
Abdul Qadir Khan lay back on his pillow, the centre of it all, as at
birth, or marriage, or death: but not quite at the centre, because he
was not the only one, it seemed.

"You know, you know, you have heard?" they were asking, filled
with news, spilling over with it. "Roshan—he's already dead! *And*
Mahboob! Sadiq Khan did it! And Sadiq Khan's cousin-brother
helped as guard and to carry the chopper . . ."

" . . . and you heard how it was? How can you not have
heard!"

" . . . they were hiding by the road, where there is a little bridge, and
trees. Sadiq and his cousin-brother. Sadiq had his revolver. *T-hung!*
T-hung! Two, he got, quick as a falcon! Roshan and Mahboob—
before anyone knew what he was going to do. And then Abdul
Qadir Khan, here! *T-hung!* Three! That was Abdul Qadir
Khan, you see, and . . ."

" . . . and then what? *Ah-h-h-h-h!*—what a thing! Listen to
me! Keep silent, Abdul Qadir Khan! I am telling this. Listen,
Peter sahib! Abdul Qadir Khan saw everything—he was lying
there, but he was not quite dead yet. Sadiq took the chopper from
his cousin-brother, it was a chopper for wood, and with it he cut
through Roshan's neck so that the head came off—*B-hang!* Blood,
blood everywhere spurting! Then Sadiq Khan drew a big handkerchief from his pocket, slowly he drew it and held it out before him and
then he kissed it—and then he took the head and wrapped it in this

handkerchief. Then he went away silently, paying no attention to Mahboob lying there dead, nor to Abdul Qadir Khan nearly dead too."

"There is more to tell, Peter Sahib. Listen! Sadiq Khan went to Roshan's village—can you imagine the madness? Roshan's friends —me and him and him and him—would surely be coming soon, coming quickly to the sound of the revolver-shots, but Sadiq cared nothing. He went to the village and outside it he found a child to whom he gave the handkerchief with the head wrapped inside. 'Give this to the wife of Roshan Khan,' he said to the child. 'Tell her it is the gift of Sadiq Khan.' And the child says that Sadiq's hands and his clothes were covered with blood and that his voice was clear and loud, so that it frightened him and compelled him to do as he was ordered, and he did it."

They nodded at each other and at me, and Abdul Qadir Khan lay silent on his pillow.

"Three of them, he got. Roshan, Mahboob—and the third is Abdul Qadir Khan. It was written."

"It was written," Abdul Qadir Khan said from behind his shuttered eyes.

"Sadiq has taken refuge in Tirah, people say. With the Afridis. He is *mafrūr* now."

Yes, Sadiq would be an outlaw now. And Gul Khan was already dead these several weeks, his death avenged. And now it was some-one else's turn, and it was the death of Roshan and Mahboob that must be avenged. I was becoming used again to the idea of friends' dying violently. I don't know what I felt, if indeed I felt anything as I stood there in the ward—unless it was perhaps that death in war-time, from an unnamed bullet or an unnamed bomb, was one thing—and that death at the hands of your own, personal, sworn enemy, today, or next spring, or whenever the time might be fully ripe and you had, for once, not taken the proper precautions—that was another thing.

I stayed on for a minute more, embarrassed and silent, and then turned to go.

"I will come and see you when I return from Swat, *Insha' Allah,*" I told Abdul Qadir Khan.

"Good be on your way," he said, "but I will be gone when you return," and the others nodded.

I left Peshawar next morning.

*　　　　*　　　　*

There was a big box on the roof of the bus, just over the driver's seat, and wording stencilled on it: 'Someone's Special Air-Conditioning Unit'; and inside the bus there were two taps, one in the front and one farther back for the lower-class passengers, with more wording, in Urdu and English this time: 'Iced Water is available for the convenience of passengers.' I was then told that the air-conditioning unit operated with blocks of ice loaded into it. I did not need to be told that no one had put any ice into it that day.

We trundled through the countryside, orchards veiled with dust, sign-posts—Charsadda, Mardan, Shabkader. The mountains lay fainting against the skyline, formless to west and north of us. I tried not to think as we trundled through the furnace and when, hours later, we reached the foot of the Malakand Pass, I did not even get out of the bus. They were checking the bus and its passengers at Dargai, where there is a barrier between the administered districts and the Malakand Agency.

"Are you Peter Mayne sahib?" a Malakand Levy-man asked me through the window. The Levy forms part of the Frontier Corps.

"Yes."

"They wish to know if you are stopping to visit the Political Agent sahib in Malakand."

"I don't think so. Does he want me to?"

"I don't know. His clerk is asking on the telephone. What shall I say?"

"Say that I am going straight through to Swat—that if I get out of the bus I shall have no means of reaching Swat till tomorrow."

The bus waddled on up the pass road and behind us the vale of Peshawar stretched in its haze of impenetrable heat, waves of it, fingering for us still as we climbed beyond its reach.

At the village of Butkhel I had to change buses. It is a gay, decadent little village, and quite a number of its ladies have in the past found employment in the whore-shops of Lahore. I don't know what whores are supposed to do in Pakistan today, except sing endless songs to which their visitors scarcely trouble to listen. It all seems rather dull to me, like dinner-parties with no drink. But I like Butkhel very much. I like its river and its canals, and the waving valley corn and the olive-trees, and the brightly-coloured buses that hang about outside the tea-shops in the main, indeed the only, street.

I was looking for a bus to Swat. There was no definite service, and

N

certainly no time-table, but people said there was quite a chance that sufficient passengers would be found to encourage a bus to set off. I ate a late breakfast, sweet tea and *parathas*, which are unleavened wheat-cakes fried in *ghee*, which is clarified butter. Very filling and nutritious. It was too hot for talk. We had slithered down from the high-point of Malakand and its pass into another valley by now—but the air was filled with the booming of Eastern music played too loud on loud-speakers. I watched passengers taking their places in the bus for Swat. I had already staked my claim to a seat. The bus was painted white and all over its flanks were medallions in colour, fortresses grimly granite, flowers and flower-pots, and aeroplanes—or were they birds? We started.

We were stopped at the next check-post. On the far side of the river was Chakdarra with its main fort and, above it on a hill, the little fort to which Gunga Din had carried water for the soldiers under the gun-sights of the enemy. Kipling made a verse about him. That had been in the days when the people hereabouts were fiercer, more violently Pakhtun, than they are now. We were held up while a Levy-man came to look for me.

"Are you Peter Mayne? Where are you going?"

"To Swat. Saidu Sharif."

"For how long?"

"If I am welcome and happy, I shall stay some days. If I am not, I shall not."

"And after Swat, where?"

"I haven't stopped to think yet."

"Oh."

On again. The river flowed past us on the left, very full at this season, so that the rocks and the rapids scarcely showed themselves in the general turbulence. A friend from one of the villages had taken me down this stretch of water on an inflated skin some years before —but at a season when you could see what you were doing.

At Thana, another village, we stopped for a little, and I asked after a friend—but he was away on the pilgrimage to Mecca. On the whole the journey was not developing as I had hoped: moreover there were too many people in the bus, one of them wedged on the floor between my knees, others standing with their heads bent forward over their chests because the roofing was too low for them to stand erect. The hills had moved in on our right, cliff-like and towering over the road.

To the left I could see a curve of water, lagoon-smooth, where the logs collect and take their ease for a little before being poked out into the main flood again, on their way down-river. The bus stopped.

"You can climb on top now," the driver said.

We were quite near the Swat State boundary. The rules about roof-riding could be relaxed now. Half of us climbed on to the roof, amongst all the luggage. I chose my own bed-roll to lean against, fat and comfortable. We started off again.

This was much better, with the roar of cooling air about us, and the dust like a cumulus, well behind. Ahead I could see another truck approaching, followed by its dust-cloud. We met at speed, the two dragons swallowed each other, each into the long, white, tunnelled, rasping throat of the other, and miraculously, in a blind victory of faith, we came out again at the far end. Fortresses, like toys for giants' nurseries, were dotted about the landscape now, crumbling stone laced with wooden, horizontal members, less solid than the medallion-forts painted on our flanks. Rice-fields, water, and the air cooling round us. I was glad that chance had brought me back again.

"I shall need a bath first," I told them at the hotel when we had reached Saidu Sharif. "Then luncheon—if you can still give me luncheon at three."

"It's never too late in this hotel, sir," they said.

*   *   *

Ghazi-i-Millat Brigadier Miangul Abdul Haq Jehan Zeb, Wali of Swat, prefers to wear quite ordinary clothes, and Jehan Zeb as a name —but his sonorous titles fit him very comfortably when he chooses to put them on. He is a complete autocrat and could, if he wished, cut off a subject's head without a by-your-leave, or even a second thought. He does not. He does not even need to. In fact Swat State is an example of how very benevolent an autocracy can be. It is an anachronism, I suppose, but it is interesting to see that an auto-cracy can work admirably at best, just as a democracy can work abominably at worst. Swat State is quite small, which makes it easier—a population of about half a million—yet quite big enough to make a tyrannical mess of, if Jehan Zeb were a tyrant.

It had started with Jehan Zeb's father, in 1917. The family of the

Akhunds of Swat, as they were called, spring from true Pakhtun stock and generations before they had produced a very considerable saint, who was buried here. The people these Akhunds found themselves amongst when they first came to settle in Swat were not Pakhtun. Miangul Badshah, Jehan Zeb's father, had been—still is, in fact— a remarkable man. He invented this valley state, and became the first Wali of it. He was deeply religious, ascetic, with a passion, a strange one, for running up and down hills. This he would do, and still does, every morning, followed by courtiers of all ages breathing prayers for breath to reach the summit behind their lord and master. Miangul Badshah was good, and ruthless too. Slowly he extended his power further and further beyond the group that owed him spiritual allegiance because of his ancestry, and, in gaining power himself, had necessarily to destroy the power of the local Khans, or headmen. The Khans complained bitterly, but that was as natural as the groans of the people had been before. Having grown old and nearer to God, Miangul Badshah has retired to a life of contemplation, and has relinquished temporal sovereignty to his son, the present Wali, Jehan Zeb. In 1949, therefore, Jehan Zeb took over a scale-model of a country. He administers it wisely, with humanity and no nonsense. He can be ruthless too, when there is no alternative, and his people have prospered still further. The valleys are rich in rice and wheat and maize, there is fine timber felled in the mountains. There are motorable roads everywhere, and those who walk on them keep dutifully to the left, leaving the centre free for fast-moving wheeled traffic. That this should be so in the East is far more remarkable than a westerner might think. Ugly little villas are springing up over the countryside out of the profits that resourceful State-subjects are raking in.

I had not told Jehan Zeb that I was coming—as I should have done in terms of good manners and protocol—so I went straight to the hotel because I had heard that an hotel was now open and receiving visitors. It proved to be delightful. It is housed in what was once the residence of the Wazir-i-Azam, the Prime Minister of Swat. He had built it for his own residence. He had not a great deal of taste, perhaps, but he had amassed an acceptable fortune during his tenure of office, and in due course they had had to expel him not only from State service but also from the State itself. So his residence has become an hotel and, I should like to add, the least pretentious and best-run hotel in Pakistan—in the whole of Pakistan. Like Swat, it is small, and efficient management on a small scale is easier than on a large, but this fact does not diminish the truth of the hotel's excellence. It's a pity for tourists that Swat is so very remote, but it is worth anyone's time and money to get there.

I arrived unheralded, so I was pleased to find that the manager of the hotel was an old friend—Mr. Bhatt, who had for years been at Dean's, in Peshawar. I knew his staff, too. There was another old friend, as well, a very important one this time: Ataullah, who had been the old Wali's secretary and was now Jehan Zeb's. He lived in the house next door and I at once called on him. Together we went to see Jehan Zeb, and there I found that the Political Agent had come in from Malakand to Swat too, and no one said a word about how improperly I had behaved in arriving without invitation or permission, so I was completely happy.

"You're my guest, of course, Peter," Jehan Zeb said, and Ataullah whispered:

"Except for drinks—alcoholic drinks, I mean. You can get whisky at the hotel, if you want it, but we couldn't have whisky bills coming through on the Finance Department files. It would look so bad. So you will have to pay for whisky yourself."

I laughed and said that I hadn't realized I would be able to get a drink at all. Swat State is strictly 'dry'—but they no longer expect unbelievers to fall in line with orthodox Muslim ideas about drink. Once, when I had come to Swat, bringing with me an English friend, we had smuggled a bottle of whisky in with us. We were guests of the old Wali at the time. There was no hotel then, and we were housed in a little palace and provided with an armed guard at the four cardinal points of the compass, because it looked honourable and nice to have a guard. Before dinner, in the privacy of our rooms, I had brought the bottle out, but had opened it clumsily and broken the cork. I had to push the cork into the bottle so that we could have a quick nip and go fortified into dinner.

"We'd better hide the bottle," Antony said, as we were leaving the room.

"Oh yes, I was forgetting."

The little palace was stiff with servants. We didn't want them to discover the bottle.

"Lock it in a suit-case."

We couldn't. Neither of us had a suit-case deep enough to hold a bottle standing upright, nor could we lay the bottle tipsily on its side because the cork that should have stoppered the contents was bobbing about inside it. There was no lockable cupboard in the room, nowhere in which the bottle could live out its secret life.

So we sat down again, resourcefully determined to drink it down to the point where it could be propped diagonally on a bed of socks and shirts, in a suit-case which could then be made to close over it. Then we hurried in to dinner.

The effects of this sort of thing are visible, however. 'Your eyes swim with intoxication—how beautiful they are!' There is a Pashto song that says this, the imagery of wine being traditional amongst the Muslim poets. You are expected, however, to think of 'love' as the intoxicant, and I don't believe that my swimming eyes made me beautiful that night at dinner; Antony's didn't make him beautiful either. No one quoted the verse, and I never told Ataullah, but of course he knew.

"What do you want to see?" they asked me now, so many years later.

They are used to receiving State guests, and I even suspect that the model prison in this model town of Saidu Sharif has been built in order to please visitors, it is so neat and clean and the property-convicts look so contented as they walk along to their work on road-mending, laughing with their warders and clanking their chains. I suppose that there are other unseen convicts who like it less. Schools, hospitals, dispensaries, prison, mosque, animal-husbandry centres—most visitors like them very much.

"Listen," they said. "We'll give you a car and a driver and you can do whatever you like."

"I know what he would like," Ataullah said, smiling.

"What?"

"To go up to Shokhdarra and see Amin Khan. Is that it?"

"How do you remember that?"

"Ataullah remembers everything," Jehan Zeb said, laughing too.

"Yes, I would like to, then," I admitted.

It was quite true. Swat for me meant Jehan Zeb, and Ataullah and Amin Khan. Amin was someone of quite a different kind, all the same, and very much someone I wanted to see again. Antony had had news of him by letter—the same Antony who helped with the whisky bottle a page ago. So we knew that things had gone wrong with Amin's family fortunes. He had never been rich, but it seemed that he was rather poor now. He had had to sell off much of his property and was involved in shrill-voiced litigation over what remained.

"Are you stopping in Malakand on your way back?" the Political Agent was asking me.

"I'd like to. May I come and see you?"

"Do. Come and have luncheon. Tell them to telephone me when you know the date and time. I'll send you a jeep, if you like—and if you feel like going to Dir, you can have the jeep to take you there."

"Really? You mean that? You're very kind."

"And what about Chitral?"

"I haven't time to go to Chitral, alas," I said.

We discussed details, leaving Chitral out of it.

The next day I did nothing, and they found nothing strange in this, Why, in the west, must one always search for something to do, and compel one's guests to do the same? And the day after, deliberately sending no advance notice to Amin Khan, I set off in one of Jehan Zeb's cars for Shokhdarra. Ataullah had told the hotel to provide me with a picnic, Muslim style. They carried it out to the car and the driver stowed away the baskets and the little bowls—curries and *parathas* and *mastah* (which is curds), and big béret-Basques of *nān*, the Pathan bread. There was a fat chicken, roasted and stuffed and soaked at some point in the cooking with yoghourt.

It was a long way, with the rice-crop sharply green in the valley, and olive-trees that bore a wizened fruit. Romantics like to think that Alexander the Great who entered India by way of the Malakand valleys nibbled his Greek olives and spat the stones over his shoulder. I rather like to think so too. We crossed a tributary of the river and made our way up a side-valley. I could see Shokhdarra some time before we came to it—it is only a little village, but it stands up above its valley in a grove of trees. About a mile short of it we passed a group of villagers, striding along, rifles slung over their shoulders. I swung round in my seat and stared. One of the villagers stopped abruptly and then started running.

"Stop!" I shouted to the driver.

I got out and I think I started running back myself, and the man came panting up to me. It was in fact Amin Khan. We didn't speak, at least not for a moment or two, and then he started:

"Oh, Peter sahib, what are you doing here? Why did you not say? You must come to the village—now. Was it to our village that you were coming? Are you going to stay with us . . .?"

His companions had joined us by this time. One of them I knew.

"I have come to see you, Amin," I said.

"And Antony sahib . . . where is he? Is he not with you?"

"No. He is in Africa."

"Not here with you? But why . . .?"

"No. He is far away, in Africa."

"Come to the village," he said.

They all got into the car, Amin, his three companions and the young mullah of the village, all with rifles except the mullah, and clumsy legs and arms unused to riding in a car, but unaware that it made any difference, talking and laughing. As soon as I could, because I felt instinctively that there would be little to offer an unexpected guest in their homes, I said to Amin:

"I would like to have some tea in the village. And perhaps a *biscoot*." There is generally a tin of tired, crumbling biscuits that comes out when a villager receives guests. "The Wali sahib has sent all this food with us so that we can have a picnic up the big valley near Madian, or perhaps near Bahrein, where the two waters join. Will you come? Please come. You see, the Wali sahib has arranged all this."

"Yes. I will come—if that is how it is. But I would have liked to make a feast for you."

"Do you remember the last feast—the lamb, and the chickens with the sour cream and the sweet cream, and the apricots? Our picnic today will not be so fine as that feast, but never mind.".

"Yes. I remember."

In the village they pulled out the string beds and we sat under a chinar tree. They gave me a little decorated wooden footstool as an addition to honour. They also gave me an immense cushion with fringes and tassels—but they made me sit alone on my big bed and squeezed themselves on to the others. The driver had a bed to himself, too. Tea takes so long, and you never know why: in this case, perhaps, because they wanted to iron and press the embroidery that made a ritual covering for the tea-service. The *hūjra*, that is to say the little village guest-house outside which we sat, seemed different. Amin saw me looking at its façade.

"We have had to divide the *hūjra* into two—because of the trouble. We have half now, and the others have the other half. We have had to build that wall between us, as well."

"And the other chinar? The huge, beautiful one?"

"*They,*" he said, "the others have cut the poor beautiful thing. It has gone."

Amin Khan was changed too. He was thin and he looked ill. He had been straight and firm before, with a proud bearing. He still kept his proud bearing, but his body had shrunk away. I felt sad, almost as if it would have been better not to have come here. A man passed, fifty yards distant, through the maize crop. My hosts kept their eyes sternly fixed before them, and no one said anything till the man had gone. I didn't ask who he was. A brother, I think, from the resemblance in the set of his eyes, and in his gait. There is trouble in that family.

We motored up the main valley and spread our picnic, well above the junction of the two rivers. There were big grey rocks by the riverside, and the water was coming down ice-blue. Three children and a water-buffalo appeared magically and watched us. When we had finished we gave them what remained: food must never be thrown away. We gave them tomatoes, bits of *paratha*, a chicken-carcass, and Amin added what was left in the screws of paper that had held salt and pepper and another spice.

"Their names are Bibi Almi and Bibi Aveli for the two little girls," he said. "And Mobin for the boy."

"Do you know them, then?"

"No. But they have told me their names and I have told them ours."

"What did you say for mine?"

"I said 'Peter *ferangi*'. They are guarding the water-buffalo."

The water-buffalo stood swinging its head from side to side, beyond an olive-tree. It was shiny as a black patent-leather suit-case, and more durable.

On the way back to Amin's village we met another of his brothers, one that I had never seen before.

"Do we greet him, or do we not?" I asked, when Amin told me who it was striding towards us.

"We greet this one. He is a good one." We greeted him and passed on again, and Amin said: "You know that I am marrying again?"

"No. I didn't know. How many wives have you got now?"

Muslims may have up to four, provided they can be certain to treat all of them with equal fairness: but you must be a rich man to support more than one.

"I have had two, but they have both died. They were not strong enough. And my child is dead, too. I must marry again and have another child, *Insha'Allah*. But it needs about eleven hundred rupees[1] to get the silver jewels for the new wife. I don't know when I shall be able to marry her."

He got out of the car, and I said good-bye with a nagging sense of yesterdays uprooted. Perhaps it was wrong to see old friends again: wrong, in any case, to meet just once for a few hours and then go away, leaving the past shaken out of its ordered and happily-remembered frame, and the present fluid, with nothing to hold it in.

At dinner that night with Jehan Zeb, he asked me about Morocco.

"Wonderful," I said. "Take a holiday. Come and see for yourself."

"I must stay in my country," he said, shaking his head. It was almost as if he said: 'I am Swat.' He went on: "I sink or I swim with Swat." Jehan Zeb, the Pakhtun, is today a Pathan king, but I don't think he will disintegrate as have all the Pathan kings of bygone India, because his life is still in the mountains. He is still bounded by Pakhtunwali to which, with a mixture of skill and humanity, have been added western elements.

*   *   *

We went to Dir—but there is little I shall say about it. The country is beautiful with high, hard mountains, and the capital of the State, the town of Dir itself, lies in the entrance to a valley that leads vertiginously up to the eleven hundred foot Lowarai Pass. Beyond Lowarai is Chitral. This is the way that I have taken on visits to Chitral, and I have never done more than spend a short night at the Levy Post and departed at dawn, on horseback, up to the Pass.

[1] Approx. £110.

He likes falconry

Dir is a sad, furtive, enclosed little State for all the beauty of its valleys, and the ruler's subjects emigrate if they can, becoming dock-workers, engine-room workers in ships, watchmen for down-country factories—they become anything their limited experience fits them for, provided it enables them to leave their homes. They are tough and strong, and the strange thing about them, as about the tribes throughout this particular frontier area—Bajaur, Dir, Swat too—is that they submit to the rule of a leader. They are accounted Pathans, but in some fundamental sense the 'sturdy individualism' is lacking. Bellew, a nineteenth-century student of the tribes, claims that these peoples were first carried right through into the plains of Pakistan on the tides of migration many centuries ago. Then, to escape the threat of a subsequent migratory wave, they were forced to uproot themselves once more and move north into the mountains. They joined a kindred people in the vicinity of Kandahar, perhaps, and later still moved east, to the country they now inhabit. Is this true? Again, no one seems certain—but if it were true, it might explain the fact that in those parts of the frontier alone will you find little kings ruling over a people claiming to be Pathan.

There is nowhere for an ordinary visitor to stay in the little town of Dir—not even a tea-shop to which he would be admitted for the night. The ruler, the Nawab, has a palace and many dogs, and he likes falconry, but he does not much like visitors. He particularly dislikes visitors walking about the little town, looking at things—the roofless building that is described as 'the hospital', for example. Possibly the walls of the hospital will have collapsed by the time the roofing material is brought, so the Nawab will be spared the expense of furnishing it with beds and doctors, or even with patients.

I stayed at the Levy Post. I knew one of the levy-men, and we all ate together and I politely said nothing about dogs and falcons. Dir has a feel of sullen nothingness, and I was glad to go, though glad to have seen the levy-man again.

This, at least, I can say—that in summer the mountains of Dir are cool, which is nice for the people of Dir, and that it was nice for me too.

On the way back to Peshawar through Malakand (where I lunched very well with the Political Agent) I met a party of nomad Ghilzais. We stopped and talked for a little, and they told me they were Aka Khel Ghilzais. They sang the Walton Symphony opening-phrase, over and over again, and this is why I suppose that the singers I had heard in Kabul were members of the same tribe.

*   *   *

I had regained Peshawar after this short diversion. It was hotter than ever, and once more I was sentenced to the little white-walled furnace of a room in the club. Fateh was there to greet me, but he was leaving the same evening for his village. With him was an Afridi.

The Afridi said: "Peter sahib, I am coming with you to Waziristan. Fateh Khan says that you are travelling alone. This is not at all proper. What will people think?"

A room-bearer brought us tea. "Abdul Qadir Khan is dead, you know," he said to me, as he stood there, pouring out the tea for us. "He was right and the hospital doctors were all wrong."

*   *   *

I went to the hospital with an unreasoning distress in the back of my mind. Abdul Qadir Khan had never been a friend, and I owed him no duty, yet I felt linked with what had happened. I questioned the house-surgeon.

"He just lay back and died," he said. "Medically there was no reason for it at all."

Abdul Qadir Khan's family and his friends held that he had died in the noble cause of *badi*—and this is a real thing, whatever it may seem to outsiders: but he had died also, I was thinking, because he could not face a second death. It was enough the first time, when Sadiq Khan shot him—*t-hung!* It was better to lie back and stop living, than to await the inevitable day all over again—poor Abdul Qadir, with the dominant Pathan gene missing, so that he was left defenceless in his awful world. I said nothing of this to the others.

I found a letter waiting for me from Chainak Khan. I had been wondering what had happened to him since I had left him in London, months before. I had written before going to Kabul, and had left the letter, as instructed, with the proprietor of a little shop just inside the barbed-wire perimeter at the Bara Gate, where the road leads out to the Bara Plain, south-west of Peshawar. Chainak had been to Peshawar during my absence, he now wrote—but he seemed to have forgotten about the chance of letters at the Bara Gate shop, and complained that he had not heard from me:

"I have a contract for supplying material to the Military Engineering Services" the letter went on, and he mentioned a town in the deep interior of the Punjab. "I came to Peshawar to collect my men to work with me there. Where are you? People say that you have gone to Kabul. Why do you not come to meet me? My mother is asking where is our *ferangi* Peter."

He gave me a new address for my reply: a restaurant of some kind, in Lahore. So I wrote to him, telling him my plans, that I was due to leave Peshawar within a day or two for Kurram and Waziristan, and that I expected to leave Waziristan by way of Baluchistan, that this would take me farther away from the Punjab than ever. It did not seem that the prospects of meeting were very hopeful at present.

I could not change my programme again.

I posted my letter and went back to the club. Muhammed Farid Khan, with whom I had stayed on my first arrival from Karachi, was said to be in the mountains, touring. Fateh was in his village by now, performing a little duty towards his wife. Said Akbar, the Afridi whom I supposed I would now take on as my orderly for want of the energy needed to beat him off, and also because I had always liked him and liked too the idea of his accompanying me on my journey—Said Akbar had gone to offer prayers for something at the tomb of his spiritual adviser, Kaka Sahib, beyond the Cherat hills. He would be back the next night, he had said: in time for our morning start for Kurram.

It was so very hot, and I was depressed. I had wanted to see Chainak Khan. There was no seeing Gul Khan under his gravestone. He was finished now: Roshan and Mahboob, too, though they had only been dim shrouds in the background of my past. Now Abdul Qadir Khan was dead, another shroud. Had Shah Nawaz gone as well? I had written to him to his village in Waziristan long before—and to mutual friends, asking where he was to be found—but I had heard nothing. I kept thinking of what was gone, when I ought to have been content with each day as it came. In my little room, with the table-fan roaring and a stream of white sun through the skylight, the afternoon sagged by and I wondered about these things.

What else was it that had died? My love for this country, or I who had loved it? If I waited a little, if I kept watching through the split-cane screen of my doorway, would I come through the garden looking like a faded passport-photograph, and with me friends of another era young? Would they take no notice of the man behind the screen and pass by uncaring?

Where would I be going at this hour? To lunch at four, as the bar-boy had said? Or possibly out into the silent countryside, beyond the canal and the polo ground from which you can see Peshawar City rise in the distance, as Toledo for El Greco? There was a peach-orchard, and a pool surrounded by a broken wall in which the serpents hid—or so I had supposed, without ever seeing any. Would that snuffling woolly dog come waddling behind, shaved for summer but still far, far too woolly, poor thing? Had she still her feathered legs, Kerry-Blue curls and a spaniel-face? Out of the past came Fateh Khan, more jaunty this afternoon—fan, friends and smuggled cloth—and Shah Nawaz with his fine Wazir head and the gold shoes he had presented to me for some special occasion (though I forget exactly what) and had had made to his own foot-size so that in the end it was he who wore them. He was the same as ever—but where...? And Gul Khan again . . .

Did it matter to me so much? I really don't know, but I suppose it did. I only knew that after all reaching back was impossible, and that I should destroy these images once and for all time. I must exorcize the ghosts, amongst them the faded ghost of me so long before. I ought to have been able to laugh at them by now—and they could certainly sit back and laugh at me, because in the end the most I could do to them was to make a symbol of the deaths they should have died in whatever year it was.

*   *   *

There were a few whites left in Peshawar even today, even in high summer. A man I thought I recognized turned up at the club on the second night of my visit. We eyed each other across the empty bar-room as he passed through on his way into the garden. He stopped, not recognizing me, and said:

"Have you told anyone you're here?"

"No."

"Well, you won't get a bar-boy inside unless you call one in. Everyone sits on the lawn in the evenings."

"Yes. I know. I was just sitting here and pretending it was winter for a minute."

"What a strange thing to do."

"Yes. Isn't it? I like to think of the place being full again, and of the noise of that awful dance-band coming in from the ball-room."

"Hm-m . . ." he said, uncertainly, staring at me. "But we know each other, don't we?" We exchanged names. "Yes. I thought we'd met before, somehow. Hm-m, yes Jolly, wasn't it, in those days? Nobody uses the club much now. Many of the Pakistani wives keep purdah, and even those that don't, don't drink. And drink helps, I always say. Hm-m, yes, it helps. There doesn't seem to be any provision for clubs in the Muslim world, that's the trouble, you see. Still, there's the cinema—they've got a show this evening, out there on the lawn. Probably there'll be quite a crowd. But it's not like the old days. When did you leave? I lose track of things."

I told him.

"Oh yes," he said musingly. "That was the year before Mrs. Transom shot all the hounds, wasn't it?"

"I hadn't heard that. Who was she?"

Another man had come in, and my friend introduced us. He was English too.

"I was just telling Mayne about Mrs. Transom . . ." And then he turned to me again. "Mrs. Transom. She was Master of Hounds, the Peshawar Vale Hunt, the good old P.V.H. She's the only woman master we ever had—except, of course, Mrs. Gutch."

"I think I remember Mrs. Gutch."

"Yes, well . . . poor dear Mrs. Transom. A good woman, and a terror in the field, she was. Voice like a . . . like a . . ."

"*Cor anglais?*" I suggested.

"Yes, that's right. Voice like a fog-horn. Well, before she left she shot all the hounds—couldn't bear to think of them falling into the wrong hands. Adored animals, you see, really adored them. Crying like a child, she was, but she shot 'em all right, every man jack of them."

"But whose hands could the poor things have fallen into?" I asked him. "Did the tribes want them, then?"

"Oh no, not that! But she feared her successor as master might be someone she wouldn't quite . . . anyway, that's what she felt. So she shot the lot. Every one. *And the horses*, a horse of her own amongst them. Well, well, stirring times, old fellow, stirring times. Old Colonel Plangent says he hasn't known such a weeping and gnashing of teeth since the Afridis invaded Peshawar." He paused and then said: "She spared the hunt servants, of course."

The other man hadn't quite heard, perhaps. He looked up with interest.

"Rode 'em down, you mean, ? With a hog-spear ?"

"What ? What's that ? With a *hog*-spear ? What *are* you talking about, old man ? Steady now !"

I felt I ought to intervene. "I think the word was *spared*—not speared."

"Oh-h, I see ! Sorry, old chap. *Spared* the hunt servants. Well, that's more merciful, anyway."

I looked over my shoulder at the photographs of the successive masters of the Peshawar Vale. They had been tinted pink—almost like flesh and blood—and their coats were pink, too.

"There she is," my friend said, pointing. "Under the Ovis Poli. Nice head it is, too. See her ?"

"Mrs. Transom ? Which ?"

"Right under the Ovis Poli, there."

"But the moustache . . . ?"

He coughed nervously and said: "That was the work of a member who is a member no more. The Committee had to take disciplinary action. But we couldn't get the moustache off again, all the same, try as we might. We had to put it to the vote—whether to hang Mrs. Transom as she was, or not, and the majority voted for hanging her. So there she is, with the rest of them, but it's a pity about the m . . . I say, I suppose *you* don't happen to know a solvent for Chinese Black, do you, old fellow ?"

*　　　　*　　　　*

I sat on the lawn which had been sprinkled with water to give it the fiction of coolness, and my shirt dissolved round me. Little runnels of sweat collected behind my knees and every minute or two I would tweak the cloth of my trousers away from the skin, and it would slowly attach itself again. From where I was sitting I could see another lawn set with a dozen empty tables waiting hopelessly for diners, and I could hear the tornado of sound that the big, standard-fans made, whipping the table-cloths like sheets on a wash-line. Melba toast spun in the air as if it were tumbler-pigeons, and the servants had a strained look. A little later the cinema started behind a canvas screen thirty feet down the lawn. They were showing 'Bring 'em back alive', I think. An American voice was speaking its commentary in a fury of snarls and growls and the snap-snap of crocodile jaws. My friend had left me, and I was quite alone amongst all that noise and horror. 'I must close my ears and eyes and pores against all this,' I thought to myself, 'and not open them again till I start for Kurram, and then only just enough to make sense.' I supposed that it had been like this when it had been part of my life—but if so, then I had changed a good deal and my tastes with me. And then my mind revolted—— No, no! It could never have been like this!

*   *   *

Said Akbar had come back from the visit to his spiritual adviser, and I felt that, before we started, we should get the question of salary settled between us. I explained that I could give him such-and-such a sum daily—that this was to represent his pay, and had to cover his feeding too.

"We will probably be the guests of various people in the tribal areas," I said, "and when that happens, they will naturally feed both of us. So you will save a lot at such times. And when we reach Quetta, *Insha'Allah*, I will send you back to your village."

"Where will you go from Quetta?"

"To Karachi."

"I wish to come to Karachi, too. They say there is a huge sea there."

"No. I won't take you to Karachi. I shan't need an orderly any more then."

"Nevertheless I will come with you, please, as I wish to see that sea."

Fateh, who was with us, said to him: "Yes. Go with Peter sahib to Karachi. It is a big city."

"Very well, I will," Said Akbar said. Then he turned to me: "And tomorrow you give me your revolver to wear."

"But I told you—I haven't got one. I thought *you* had one."

O

"Me? No. Haven't *you* got one? What *will* they say?"

"What will who say?"

"The people, of course."

"Peter sahib does not like revolvers," Fateh commented.

"Well, it isn't that I don't like them, but I'm very dangerous with them, and I always think that in the tribal areas someone will want to steal it from me more than I shall want to use it. So I never carry one at all."

"And me, your body-guard?" Said Akbar asked.

"You'll simply have to pretend that we've got one somewhere."

"It's rather a *sharm*," he said. Rather a disgrace. "And your clothes, Peter sahib. Fateh has told me . . . You will not be wearing that awful mechanic, will you?"

"He speaks of those blue horribles you were wearing when you came in the aeroplane," Fateh said, explaining again.

"The jeans? I had certainly intended to."

"Then I pray that you will not. How will they believe that you are a colonel-sahib"—colonel is spoken as if it were spelt '*kerrrnail*'—"if you look like a mechanic?" Said Akbar was very distressed.

"Do you mean to tell people that I am a colonel?"

"Of course—a full colonel. If I am your body-guard, Peter sahib, it is necessary for the people to respect you."

He has strict ideas of what is proper in an officer, and what is not.

*   *   *

It was five in the morning when we set off. Said Akbar's little son had come to wave good-bye to us. He stood, holding Fateh's hand, waiting.

Fateh was saying: "You are going and I do not think that you will come back, Peter sahib. What will happen to you, and what will happen to me?"

"We shall remain friends always, Fateh, whatever happens."

"It is not of much good to remain friends, with those huge seas lying between us. You will not, I suppose, take me to Morocco with you?"

"And your family—your wife and your sons, and the property in the village?"

"The trouble is that I do not care about work," he said. "I like my friends, and chillums, and no work, and I do not require much money."

"I have no money, you see, Fateh, my dear Fateh."

"Oh Peter sahib, God help you and me, what a mess we have become!"

Said Akbar stood beside me looking very downcast, because after all I was wearing the blue horribles.

Chapter 17

WE were careering through the Kohat Darra where the Adam Khel Afridis live, our engine roaring, tappets clacking like castanets and the camel-tassels flying in the wind we made. There is something to be said for so early a start, when to delay would mean submitting to the sun too soon. There was plenty of heat to come, but at present the hills cast their shadows across the valley. The final climb to the Kohat Pass itself lay ahead of us. The Adam Khel villages made me think of gunsmiths, gunsmiths of rifles, rifles of the tribesmen's need for them, and from there it was only a short step to Chainak's aunt, the poetess.

> "*Shné stargé, laré pozé,*" I sang:
> "*Rabb' tol war-pasé bozé!*"

Beside me, Said Akbar the Afridi said: "Tch-tch. Very bad."

I wasn't really paying much attention to what he thought. I continued to think about Chainak's aunt—or was she, possibly, his great-aunt? She was evidently a very old woman, though living still. She had never been a poet, in the full sense of the word, except on the morning of her inspiration. It had happened in this way. Her husband had for long desired an authentic British .303 rifle in place of his *darrawal topak*,[1] and he had finally got his wish. There had been trouble and there were British troops about, and it had meant lying up in the hope of a straggler so as to get his rifle. In Chainak's family they say that they brought the body in as well, but I can't think why they should have done so, and I suspect that this detail is no more than an artistic embellishment, so that they could describe how the divine afflatus thereupon got Chainak's aunt, and how she sank on to her

[1] *Darra* for valley, *topak* for rifle—hence 'valley-made rifle', the manufacturers being the Adam Khel Afridis of the Kohat Darra.

204

knees over the poor dead British youth and how she was inspired to sing over him, her hands weaving about in the air:

'Blue eyes, long noses!

May the good Lord gather them all unto Him!'

This was the song I was singing softly to myself that morning when Said Akbar clicked his tongue and made his objection. For me it was as if I had been carelessly singing 'Over the sea to Skye', without even a thought for the Jacobites—it was just a fine song. But Said Akbar sitting beside me in the bus as it raged and bounded through the valley, was shocked.

"Tch-tch," he said "*You* should not sing such a song."

He is very large, and gentle as Pakhtuns go, and he has a bullet-head, which is unusual amongst Afridis who more often have long horse-faces. He comes from the Aka Khel section of the Afridis, up in the Tirah, and his mother had taken him away as a child, to escape blood-feud enemies who had already killed his father, I gather. In any case his mother had managed to get Said Akbar away some twenty-five years before, and they had settled down as *hamsayas*—dependants—in a village not so very far from Peshawar where they gave her and her child refuge. In due course Said Akbar joined the Tochi Scouts who were officered by the British in the old days. He grew to love them dearly and during his service with them absorbed a strong feeling for etiquette—what is, and what is not, done. Being on the side of the angels, he was shocked by my song. He thought it treachery to my kind for me to sing it.

I explained that it was quite all right: Chainak's aunt had only meant to sing that if every member of the tribe could kill a British soldier, as her husband had just done, then they could all have a good British .303 in place of their *darrawal topaks*; it was British rifles she was praying for, not British blood. And having established that point it was easy for me to switch the conversation to rifles in general and to *darrawal topaks* in particular, and in this way to calm Said Akbar's sense of outrage.

"How are they doing these days, the Adam Khel? Are the arms factories thriving? I hear they're making Sten-guns as well, now."

"Yes. Quite nice, but not very nice. *Revolvers*, too." He gave me a stern look as an underlining of the word.

The arms factories are housed in the villages we were careering past. It has been a profitable industry for years, though there had been a moment in the first decade of this century when things threatened to go ill for the Adam Khel. There they were, as usual, industriously making weapons for the other tribes to buy from them, and making them very competently, even if one would occasionally explode and blow its owner to pieces. The Adam Khel were very docile for Afridis, Pathans almost. Their raw materials were bits of steel and wood, and they had their agents out, cutting the excellent copper telephone-wire that the British were busy stringing up between their frontier settlements. Then, suddenly, round about 1907, an enormous consignment of Martini-Henry rifles started coming in by way of the Persian Gulf. This was equipment originally intended for the South African War, but discarded on the introduction of the new-fangled .303. European dealers had bought the discards and now had found a sale for them amongst the Pakhtuns. The bottom fell out of the market for *darrawal topaks*, as can be imagined, and the Adam Khel came running to the British with their protests. How could they possibly, peaceably, follow their calling as gunsmiths to the tribes if the British allowed such things to happen? Shame on the British! Shame on them, and let them at once pay the Adam Khel compensation for their commercial losses!

It may seem a little dotty today, perhaps, but at the time the British entirely agreed with the Adam Khel point of view—except for the bit about compensation. The tribes had to have fire-arms to shoot each other with and, if it came to a show-down between the British and the various tribes (as it very often did), the British much preferred that the tribes should be armed with *darrawal topaks*, outmoded in pattern and of limited efficiency. The Martini Henry was not the very latest in small arms, but it was a good weapon, well-made and unwelcome.

Despite British efforts, gun-running continued on a scale too large to be comfortable and for a time the tribes were dangerously well-armed. But everything has its day and in due course the Martini Henry had served its turn and the Adam Khel were producing a *darrawal* version of the new .303. Quite good it was too, though in the early stages they had difficulty in copying the bolt. Tribesmen still preferred a true British .303, but not all of them were as resourceful as Chainak's aunt's husband, and most men would have been content with a compromise: they would try to steal an authentic .303 bolt and have it fitted into a *darrawal topak* in the Kohat Pass.

"'Blue eyes, long noses . . .'" I started again, but Said Akbar stopped me this time.

"Please don't," he said. "If you wish to sing, sing some other song."

So I sang one to him that starts: "'Young man, what are you doing under my bed at midnight . . .'" He turned away from me in awful embarrassment, and I spared him the rest of it.

The bus had scrambled to the top of the pass by now and we crossed the saddle. Three thousand feet below us, almost vertically below as it seemed, though several miles away in reality, lay the district-headquarters town of Kohat. The pass is not so very high, but it is sheer and craggy, and as exciting as any pass I have crossed. Most passes are a disappointment when you come to them. They so often flatten out when they should reach a precipitous climax.

On we bounded, through Kohat and into the Hangu valley. The Adam Khel Afridis had been left behind and we were coming to Orakzai and Bangash country now. There would be Khattaks to the south of us, and beyond the first range of mountains to the north would be the main body of the Afridis, Said Akbar's Aka Khel amongst them, up in the Tirah. It was to be a day-long journey by bus. Soon the mountains of the Ahmedzai Wazirs were running parallel with us on the left—a strange, eroded formation called the Ahmedzai Salient. The Salient is traditionally the home of brigands who recruit their bands from tribal outlaws, plus a very occasional deserter from the 'Scouts' or from some regular army unit. Such men would be welcome if they brought their rifles with them, and more welcome than ever if they could bring a light machine-gun—but that was rarer still. Outlaws and deserters of this kind would be expected to earn their keep by organizing hold-ups and ambushes. There was a good stretch of ambush-country just down the road we were taking that day—where the Ahmedzai mountains trail their skirts right into the Hangu valley. But there had been no ambushes since the British left, people said, and that day, certainly, we went through in peace and unarmed.

The fortress of Thal stands at the far eastern end of the valley, ugly and widespreading. The village that lies under its walls is about as nasty as a village could well be, and seems to exist only as a dependence of the fort, and as a staging-post for travellers. It has its bus-stop and its hand-operated petrol-pump, and caravanserai—which Pashto shortens to 'serai'—for those who break journey here, and a feeling

207

of dusty, slightly ill-tempered discomfort. No one is likely to stop unless he must. We had to, because our bus went no farther, and we had to find transport for what remained of our journey. By the grace of God a friend of Said Akbar's, met accidentally in a Thal tea-shop, had a relative who owned a smart American saloon, and though he had not thought of doing so till it was put into his head, he was easily persuaded to take the car to Parachinar. We were invited to push each other into the saloon with him and his relatives and other friends, and somebody else was asked to telephone to my host, the Political Agent of Kurram, to say that I was being brought to him, and in this way we set off again.

From Thal, as you strike north up the Kurram valley, you can already see the Sufed Koh range with its snow, like a mirage floating high beyond the dust and heat. The Sufed Koh forms a wall between Pakistan and Afghanistan, but the wall has collapsed by the time it has turned the corner and started southwards, parallel with the Kurram valley. You could stroll into the Khost area of Afghanistan from Thal or Kurram with the greatest of ease, if you avoided the points covered by frontier posts. Fifty miles ahead of us, up the valley, was Parachinar, the agency headquarters. I would need a blanket on my bed that night. The gardens would be filled with chinar trees and flowers.

Meanwhile the smart American saloon was filled with Pakhtun bodies and baggage. I sat in front with the driver, our host and another man. Said Akbar was behind with the rest of them, and I could hear him explaining about me. It sounded very different from the explanation that Major Mir Badshah had been accustomed to give inquirers. I had graduated, evidently, from the penniless, weaponless, car-less, alone-and-unprotected person of that Mahsud visit. I had become, overnight, a man of some consequence. I heard it all with mounting embarrassment.

"Yes, a *kerrrnail*, of course, a full *kerrrnail*, crown and two stars and a piece of red on the turn-back of the coat—though not today. He is enjoying leave, you see. Resting, you see, from wars here, there and everywhere. He wishes me to remain with him always. I am his gunman and his friend. Ah yes, *very, very* important. We will go where we please, everywhere we will be invited—but perhaps we will not always agree to the invitation. That will depend upon the inviter, of course. You see how it is?"

Mir Ajam

I decided to make no comment, now or in the future, so long as Said Akbar was believed.

Kurram is beautiful. Willow trees line the streams that come tumbling down the hillsides to join the main body of the Kurram river, but the hills are for the most part bare, as if they belonged to a world separate from the watered world of the valley. The road climbed steadily up-river and with unexplained suddenness the vegetation stopped, and we came out on a wide plain, stone-covered. Beyond it lay the little town of Parachinar, only a few miles off now. The Sufed Koh rose like a wall behind the town.

The owner of the car insisted on handing me over in person to the Political Agent, whom we found under a tree in his big garden. He had a number of tribesmen with him, and an orderly stood alongside, holding a silver tray with a silver ink-pot and an elaborate kind of pen—symbols of governance. He got up and came towards us.

"My name is Mir Ajam," he said. "You must be Peter Mayne. Is this your man?" He looked towards Said Akbar and shook hands with him too. "You will be my guest, of course: but I've given you a separate little house at the end of the garden. It is quiet and it has a good view. Come along, I'll take you to it. I expect you will want to wash off the dust of your journey. I think you will prefer to be independent of me and of my family—though we hope you will take all your meals with us. My orderly will look after your man." He smiled and took me by the arm.

The emergence of Pakistan meant spectacular advancement for many young men in the administrative services. At little more than thirty—as I judged Mir Ajam's age to be—he was already a Political Agent, an officer with a senior and very important charge. I liked the easy way he greeted me, and as I got to know him, I liked everything about him and grew to admire him as an officer. He is a Pathan, with intelligence, strength of character, and a determination to do all he can for the people he is responsible for. I soon learnt that these people recognized his qualities too.

I was very pleased about the cottage he had put at my disposal, also. Someone had filled it with flowers: probably the gardener who stood at the door with a tight little bouquet held in front of him.

When I went over to the main house for dinner, I was shown into the drawing-room. Both the exterior and the inside of the house gave the impression of a late nineteenth-century English village rectory—a small one. But when Mir Ajam's wife joined us, this impression went up in smoke. She had the beauty and elegance of a woman you might meet in any of the great capitals of the world: tall, with hair on the chestnut side of black, very rich and shining and worn over her shoulders. Her features were almost Greek, and she had a tremendous natural dignity.

"My wife keeps *purdah* in the ordinary way," Mir Ajam explained. "But we make an exception with the guests who come to stay with us."

I turned to say something to her. She wore Punjabi clothes of a type that have become more or less standardized for women of the leisured classes in western Pakistan: a long shirt over baggy trousers, both of silk. She had a gauzy scarf, called *dupeta*, the two ends hanging loose down her back, with a loop of it in a loose swag over her breast. I knew she was a Pathan girl: I even knew who her father was, in the way that these things are known to everyone in a tribal world.

"You have made me very welcome and most comfortable, Begum sahiba," I said to her in English. "Thank you."

"Are you sure you've got everything you want? If there's anything you need you have only to ask for it, you know. I told my husband I thought you'd be happier, there in your cottage."

She was just as much at home in the rôle of English hostess as she would be in her Khattak village.

*   *   *

I spent the first morning with Said Akbar, absorbing again the look and sound of Parachinar. It is a little town at this high upper end of the valley. Like most towns that serve as district or agency headquarters, it is in two parts: the residential part laid out in a more-or-less western manner, and the bazaars. During its fifty or sixty years of life it has had time to grow beautiful with trees and gardens. To one side of it lies the headquarters fort of the Kurram Militia, which is yet another of the elements of the Frontier Corps. There is an airfield, no more than an emergency landing-ground, that slopes more abruptly than aircraft find comfortable, alongside. A saint's tomb sleeps under the trees that border it. Said Akbar has a feeling for saints, and I have too, so I stood with him while he said a short prayer in his head. When he finished he said:

"You know about this *pir*, this saint, Peter sahib? He used to have his tomb over there, in the middle of the aeroplane-ground, but he was not content with no shade. He placed a dream into someone's head, saying that he would prefer to be moved, with his tomb, to under these trees. So they moved him."

I looked at Said Akbar for a moment, wondering if he had heard as much as I about all this—but he stood there, nodding wisely and innocently. It was, of course, quite true that the saint had always been in the middle of what eventually became the landing-ground and, when the authorities were planning to provide emergency facilities for aircraft, his tomb was more than inconvenient. If the saint had not himself caused a respected citizen to dream the dream which made possible the removal of his tomb to where trees would give it shade, nothing could have been done about it—least of all by the aeroplanes that wished to land there from time to time.

"He is a good saint—but, for my Afridis, Kaka sahib is the best one," Said Akbar said thoughtfully.

Kaka sahib is indeed the best saint for the Afridis and, although his tomb is inconveniently distant from the Tirah, he has a great number of Afridis amongst his followers. His tomb, or *ziarat*, is beyond the Cherat hills in Akora Khattak country, south-east of Peshawar. The family that produced him had already, before him, produced a whole succession of saints in their own right as the centuries have unrolled themselves—Abak sahib, and Mast Baba, and Ghalib Baba, and Adam Baba, and Musa Nika and so on, backwards, the tombs of each marking a passage through time and space back to the early Islam of Arabia, by way of Waziristan, Baluchistan, Iran, Iraq. Kaka sahib has an especial appeal for the Afridis, as Said Akbar admitted. Wali Khan the Kuki Khel whom I had seen in Kabul, had intended to offer thanks to him for his victory over Pakistan, but when it came to the point there had been no victory to be thankful for—but that was a different matter altogether.

The point is that there is a shortage of acceptable saints amongst the Afridis. Other tribes laugh at them a little on this account, but worse even than the laughter is the material disadvantage that follows. Quite often a man will want to swear on his particular local saint in order to convince someone else that he will do what he says he will do

—or that he has not done what is alleged against him. The Zakha Khel Afridis, a section of the tribe with a particularly bad name, complained that no one seemed ready to believe a word they said, somehow. One day it happened that a stranger crossed into Zakha country—which lies at the approaches to the Tirah from the Khyber Pass—and asked for safe conduct through the hills to his destination. This was normal enough, and an escort was granted to him. But the Zakha Khel escort had not taken the old gentleman far before they realized that their guest was outside the usual run of men. He bore the stigmata of sainthood—even the Zakhas could see that. As a matter of fact he was a descendant of Kaka sahib and he told them so, and this much increased the chances of his eventual canonization. When they had gone a little farther, the Zakhas started thinking that if the old gentleman should chance to die within their territory, he might become their own personal saint and they could then build a shrine over him and embellish it suitably, and then start swearing on him. Pilgrims would come to his *ziarat* too, and that would be good for business. In fact the sooner the old man died, the sooner could the Zakhas start swearing on him. So they killed him (if certain other tribes are to be believed) quickly and neatly and as far as might be painlessly, and made a shrine for him—the Ziarat of Gurgurra, which means the Shrine of the Sloe Tree. The Zakhas don't admit the truth of this story, however: they say that wicked Shinwari tribesmen (Pakhtuns, but not Afridis, living on the other side of the Khyber) killed the old man. On the other hand the neighbouring tribes don't admit that the proper degree of sanctity resides at Gurgurra—the old gentleman may have been a martyr, they say, but he was not a full saint. So no one is pleased, not even the poor old gentleman who died to no purpose. The only thing that lives is the shrine itself and this story about it. It goes to show, I suppose, that you can't invent a Pakhtun saint, any more than you can invent a Pakhtun leader.

"What about the Ziarat of Gurgurra?" I asked Said Akbar maliciously—but the Zakhas are cousins to the Aka Khels and Said Akbar did not choose to reply to my question.

*　　　　*　　　　*

The noise of constant water is in your ears as you stroll through Parachinar. The gardens are divided from each other by little stone walls, the houses are festooned with flowering creepers. It reminded me of the gardens of Paghman, up beyond Kabul, but with the ghosts of British gardeners in the background. The biggest house is reserved for the Governor's periodical visits, and the next biggest is the Political Agent's 'rectory', and the third biggest is for the Commandant of the Kurram Militia. Others are reserved for the various civil and militia officers.

I returned to Mir Ajam's house before lunch to find him receiving a *jirga*, or tribal council, of the Parachamkanis. This is a violent and rather tiresome little Pakhtun tribe who live in the mountains above Parachinar to the east, a buffer between the Afridis of Tirah and the Turis of the Kurram valley. The Parachamkanis are not my favourite people, possibly because I have never known any: but apart from that I feel instinctively that violent and murderous people should romantically look the part. The Parachamkanis are smallish and rather scruffy to look at, but they can evidently be entertaining when they are in a lighter mood. Mir Ajam motioned me to sit beside him and then explained to the *jirga* who I was and what I was doing here. They nodded politely.

A *jirga* is an interesting phenomenon: any adult male member of the tribe can sit in it (except mullahs). It is very democratic and it provides a good deal of interest and steam-letting for everybody. When the *jirga*-members leave they expect to be granted *kharcha*—expense-money—and the distribution of *kharcha* is often the most ill-tempered moment of the whole session. I arrived as they were already finishing the business of the day, and Mir Ajam turned to me.

"Shall we ask them how they used to behave in the time of the British?" he suggested. His eyes were twinkling.

I agreed readily, and the Parachamkanis were taken with the idea too. It seemed to offer all sorts of possibilities. Everyone wanted to speak, each tumbling over the other in his anxiety to get to the front to say his piece.

"We used to shoot at them and steal their guns," one of them began, breathless with imagination. " . . . and then the Political Agent sahib would complain to our *spin-girai* (grey-beards) and our *spin-girai* would stroke their beards and say 'But these are only pranks of the hot-heads, the young men, the *kashars*. Leave it to us. We will see to it.' And they would hold out their hands for the *kharcha* and then complain that it was not enough . . ."

"... or," said another of them, talking at me this time, "we would shoot—*t-hang-t-hang*—over the head of the Political Agent sahib as he went on his horse, from afar we would shoot, and he would have to take notice from pride, and try to stop us, and then he would angrily demand explanations and we would explain that in some way or another he was treating one of us unfairly and that he must put things right for that person, and where was justice? Where was it? we would ask him. And the journey in to Parachinar to ask where was justice would mean more *kharcha* and we would go away laughing again."

"But now," said an old man sententiously, his eyes fixed upon Mir Ajam, "all that is changed. Now we have our beloved Pakistan, and our *beloved* Political Agent Mir Ajam sahib who is our father and mother, and we do none of these things because of our love for him...." And somebody tittered a little, and when I myself looked sideways at Mir Ajam to see how he was reacting I caught his eye because he was looking at me for exactly the same purpose, so that we both laughed.

"Then," resumed the same oldish man, warming up a little now, "we would swear on the Qoran, we would, that we would not do something again—and the Political Agent sahib would believe us! Can you imagine it? Did he not even know that to swear on the Qoran Sharif before a Christian did not count at all?"

I was rather shocked by this, having lived surrounded for so long by people to whom the Qoran counted a great deal. "What sort of Muslims are these?" I whispered to Mir Ajam.

"Well," he said, coughing nervously, and laughing too. "Well ... yes, I agree. It's going a bit far..."

"And then ... Wait. I am coming closer. I am deaf, you see." A very old Parachamkani had shuffled forward towards Mir Ajam's table. "I want to say something in your ear." So Mir Ajam inclined his ear and the old man leaned forward and whispered into it at the top of his croaky old voice which was in any case collapsing with laughter, with tears, almost: "And in the time of the British devils attacking the Tirah,[1] you know what we did? We captured

---

[1] He must have been referring to 1897 when a very considerable British expedition entered Tirah from several points simultaneously, one of them through the Hangu valley and up towards Parachamkani country. The old man was vague, and it was difficult for us to check dates and places. His story had already become lost in the happy imprecisions of a myth.

a British *kerrrnail*, a *kerrrnail* with sword and gold and red, and we put him into a pot, and we . . . we"—the poor old thing was almost speechless with tears and laughter—"*we cooked and ate him !* "

Mir Ajam and I looked at each other and burst out laughing. It was ludicrously untrue. Anthropologists may never have worked on the Pakhtuns, but no one has ever before suggested that Pakhtuns are cannibals. But it would have been absurd not to join in the gaiety, so we nodded at each other and at him and smiled happily:

"Ate him! Fancy that! A *kerrrnail* sahib. That's good!"

They were showing off now, and enjoying it heartily, like children, but luncheon was probably ready and waiting to be served, and the best parties have to end sometime, so Mir Ajam called for his silver tray and the elaborate pen and started writing out the *kharcha*-chits. There was an instant riot, with tribesmen running about to complain and to check their *kharcha*-chits against those given to others. In the middle of this a mullah, who had been compelled by his 'cloth' to remain a hitherto-silent spectator, stood up and, in a voice like a fire-alarm, started to harangue me.

It was rather disagreeable. I don't think he meant half he said: I think that his principal concern was to restore the balance between himself as a nonentity while the *jirga* was in session, and himself as an important, even a feared, member of the community at other times. He was a youngish man, handsome, with his full black beard and his wild eyes. He attacked me as a *kafir*.[2] Mir Ajam, looking up from his chit-scribbling, was upset on my account—but I signalled to him not to interfere. I don't think I minded much, and it lasted for no more than thirty seconds, because another tribesman came up and took the mullah away.

They started to disperse, grumbling about their *kharcha*. A Parachamkani was coming towards me, dragging the young mullah unwillingly with him. The mullah looked sheepish. The other made him take my hand and I took his readily enough and then, without warning, the mullah leaned forward and laid his head against my neck. I believe I was more touched by this strange apology than I had been

---

[2] Christians—like the Muslims themselves—are counted as people 'of the book', that is to say, a people with a revealed religion distinguishing them from the *kafirs* to whom God has revealed nothing, no Qoran, no Bible. It is only by extension that the term 'Kafir' has attached itself to the South African tribe of this name.

angered by his insults. He stood like this for a moment and then walked away without looking back.

I rejoined Mir Ajam. "They're making rather a noise about their *kharcha*, aren't they?"

We were walking across the lawn, in the direction of the house. Shouts and wrangling came to us over the sleepy, midday air, abuse and shouts and angry cries.

"It's always such a business," he commented. "They're quite content—that is, each individual receiver of *kharcha* is content enough, but it maddens a man to learn that someone else, whom he considers his inferior, should have received the same sum: or that another, whom he thinks of as barely his equal, should have received a little more, perhaps. It's impossible to get it quite right, of course."

"*Murghi moghlai* for lunch," the Begum Mir Ajam said to us as we joined her up at the house. "I hope you like it."

I can eat it till I faint—young chickens, cooked in an elaborate sauce that the Moghuls loved.

*　　　　　*　　　　　*

"I think you said there were one or two villages you wanted to visit," Mir Ajam reminded me. "Which ones, in particular? You can go wherever you please, naturally, but we'll have to let them know you're coming."

I told him. Shalozan, for one, at the foot of the track that leads up to Peiwar Kotal, the pass on the Pakistan-Afghanistan frontier. Shalozan is a Turi village, but a bit farther up the track the territory of the Mangal tribe begins. It was not that I had any special friend in Shalozan—indeed it is a village that I knew only from a brief visit in the past: but it was beautiful, and I remembered that one visit with pleasure. "And after Shalozan perhaps I could go to Ahmedzai," I suggested. Ahmedzai, south of Parachinar and the stony plain, is the home of a leading Turi family that I would be glad to see.

"I'll arrange it then. Do you want me to come too, or do you prefer to be alone?"

Mir Ajam was very understanding. It may well be that he hadn't time to come with me himself: that was a different matter. But he knew that the atmosphere would be rigid if an official were present . . .

and how a tribesman at once modifies his behaviour in such circumstances. From my point of view, it was good to be trusted, and it occurred to me that his trust must be reinforced, at a deeper level, by his knowledge that he had his tribes well in hand, and could trust them too. The Turis are a relatively peaceful people, of course, but most political officers in far-off places where trouble is never so very deep below the surface, like to keep a watchful eye on their visitors.

So I went to Shalozan, beautiful Shalozan with its Persian-sounding Moghul name. Their women have long been famous for their beauty, so that the Moghul emperors would send for a daughter of this remote and lovely village as wife or concubine—for a '*dukhtar-i-Shalozan*'. Shouaib, a present-day headman, had had a grandfather whose sister had been married to the great Amir Dost Muhammed of Afghanistan. That was a hundred years ago, when the Kurram valley was ruled from Kabul. And there had been a still earlier daughter of his family who had married the Moghul emperor Shah Jehan. Shah Jehan, who built the Taj Mahal, had also built a little shrine above Shalozan, to shelter the bones of a holy man who belonged to this village.

But, with all that, it would not have surprised me if Mir Ajam had stalled and headed me off from Shalozan, because the Turis were scrapping with their Mangal neighbours a little bit farther up the track to the Peiwar. A section of the Kurram Militia had had to intervene, and the incident was not yet closed.

Twelve chinar trees, rising proud and lovely on the banks of a little stream that rumbles down through the village, laid their shadows on us that evening, soft shadows like gauze—grey and green and a dusty yellow. The villagers were building a mosque at the time. It was alongside the village *hujra*, where guests would normally be received. The ground had become a builder's yard of material for the mosque, stones and pine-trunks, and lime for plaster. They had spread the carpets between all these piles, and food took even longer than usual because of the chaos. A very old man was carried down from his house to sit with us, but he was deaf and almost blind, and we could make very little sense of what he said. But they were proud of him, and he had a certain nonagenarian beauty. Even the village dogs were quiet and restful, once they had had a first threatening of stones.

Late that evening the skies opened and rains came down on us in a torrent. We had climbed a track that leads to the *ziarat*, difficult

P

enough in dry weather, but impossible once it had been transformed into a stream in its own right. Having got there, we had to stay there for hours. I sat in a little alcove set obliquely at the entrance to the tomb itself, and sheltered by an overhang of corrugated-iron sheeting. It was convenient as a protection, but the Emperor Shah Jehan would scarcely have approved of it. From the high-set *ziarat*, with Peiwar Kotal towering over us to the west and heavy with the storm that clattered and banged about its summit, we could look down into the valley. Huge wet steel-grey clouds had gathered over the countryside, and had parted here and there to let the light through. Where the light struck, the valley sparkled with the silver of rain.

We were soaked to the skin when we reached the village again, and the carpets outside the *hujra* were soaked too.

*   *   *

When Mir Ajam told me of the action he had had to take to control pro-Pashtunistan propaganda amongst his tribes such as the Parachamkanis who live on the borders of Tirah, I suddenly realized that this was the first mention of Pashtunistan I had heard made since my return from Kabul.

"What is the tribal attitude towards Pashtunistan?" I asked him.

"You know very well what they're like, my tribes. If somebody offers them money, they take it. Accepting money doesn't necessarily mean accepting what it is supposed to represent. It could be the same when they accept my money. But even a backward tribe like the Parachamkanis can see which side their bread is buttered. It's sufficiently obvious, I should say, that their advantage lies with Pakistan. They aren't fools, the tribes. They're concerned to live as best they can, that's all. There have been agents for Pashtunistan working up there in the mountains, all the same."

"How do you deal with the situation?"

"It's not difficult. I tell the tribes to get rid of them. I don't mind their taking Pashtunistan money, wherever it comes from, of course: but they know very well that if they were silly enough to play the Pashtunistan game, they'd have to play it alone—with no more help from Pakistan in the way of allowances or anything else. A tribesman of mine got killed recently, in the process of getting rid of an agent. I

218

felt bound to pay compensation to his family. And it has happened that a tribesman of mine who agreed to work for Pashtunistan and actually started to do so was killed himself, by one of his fellows who interpreted my orders over-zealously. In that case I had to arrange to pay the killer—no, no, not as a reward! Nothing of the kind! But to enable the killer to find blood-money with which to settle with his victim's family. There is provision in tribal *riwaj* (custom) up there for settling a feud with blood-money, if the family accept—and they accepted it. I couldn't have my orders resulting in a new blood-feud, after all." He paused momentarily, and added: "It wouldn't make much sense in England, I'm afraid. But it isn't England I'm concerned with, when you come to think of it."

"It makes sense here, all right," I said.

"What impression did you get about Pashtunistan in Kabul?" he asked.

I started to tell him and he listened patiently enough but it all seemed rather dull. "To tell you the truth," I said, "I'm rather tired of Pashtunistan—it's like everything else that fails to make much sense: you get sick of it, finally: and it's been a relief not to be made to talk about it since I returned to Pakistan."

This was, in fact, the truth. I could, of course, understand Kabul's irredentist yearnings: and I could see that even if they struck little or no response from Pakistan's tribes, yet, in Afghanistan, propaganda about a homeland for the Pakhtuns beyond the Durand Line could be helpful in diverting the Afghan tribes' attention from deficiencies at home. I could see, too, that it suited India to support the Pashtunistan campaign for so long as Kashmir remained to poison her relations with Pakistan. I said something of the kind to Mir Ajam.

"Yes," he said. "But ultimately what matters is the reaction of our tribes."

"And they seem to have decided that Pakistan has more to offer them than Kabul, or Pashtunistan?"

"Well, it is so. Don't you think that, if it were not so, you would at least hear murmurs? We couldn't control Pakhtun tongues and actions, even if we wanted to. Our tribes are realists, you see. They are a very sensible lot when it comes to seeing what is to their advantage."

*　　　　*　　　　*

Mir Ajam provided me with a car in which to reach the village of Ahmedzai. They had built a rough road that made it possible to drive right up to the village walls, and I was amused to find a tumbledown Chevrolet belonging to a prosperous villager already standing there, like a patient mule.

My hosts came out to greet me. One of them I knew—he was the reason for my having chosen Ahmedzai—and another I had at least met before. The others were strangers to me, as I to them. But they took me in as if I belonged here, leading me at once to the *hujra* where I was to be lodged.

It is a charming *hujra*. It is built out on a roughly-cantilevered balcony above the level of the village walls. There is an interior room, quite large, with a closet alongside it, and this fine, wide balcony in front, half of it covered by a roofing of wooden slats, and half open to the skies. A low wooden parapet borders it, the paintwork powdery-green with age.

"We have had so little warning of your coming," they said. "You must forgive the poorness of the welcome we can make for you."

There was nothing to apologize for. On the contrary, there was a great deal to thank them for. They had set chairs on the balcony, and decorated them with rugs and cushions. The floor itself was spread with carpets, one of them an excellent Bokhara, a Tekki, bigger than is normally seen, and of a beautiful slightly rusty red. Tea came in, served in the traditional Gardner china from Russia, and we all sat round, fencing with words at first, till each knew all that seemed essential to know about the others. Said Akbar was with me, of course. I prayed that he would not overplay his part, but I expect he did. They treated me as if I were a *Genail*, instead of a simple *kerrrnail*.

Out beyond the village walls, beyond the wheat crop and the river that slithered silvery and slow and curled away behind a clump of trees, lay another village, less than a mile away: a poor-looking affair of mud; treeless, mean and ill-cared for.

"The Malli Khels," they said bitterly—and I remembered that the Malli Khel, who are believed to be a Ghilzai people in origin, were at feud with my hosts, the Turis of Ahmedzai.

"Hasn't there been trouble about wood-cutting rights?" I asked.

"For a long time now we have been unable to cut wood on our

220

hills," they admitted, pointing beyond the enemy village. "And this has been getting worse. We are stronger than them, but they stand in happier relation to our hills than we ourselves who own the hills, and they can send in a party to cut wood, while we cannot spare enough men to mount a permanent guard there to prevent them. And if we go to cut our wood, they can snipe us and there is fighting and the Political Agent sahib has to send the militia. Now we have Mir Ajam sahib here and we have told him: 'You must beat the Malli Khels for us—or allow us to beat them. You won't let us beat them? Then batter them and beat them yourself!'"

"And will he beat them?"

"We fear that he will not," one of them said. "He says that the Malli Khels must be allowed to live too, and that to live means that they must have fuel for their fires, and that the only fuel in this part is on our hills. I think he wants us to divide our wood."

"Is there enough wood for both villages, there on your hills?"

"Oh, there is plenty of beautiful wood there! It is ours, ours! More than enough, but till this affair is settled neither we who own it, nor the Malli Khels who desire it, can have fuel without fights. Look down there—just below our wall. You see that big chinar? That big one with its head cut off? You know why that tree has no head any more? You know how thick that tree is? One and a half turban lengths round its thickness. And we have been obliged to cut off its head in order to supply us with fire-wood."

"What would you do about it, if you were Political Agent?" another of them asked me.

"I would tell you to leave it to me to settle in the proper way, by agreement with the Malli Khel."

"The Malli Khels are devils."

"Of course. But that does not make any difference."

"Every difference. Devils will never, never agree."

"And you Turis of Ahmedzai will never agree either, I think, because you are obstinate about this wood question."

"You ought not to say that!"

"I have not said it. It is what I *would* have said, *if* I had been the Political Agent sahib. We are talking in 'if's' and 'would's'."

"Ah-h," they said and started smiling discreetly. "It is what the

Political Agent sahib himself says already, without an 'if' or a 'would'."

*   *   *

They told me many things that first evening as we went walking by the river and, later, sat out on the balcony. They spoke about themselves, about the fighting in Kashmir and about other tribes who had been in Kashmir too. I was told, for example, that second in valour to the Turis (for the Turis had come first, according to local report) had been the men of Dir State, and I remembered that in Swat too I had been assured that the men of Dir had come second—second to the Swatis, in that case.

"And the Sudhans of those Kashmir hills? And the Mahsuds and Wazirs, and the Afridis?"

"The Sudhans were brave and their fighting was good. The others were brave and . . . greedy for loot."

Britannia did this, Britannia did that . . . the talk went ranging from Kashmir to the British, from the British to the Malli Khel for the second and third times and back to the nineteenth century and the Afghans who had held Kurram then. There had been a resident Afghan governor: Sardar Muhammed Azam Khan. His name was remembered, though—as I have read—he left the valley as long ago as 1864. It was he who had built the fortress of mud and stone near the village of Ahmedzai, the same fort that I had passed on my way here. Today its crumbling walls enclose a half-acre of artemisia. Close by it is a grove of immense chinars.

"Sardar Muhammed Azam Khan made us feed milk to the roots of those trees when first they were planted," they said, as if 'we' a hundred years ago were still this group of 'us' sitting in the *hujra* today. "He needed a shady place for the holding of *jirgas*. Milk, he made us pour. Chinars like milk very much indeed, and horse-flesh."

The Afghan governor had treated the Turis harshly. No one in this part of the world would have expected a governor to be other than harsh, but by 1860 the British had pushed their way through from Kohat to the Hangu valley, and the Turis were able to observe that harsh as the British might be, they were less harsh than the Afghans, and moreover there were other reasons for preferring the British, as well. The Turis were different from most Pakhtun tribes in one very important respect: they were Shiah Muslims, of the same heterodox sect of Islam as the Persians. The tribes around them were orthodox Sunni Muslims. The Turis' heterodoxy, coupled with the richness of the Kurram valley—which they had wrested from the Orakzais some centuries before—made them objects of dislike and envy. The Turis put their heads together and decided to ask the British to protect them. My hosts' forefathers had been leading members of the group that had signed the petition addressed to the Deputy-Commissioner of Kohat by name, and 'to the Khans of ancient lineage, high degree and great courage, and to all the English people'.

The petition seems to have been drafted in English for them by someone, but I don't know who—perhaps a street petition-writer in Kohat, or even Peshawar. The prose-style suggests it:

> 'Oh, English gentlemen!' [it read]. 'We appeal to you in God's name. By the Durranis we have been ruined and reduced to the last extremes of distress. They plunder us without restraint. With sighs and tears we appeal to you to free us from these oppressors. . . . Durrani rule we loathe. For British rule we yearn!'

Tears and sighs—no doubt the Turis had been advised by the petition-writer that the idea would flatter the British.

> 'Kurram is a well-favoured and fertile country'

the petition went on, temptingly:

> ' . . . Move but a step forward and you will free us from the burden,'

and it finished up with a little blackmail, along with a description of the man who would present the paper to the British on their behalf.

> 'If ye refuse to aid us, rest assured that at the last great day of judgment we will seize the skirts of your garments and accuse you of this injustice before God himself! A tall man with a silk turban will deliver this our petition. Treat him kindly. . . .'

It suited the British very well to treat him kindly. They had plenty of truculent tribesmen glowering at them at the time, and this pact with the Turis, a pact based on mutual benefit, was highly satisfactory. It worked very well and the Turis, that minority of Shiahs amongst Sunnis, prospered too.

But that evening the subject that held us with much more immediacy than the arrival of the British in Kurram or the Second Afghan War, or even the Third, was a man called Qasim. Qasim was the son of a very famous local bandit called Chakki, who had been a Robin-Hood figure, operating over a very wide area in his time. Qasim, the son, would like to have taken over his father's business, but for the moment he had fallen in love. Love and banditry are mutually destructive, despite Hollywood.

"A bad woman she is, that Qasim loves—a Jaji tribeswoman who came hurrying over Peiwar from Afghanistan a little while ago with a baby in her stomach. Her mother came with her, but the baby's father was uncertain, and the Jaji people of her village were chasing her in order to kill her. She reached Parachinar in safety, however, and in due course, when the baby was born, she 'threw' it."

"She was beautiful. Qasim saw her and promptly loved her."

"Yes, he loves this almost prostitute-woman, and has recently been making negotiations with the girl's mother. For marriage."

It appears that the girl's mother was considering Qasim's offer when a gentleman called Bulbul knocked at the door of her lodging and asked to see her. 'Bulbul' is generally, but quite wrongly, translated 'Nightingale'. It is a very popular bird with poets, who write ceaselessly about 'Bulbul and the Rose-flower'. In this case Bulbul was a plumpish, richish, oldish merchant of Kurram. He had come to say that he wanted the Jaji girl for his son. The mother, seeing at once that she had here a chance to stimulate competition, agreed to consider Bulbul's offer as well. Bulbul thereupon deposited the sum of rupees one thousand as guarantee of his honourable intentions, and left. A good bargain must be given time to mature. I suppose he intended to come back to the Jaji woman within a day or two to speak further on the matter.

"But you see, Qasim has a *ghag*[1] on the girl," one of the Turis went

[1] A *ghag* is a lien, and when a man has a *ghag* on a girl, it means that no one else can enter the lists till the *ghag*-holder has decided whether to take her or not.

on. "So, of course, when Bulbul discovered that Qasim already had this *ghag* on the girl, he became scared and hastened back to the mother to demand the return of his rupees one thousand. You understand that he did not wish to annoy Qasim, who starts to shoot when he is angry, and he did not wish to lose his rupees one thousand either. This is often the trouble with merchants: they like money very much, and guns not at all"

We were at dinner by now. Said Akbar reached across and put a second little spatchcocked chicken on my plate, and a second on his own.

"However, the girl's mother declined to return the money, and by her refusing to return it, it meant that poor Bulbul had spoiled Qasim's *ghag*. He had not intended to, but nevertheless he had spoiled it."

"What a situation," I agreed, thinking that for plumpish, richish, oldish Bulbul, it was a very awful situation indeed, especially if he did not care for fire-arms.

"Worse," they went on. "Qasim, having learnt about his spoiled *ghag*, at once decides to do some spoiling himself. Do you know what he does?"

"Shoots poor Bulbul?" I suggested. "In the stomach, perhaps?"

"No. Worse."

"Has Bulbul a daughter? Does he catch Bulbul's daughter?"

"Worse . . . worse . . ."

"Well, what *could* be worse?"

"Try to think. What have we told you? Try to think again!"

"I can't think what would be worse."

"Worse, far! He kidnaps Bulbul's youth son and dashes him away to the mountains! What a dust from the dashing!"

"And then . . . ?"

A new speaker took up the story, sitting back comfortably on his hunkers, against the parapet. "Qasim sends a message to Bulbul, saying: 'This message is written in the finger-blood of your little son. I will return to you your son intact, if you will deliver to me not only the Jaji girl on whom I have my *ghag*, and also the rupees one thousand that you have given her mother as worthless guarantee, but at the same time your second daughter of whom I have excellent reports.'"

"Good heavens! And what does Bulbul do?"

"He cries terribly."

"Only that?"

"It is made much more terrible because many of the people are laughing at him by now."

"Crying won't get him very far, I suppose."

"He hurries to the Political Agent sahib, too."

"And what does the Political Agent sahib say?"

"This was only just now. He has made some plan, we think, but we do not yet know exactly what it will be. He is clever, and we expect that in some manner he will settle this affair."

"Yes, he is clever," I agreed "Perhaps he will also arrange your affair with the Malli Khel if you listen to him."

"Take some more chicken," my next-door neighbour said to me rather gruffly, and tried to find room on my plate for a third carcass. Said Akbar looked across and smiled. He does not talk at meals because he believes that food is more politely eaten (and in greater quantity, too, perhaps) if one remains silent.

*   *   *

The vase of wild carnations that they would carry from the dining-table to the little stool beside my chair on the balcony and then to another, bigger stool that they would put beside my charpoy at night, had had time to fade a bit before I left Ahmedzai. I was very contented with the Turis, and even Said Akbar who from the smugness of his Sunni orthodoxy was inclined to think of Shiahs as heretics, admitted that our hosts were good people.

"They treat us with honour," he said.

They did. The business of being bedded down at night was very honourably performed. I had a big charpoy with a load of quilts and decorated cushions, and a mosquito net that was quite unnecessary but proved by its folds of fusty-musty veiling and by its supports of poles lashed to the bed-legs, that this house knew what was what. Said Akbar's charpoy was set alongside mine, and three or four of our hosts grouped theirs about us, so that we lay floundering in our quilts and ringed with security.

*   *   *

The tiresome aspect of a journey of this kind was that government wanted me me to keep to a pre-arranged programme. Back in Parachinar I soon realized that it was time for me to move on—to Waziristan. Mir Ajam telephoned for me to his opposite number, the Political Agent at Miranshah in Tochi, North Waziristan. The two Political Agents screamed at each other across a hundred miles of valleys and mountains and over the heads of the Pakhtuns who lived in them. How was everything?—no trouble in Waziristan? None? Good. None here in Kurram either. And then the other must have asked Mir Ajam what I was like, for Mir Ajam glanced at me quickly, coughed and shouted: "All right. Nice, rather." I could hear a broken string of words whirring in the ear-piece.

"He says he will send an escort to Thal for you, and they will take you to Waziristan."

"That's very kind. But do I really need an escort? I have been told everywhere how perfectly safe it . . ."

"You don't really need one, but Faridullah says he is sending it all the same."

"Will you thank him for me? What day and what time?"

"He says: 'Nine o'clock on Thursday morning. At the bridge below Thal fort.' Will that do?"

"Excellently. And before you ring off, do ask him to get Guldad Khan up from Bannu—he'll know, if you don't. Guldad, the Jani Khel Wazir. I'm hoping to go into South Waziristan by way of Razmak and Mahsud country, and so I shan't be touching Bannu at all."

"By way of Razmak . . .?" he commented. "But . . . Well, never mind. I'll tell him about Guldad."

He did so and put the receiver back. "I'll drive you down to Thal. I've got one or two jobs to do down the valley. There's a kidnapping case, for example."

"Qasim and that poor plump Bulbul?"

"Do you know about that?"

"The valley's buzzing with it."

"It's rather funny, and rather a nuisance, too."

"How will you settle it?"

"The first thing to do is to insist that Qasim surrender himself to me. And then we'll see." Mir Ajam laughed a little. "They're naughty sometimes, aren't they?"

*   *   *

Bees had built themselves a nest under the floor of the drawing-room, and someone had made a hole in the foundation-wall so that the bees could come in and out without having to pass through the room. You could hear the bees buzzing and grumbling under the floor, but they were no nuisance to anyone, and every so often a bee-loving gardener would open up the floor-boards and take the honey they had prepared so industriously. It was not for honey that they were taking up the floor-boards of the kitchen on the morning of my departure, however. The garages are behind the kitchen-yard, and as we loaded the car I could see gardeners and house-boys watching the man with the pick as if something interesting were afoot.

"It's a big snake," Mir Ajam explained. "He was seen going in yesterday and, as he hasn't come out again, I have told them to drive him out."

I went over to Begum Mir Ajam to say good-bye and to thank her for being so kind to me. She called up her children, and they came reluctantly, being anxious not to miss the snake if it should suddenly make a slither for safety while their attention was politely occupied elsewhere. Said Akbar was making ceremonious good-byes, too. He had packed the 'blue horribles' at the bottom of my suit-case the night before, counting upon my being too rushed in the morning to insist that he unpack and get them out again. He had been quite right in his judgment: I was now dressed for a garden-party, rather than for a dusty drive.

Half-way to Thal we were stopped by a man who waved a piece of paper. It was a radio message from Miranshah. A storm had burst over Waziristan during the night and the road to Miranshah via Spinwam was completely blocked by a wash-out. The escort could not come through. Nothing could come through at all.

"If we hurry we can get to Thal before the bus starts for Kohat, and you'll get a connection there for Bannu. It'll take all day, but there's no other route possible. I'll signal to Faridullah and ask him to have the escort waiting for you in Bannu."

In Thal we had no time for more than the most perfunctory of good-byes—yet mine were deeply felt. The Mir Ajams could not have been kinder.

            *   *   *

I don't want to think of that journey, much less write about it. It took all day to reach Bannu and, though there were a dozen stops, we had no food. As far as Kohat we travelled in a bus called The Royal Akbar, in English. It had a tin cut-out of two smiling lions *passant* screwed to the driver's cab. The lions waved flags with their right paws. Inside the bus was a party of tribesmen who had covered their faces with their turban-tails as if they were on a raid of some kind, but they told me after a while that they were on their way to attend a court case in Kohat that interested them. Perhaps they regarded it as a battle too: or, less romantically, perhaps they were just keeping the dust out of their noses.

We changed buses at Kohat and looked for seats in one that was decorated with hands clasped in friendship, little flower-wreaths like bracelets painted round their cuffs. And another pleasant thing for me was that I found a Tori Khel Wazir from the Razmak area sprawled with a friend of his over the first bench behind the driver as if they intended to occupy all six places. When he saw me, and after a brief moment of non-recognition, he sat up and pulled me in beside him, and called Said Akbar in too, because he was with me. He gave me *naswār*, a wad of it to slip between the cheek and gums—though I don't like tobacco to chew, much less *naswār*. He also made me read a copy of a petition he had been filing in Peshawar. He wanted me to assure him that the petition-writer had correctly written in English what had been dictated in Pashto. It was through reading and re-reading this over and over and explaining it that I missed the opportunity for food. Then he introduced me to his friend. Except for this first row, in which we were only four instead of the six that were authorized, the bus was filled beyond capacity. The others tried to grumble a bit, but the two Wazirs were extremely large and fierce and they were not prepared to have any nonsense, so after a while the others remained meekly silent. For me it was a lucky meeting, and I took the opportunity of arranging my Razmak visit. We agreed that I should go up with them from Miranshah, three or four days later.

"If the Political Agent sahib lets me go," I added.

"Why should he not?"

"Because of the Wazirs and the Mahsuds fighting with each other."

"What difference does that make?"

"I want to go down into Mahsud country from Razmak."

"To the Mahsuds? How can you be a friend of Mahsuds? They are devils."

"And the Tori Khel Wazirs?"

He spat out of the window and said: "And the British? I suppose they are not devils? You know we used to tell our children that the British eat babies if they can catch them?"

Chapter 18

Bannu—despised, decadent, already decayed little frontier-town; Bannu, for all that nice to look at. Even in summer it is green. The wrong sorts of vice are freely ascribed to its inhabitants, each denigrator naming the sin that leaves him personally cold and using it as a whip to whip the Bannuchis with. The Bannuchis thrive under these whippings and manage to get the better of most people.

Bannu lies in the path of the Kurram river which, since it left the pale-green softness of Kurram, has had quite a turbulent passage through the Ahmedzai Salient amongst all those bandits and outlaws and eroded chasms. Its waters fan out over the plains with the relief of escaping from the salient and most of them sink into the sands and are lost. The Pakistanis have a scheme that is already well advanced for harnessing the Kurram and forcing it to produce not only hydro-electric power but also to irrigate the stony wastes of the Jani Khel and Bakka Khel Wazirs who have hitherto scarcely known what it might be like to grow food-crops. Guldad the Jani Khel, who was to be awaiting my arrival in Miranshah, *Insha'Allah*, proudly claims that the only tree in sight is to be found in his own village. In a little while now other Jani Khels and Bakka Khels will be having trees too and will doubtless become very high-stomached about it.

Despite its well-grown avenues, Bannu was almost as hot and dusty as were Said Akbar and the two Tori Khel Wazirs and myself, that evening when we arrived. We got out of the bus, piled ourselves and our baggage into a tonga and went searching the town for our *badragga* —as they call a tribal escort. We found their truck, a half-armoured, green-painted thing with the arms of Tochi emblazoned on it. But the *badragga*-men themselves had gone wandering away. Then I noticed that one had been left and that he was asleep under the truck. He said that he was not hungry and had stayed there, to sleep. They had reached Bannu that morning, he added.

"I am glad to see you," he said. "Welcome in happiness—but it would have been better to have arrived this morning."

"We have been travelling since seven this morning," I explained.

"Don't get tired," one of the two Tori Khels said to him.

Everyone knows everyone else in this sort of country: and the *badragga*-man replied: "Don't get old, Mirabat Khan. I suppose you have heard that the rains came in the night and have taken away your lorry."

"What! Taken my lorry away?"

"Yes. Your lorry was crossing the *khwar*"—and he named a dry water-course some miles this side of Razmak—"and then—*whoooosh!* The rains came and filled the *khwar* which swelled at once into a river like the Indus but bigger, and away went the poor lorry and fell over. It is upside-down now, that lorry."

Mirabat Khan was aghast. "Are you sure, are you sure?"

"No. I am not sure: but this is what people are saying. It is either your lorry or else it is perhaps the lorry of Shoidar Jan here." He nodded in the direction of the second Tori Khel. "Don't get tired, Shoidar Jan," he added politely.

Shoidar Jan was aghast now. He took the *badragga*-man by the shoulder, forgetting even to respond to the greeting, shaking him and shouting: "Tell me it is not my lorry! Tell me that at once!"

"Very well, then. It must be someone else's lorry, I suppose. What liars some people must be."

I left them wrangling angrily.

One of the advantages of a little town and of a remote outlying district is that when you telephone you can stamp your foot and demand a clear-line call. The line, unless it has been cut, is almost certain to be clear anyway, so that you can get your wish, and with it the warm feeling of being a personage. Within two minutes I was talking to the Political Agent in Miranshah, miles away in the mountains of Waziristan.

"Faridullah Shah? It is? This is Peter Mayne. Yes. I'm in Bannu. They're here, yes. Thank you. They say they've been here since dawn. Shall we start at once? Good. All right. Thank you very much."

"Collect the *badragga*!" I ordered in a clarion voice.

It took a very long time. Men had to be searched for and pulled out of the wrong beds and I had to telephone to Miranshah again, to this same Faridullah Shah whom I did not know yet.

"There's been a delay," I explained. "Mechanical? No, not altogether. But I think we'll be able to start very soon now. Please don't hold up your dinner on my account." I had begun to feel extremely hungry, incidentally. It was already eight-thirty, and Miranshah was not less than an hour's journey away—if all went well.

"Come as quick as you can," Faridullah shouted down the line.

We went as quick as we could. The *badragga* was all collected together now, and we started. Said Akbar told them who I was and that we had been angry because our stomachs were empty and we were tired because of the horrible, common journey in a bus all day. "We are not accustomed to being treated in this manner," he said.

They were very understanding, and two of them wedged themselves into opposite corners of the big seat behind the driver, and there offered their bandolier'd bodies as pillows, some degrees harder than feathers. The others sang to us. It was a song that had to be sung with the accent of the Turis of Kurram, and it made Said Akbar laugh. A detachment of the Kurram Militia had been sent to Miranshah to reinforce the Tochi Scouts some time back when there had been a threat of trouble. The Tochi Scouts had liked the well-mannered Turis, and the Turis had liked them, but they had not at all approved of Waziristan as country. They had composed this nostalgic song to record their unhappiness. The song was addressed to their own darling river Kurram which they claimed to be able to recognize even after the drubbing it had received in the chasms of the Ahmedzai Salient.

"'*Lāss de yāra rāka*,'" the Turis had sung, and the *badragga* now copied the sad, romantic lilt of it. "'Give me your hand, my love—and we will return to our own fair country.'"

"But they couldn't. . . ." Said Akbar had scrambled off his pillow and was shaking with laughter. "They couldn't, those ridiculous Turis! If their lover Kurram took them by the hand it would rush them down amongst the Bannuchis! It can't go back, uphill!"

Everyone was delighted at this thought and they went through the song again, so loud that we scarcely heard the back tyre burst and were aware of what had happened only when the truck swung in a mad semicircle, stuck somehow to the road and then stopped. The driver got out.

"*Punchkur shwū*," he said, laughing.

Q

Consonants get interchanged if you aren't careful.   Lecture becomes
'*letchkur*'; picture '*pitchkur*'; puncture '*punchkur*': and to say *punchkur
shwū* in Pashto is much as if an Englishman were to say: 'Well, that's
—us!'

They changed the wheel and I sat chatting by the roadside with the
badragga.   Black bobbed hair and black turbans, an exhausted hibiscus
behind the ears of those who had picked a flower for themselves in
Miranshah that morning, and a rose or some other flower more sin-
fully-fresh for those who had misspent their day in Bannu.   They were
Tori Khel and Mohmit Khel and other Wazirs, and a Daur or two,
representatives of each of the tribes through whose territory we must
pass on our way to Miranshah.   Each would have a special, personal
responsibility within his own tribal area, and all of them their collective
responsibility for the whole course of the journey.

We shall be later than ever, I was thinking.

When I had first seen the frontier it had been a commonplace for a
Political Agent stationed in Waziristan to motor down to, say, Bannu,
for an evening at the club and a change of air, and he would drive back
again to his headquarters during the night.   Later, when things hotted
up, night travel stopped: it had become too dangerous.   Even day
travel was something that involved the risk of being shot up or ambushed.   It was nice to see that comparative freedom of movement
had returned: nice, in any case, to think so as we sat on the dark roadside with the hills high and dark all round us.

"How is the road to Razmak?" I asked someone, hoping to learn
that the rains had done less damage than I had been told.

"It is closed.   Did you not hear about Mirabat Khan's lorry?"

I wanted to go to Razmak.   There would be nothing there any more,
except the looted ruins of the 'cantonment'.   It had never been a nice
place: rather the contrary, I would have said: just a dull, military
cantonment, headquarters of a regular-army brigade.   I had spent part
of two summers there, on those rolling, seven-thousand-foot down-
lands, but there had been trouble in those years, and it had been impossible to wander amongst the people.   The Wazirs would lie up on
the slope above the camp and snipe us.   This they would particularly
like to do on a night when we had a party in the open air—when the
sepoys danced for us, for example, or there were guests staying there.
South of Razmak the world drops suddenly away in a chute towards
the Mahsuds.   There was a road in the old days, dotted with scouts

234

posts, but the scouts' posts have since been closed, and the road has fallen into disrepair.

It was nearer eleven than ten when we reached Miranshah. The big iron gates of the fort were pushed open and the guard called loudly to attention. We came to a halt. There was no question of my being allowed to have a bath and go quietly to bed, however: Faridullah Shah, having waited for hours, was determined to go through with it. All the officers of the Tochi Scouts who happened to be at headquarters, and most of the officers of the Royal Pakistan Air Force detachment, were waiting in the ante-room of the Scouts' Mess, their hungry hearts hidden behind the most convincing smiles of welcome. Faridullah was in formal Pakistani evening dress, *achkan* and *salwars*, another civilian officer was in a dinner-jacket, and the service officers were in uniform. I felt dirty and ashamed.

But eventually we had fed and I was taken to my room. Faridullah came to see that I had everything. He is square and tough and has a reputation for getting things done. He and his family have been Pathans for centuries now, but their origins are Arab, the family of the Prophet Muhammed—Syeds. He is apt to call his officers and the Tochi Scouts and the Air Force 'my children'—and when he says it he half laughs, and yet you know that with the other half he means it, in a deep patriarchal sense that is rather moving.

I said: 'I'm so sorry to have kept you all up so late."

"Never mind. You must be tired. My children are, too. We'll all go to bed now: and in the morning you shall tell me what you want to do and see."

I read for a few minutes and then fell asleep, but I had forgotten to stub out my cigarette and when I awoke, rather hurriedly and perhaps an hour or so later, most of the mattress had smouldered away and there were great holes in the sheets, and the webbing support for the mattress had collapsed all down one side of the bed. The room was full of smoke and smells that hurt the eyes. I stumbled, half asleep, into the bathroom and fetched a bucket of water. It was not a very good start, I suppose.

*　　　　*　　　　*

Said Akbar pretended not to notice the desolation when he called me next morning. He was accompanied by Guldad and a *subedar* of the

Tochi Scouts who was a friend of his, and a couple of non-commissioned officers. I did my best to receive them with dignity, but they had me at a disadvantage. I sat up in bed, in a cloak of charred and ragged bed-clothes.

"May God be praised that you are safe," they said, not looking—and then I saw that there were other men in the doorway and that they carried mattresses and sheets and pillows and a new bed, and that one of them had an immense tray of tea and *parathas*. So it was to be a reception, all right.

Guldad said: "Thank you so much for all those letters from Morocco that I suppose you have forgotten to post. Thank you also for your congratulations each year on the birth of babies. I have five now."

I totted up the years. "Good heavens! That's rather quick, isn't it?"

"It is God's will. They have been coming in a stream lately, you see."

"God be praised."

Said Akbar motioned yet another man forward through the doorway, saying: "This is the tailor-master from whom already I have arranged clothes for you, Peter sahib. *Rasha*, Muhammed Khan. Show him! Look, Peter sahib, nice *qamis* and *partug*, two of each for you, and one of each for me. Nice grey *mazri*." *Mazri* is the dwarf-palm, and it is also the grey dye that colours the clothes Pakhtuns so often wear—the long knee-length shirt and the baggy trousers on a draw-string. I examined the things.

"Put them on," Said Akbar said.

"I will *try* them on when I get up."

"And we can give the blue horribles to a poor man who must spend his life lying under lorries and putting oil into their joints. He will be very glad. Nothing could be a more suitable present for him."

"Is it necessary to give him a present at all?"

"He is an old friend and I have not seen him for years."

*   *   *

So from that moment I was put into *mazri* clothes and, to flatter me, people would say that I looked like a Khan or a Malik or something grand, though it was not quite true. I looked like any other ordinary

236

person. But the clothes were comfortable and well-suited to the country and the weather, and perhaps I was secretly glad to have sloughed my obstinate loyalty to the jeans.

Miranshah is an oasis, less in the sense of trees and water than in the sense of a refuge from the cruel mountains of Waziristan in which it is set. Lawrence of Arabia, transmuted into the sad, withdrawn Leading Aircraftman Shaw, was once stationed here. He seems to have hated it—perhaps by then he hated life itself and was already searching for means to escape from it. The officers of the Tochi Scouts would beg him to come up to the Mess and visit them, but he did not wish to. Miranshah must have seemed the antithesis of what he had lived for. It was, I suppose. It is a fort, with parade-grounds and an airfield, and there is a caravanserai near-by.

Storms had wrought considerable damage all over North Waziristan. The strategic roads, such as the one from Bannu to Miranshah, are well maintained in all circumstances, but others, for example those that led to Razmak, or from beyond Boya to Datta Khel, whose importance has diminished since regular troops were withdrawn and certain Scouts' posts have been closed, matter less and have been allowed to fall into disrepair. Uncertain weather still continued, with the result that movement was very severely restricted. For a day or two I had to remain within the fortress. I was very happy to see Guldad again. He had been the first Wazir I could claim as a friend and one of the few educated Pakhtuns I know, of any tribe, who remains implacably Pakhtun despite the blandishments of western civilization. I found myself much involved with friends of his and with friends of Said Akbar's, and with visits to the *serai*, a couple of hundred yards outside the fortress gates. It was there that on my first day I ran into Mirabat Khan and Shoidar Jan, the two Tori Khel Wazirs, who were held up too till the road to Razmak and home should be usable once more. I was now told that the lorry upside-down in its grave of a water-course belonged to neither of them, so they were spared that misery, anyway.

I spoke to Faridullah Shah, the Political Agent, about Razmak—hoping to hear that the breach was being mended. His news was indefinite and rather discouraging.

"It'll be some time yet, I'm afraid. But there'd be nothing to see in Razmak, you know, even if you went there. Just the old cantonment in partial ruins, and *khassadars* camping out in it."

"Yes, but even so . . . And the track down from Razmak to the Mahsuds?"

"That's outside my agency," he said. "But if you want to meet Wazirs, I can get men in here for you to see."

As I got to know Faridullah I developed a strong feeling of friendship for him. He took me about in the motorable vicinity of Miranshah when the rains ceased, and an escort hurried along behind us. It was mostly outdistanced, however, because Faridullah drives like a mad thing. We stopped to talk with tribesmen who had requests to make, or complaints which they would emphasize not rudely or intimidatingly, just firmly, by banging with their fists on the car-roof. They would gather in a jam about the car, their faces all squeezed together at the windows, and Faridullah would deal with them firmly in his turn, with that mixture of wisdom and patriarchal authority beyond his years that I had already noted in him. For anyone interested in seeing something of day-to-day 'agency' business, this was a good object-lesson. Faridullah seemed to know his job and to take pleasure in doing it.

Yet, in coming to Waziristan again I had hoped for something other than this, however pleasant and instructive it might be. The semi-official atmosphere is no substitute for a *hujra* with its warm humanity, and the *serai* at Miranshah no substitute for a true village. At the same time I had to admit to myself that I could not expect to stay in no-matter-whose village *hujra*: it would have to be at the invitation of friends, and what friends had I now in North Waziristan? Shah Nawaz Khan was not traceable. I had had a message from his village just before leaving Peshawar. I knew now that he was 'away', but no one knew exactly where. Guldad, a Jani Khel Wazir, did not belong in this part of the country and was himself an official, as much cut off from what I looked for as anyone else in the fort. It was in fact a situation that I could have foreseen perfectly well for myself. So I had to content myself with the second-best of formal relationships, and when a party of Wazir *maliks* came and sat themselves in Faridullah's drawing-room at his invitation, the result was a village debating society, even after Faridullah had withdrawn, leaving me alone with them. We all sat hiding ourselves behind a screen of polite talk, or of talk which they supposed would do credit to the Political Agent sahib and, consequently, to themselves as well, if I had the kindness to bring it to his ears. It was not political tittle-tattle that I was after, but the sense of 'belonging'. None of us really belonged at all in the Political Agent's drawing-room.

I went to Mir Ali, and when I got there I realized that to go to a place means nothing in itself. If I had written to the outlawed Wazir who had befriended me in Nathia Gali, what could I have said? That Mir Ali was a village in North Waziristan—just a village in North Waziristan and that there was a Scouts' Post near-by, much bigger than the village?

One morning Faridullah lent me a truck because I had asked if I might go to Datta Khel. I could not go to Datta Khel because of the washed-out road, but the way was open as far as Boya. I was just setting off, through the Tochi valley with its narrow strip of cultivation and the fruit-orchards that the Daur tribe have developed into a profit-making business, when some Scouts officers and others who were at a loose end that day came along and offered to keep me company. So they accompanied me and were very entertaining. A conversation that we had started the night before in the Mess was resumed, in a moving truck now, instead of in the ante-room with its shields and silver trophies. Yet I doubt whether even alone I could have made closer contact with the valley: the country and the people are changed for you as you drive past, insulated from them by a fully-armed *bad-ragga*. So Boya was a map-name, as Mir Ali had been.

Back in Miranshah again I made for the *serai*, looking for Mirabat Khan and Shoidar. They were the closest I could get to Razmak for the moment, and Miranshah was the closest they could get to it too, as far as that went.

"Where did you go today?" Mirabat asked me. He was in rather a bad temper.

"To Boya."

"What for?"

Exactly! What for? It was a perfectly reasonable question, but I had no answer to it, so I made one up and said: "I have never shot a Tori Khel. I thought it would be nice to get one and present him to the Mess. But it was silly of me, because all the people I saw were Daurs, naturally enough—and who shoots Daurs, except other Daurs?"

He didn't laugh, and I quite see that it wasn't funny, but Said Akbar who was told later what I had said in the hearing of several others, was upset with me.

"It was a very rude thing to say, Peter sahib," he admonished.

"Well, it's true that I have never shot a Tori Khel, of course: but Tori Khels have often shot Englishmen, and I don't see why Mirabat should think it rude, even if he didn't think it funny. He was already angry about something else, probably, and attached his anger to my joke."

"It is serious and not funny to talk of shooting a man's brothers."

The days I spent in Miranshah were in fact days of insulation—from the outside world by mountains, from the tribes by battlements or the bristling weapons of the *badragga*. They would have been very happy days if I had not been seeking something else. Even the *serai* was but a property village that had probably been constructed by a movie-unit on location. Nevertheless I found there a man very much to my taste: an old Wazir with a sharp, malicious mind. He made me laugh with his pantomime of British and Pakistani and Afghan personalities, all keenly caricatured. Then he fished out a tattered leaflet from a drawer. It was dated 1929, and had been issued by King Nadir Shah of Afghanistan (as he was soon to become), calling upon the Wazirs to help him oust Bachha-i-Saqao, son of the water-carrier, from the throne of Kabul, and to reinstate the exiled King Amanullah Khan.

"But Nadir Shah snatched the throne for himself!" the old Wazir cried, making his eyes roll with anger. "He took it for himself—and where is Amanullah?"

"In Italy still, I suppose," I said.

When Amanullah Khan had made his triumphal European Progress in 1928, the King of Italy had given him—perhaps unwisely—a little decoration that carried with it the right to claim cousinship with the royal house of Italy. The Royal Afghan cousin lost his throne in 1929 and made straight for Italy and there established himself, there even outstayed his Royal Italian cousin. None of these things much mattered to the Wazirs, naturally, except that it is always nice to have a grievance up your sleeve against the need of it.

"He tricked us! Nadir Shah tricked us! He said it was for Amanullah Khan that we were shedding our life's blood, and all the time it was for him!"

I could not resist saying: "Yes, it was rather shameful, wasn't it? You would never have agreed to loot the Kabul bazaars, would you, if you had known that you were doing it for Nadir Shah? It was a cruel trick." And the old man looked at me sideways, his eyes laughing silently too.

The talk switched itself to Kashmir—inevitably—and someone said that the men of Swat had fought very well, that in reality they had been second in valour to the Wazirs themselves: but he laughed derisively when I asked where the Mahsuds came in.

"Pah!" he said, and that brought us to the skirmishing up beyond Razmak in which Abdullai Mahsuds were involved in a new round of their eternal battle with the Tori Khel Wazirs.

"No," said one of them. "I don't think they will let you go there. And in any case the road is blocked still."

"But if it opens again, then surely Faridullah Shah will let me go."

"Faridullah is a very wise man, and he is also a very strong and firm man," he commented, and I admired the neatness with which he then drew a red herring across the path and, there in the side lane, set up an Aunt Sally for our amusement: "You know that once we had a political who was so sweet and charming that if he had been a woman and not a man he would have remained all the day with his legs in the air so happy was he to please us!"

They all smiled, and I said:

"And this kind, obliging officer—who was he?"

"We forget his name—don't we?" the man asked, grinning round at the others.

"We entirely forget his name," they agreed, and turned back to me with their little private smiles.

*　　　　*　　　　*

Guldad had to return to his work in Bannu and suggested that I come down with him.

"It's no good staying on here, hoping for Razmak," he said. "And no good hoping for Shawal either." Shawal was the summer country of the Jani Khel, and part of his family would be there now, up in the mountains, beyond Razmak even. "You had better come down with me to Bannu. In any case I want you to come, so you had better come, therefore. You will be my guest."

"Very well, I will come with you. Perhaps later on, if the weather improves, I can return to Miranshah."

"Perhaps."

"And we'll send a signal to Wana, to the Political Agent of South Waziristan, asking him to signal to your address in Bannu if it is convenient to him that I go on there tomorrow or the next day."

"The Scouts already have a message from Wana to say that the road in by that long defile of Shahur Tangi is blocked. Rocks have fallen and closed it."

*   *   *

Faridullah Shah gave us a truck and an escort and stood at the gates of the fortress, waving good-bye. I thanked him for all his hospitality.

"Don't give it another thought," he said, standing there as the truck moved off. "And don't let my children get into trouble in Bannu!"

His 'children' were two Tochi Scouts officers who were coming with us. One of the two was a Bangash tribesman who in early youth had joined the Scouts in the ranks, but that had been some twenty-nine years before. Now, at the age of about forty-five, he still had the appearance of a man in his twenties. Even after partition and his elevation to commissioned rank, the name he had long ago been given by British officers still stuck to him: 'William', in place of Wilayat Shah.

William was quiet and unassuming and a first-rate soldier. He had long been a friend of Guldad's, and of Said Akbar's, and he was by now a friend of mine too, I am happy to think. We teased him. One of the others said:

"When you retire—and of course you are already very old—we will put you in a little cupboard and we will then make the recruits walk three times round you, and some of the spirit will come out of you and through your cupboard and go into the recruits. In this way we expect to be able to reduce their period of training by two months."

"William is like a tiger and like a mountain goat. He runs up hills even quicker than the old Wali of Swat and he comes down them again like a *khwar* in spate. He is our dear, dear William and we will make a splendid cupboard for him in which he can rest for ever—except, of course, when we need his help with the recruits."

William said nothing for a moment and then addressed me: "Before they put me into my cupboard," he said, "I wish to go on the *Hajj*, the pilgrimage to Mecca, and then perhaps to England where all the old officers of the Tochi Scouts are waiting to receive me as their guest. I love them and they love me."

"After the *Hajj* and the visit to England, then," they said. "Your cupboard, by the way, will be of walnut-wood which we will fetch from Kashmir specially for you."

William said: "Thank you very much, all of you."

* * *

We lunched with Guldad, the four of us, in his little house with the stream of children peeping in from a courtyard. They thought that I was a Pakhtun because of the *mazri* clothes, and when they learnt that I was English they fled to safety.

"Have you told them that the English eat Wazir babies, then, Guldad?" I asked.

"I wanted them to behave well and do me honour."

"You must tell them at once that you have lied to them."

"If they should think that their father had lied to them, their trust would be irrevocably undermined. Do you not know about modern educated parenthood? And who says that I have lied to them, in any case?"

William and his brother-officer in the Scouts left us after the meal and we went through the business of farewells. I put some money for a tea-party into the pocket of the *badragga*-leader and he pretended not to notice, just as I pretended not to be doing it. When the armoured truck moved off, Guldad and I went into the house and he sat himself down to telephone. We had had no confirmed news about road blocks farther south, and someone was saying locally that the Shahur Tangi was already cleared and open to traffic again. Indeed I hoped that it might prove true. Bannu was a furnace. Even if you have experienced great heat it is impossible to recall the true horror of it, and I had forgotten the truth during my stay in Miranshah with its mountains. Once I had reached Wana I could forget again. A telephone conversation with a friend of Guldad's in Tank, on the South Waziristan borders, seemed to confirm that the road was clear once more. I decided to leave next day, and take a chance.

Said Akbar came in, carrying a big blue and white enamel mug.

"Look!" he said importantly. "This is my present to you, Peter sahib. I am so shamed at each place we go and they say to me 'And where is the *kerrrnail* sahib's mug for shaving?' and I am obliged to say that the *kerrrnail* sahib has no such mug. If this goes on, they will no longer believe."

* * *

Another journey and more intolerable heat. The road south from Bannu to Tank was a morass from the rains: the short cut was blocked and we took the longer route through Dehra Ismail Khan: and when we came to a river which is normally crossable by an Irish bridge, I would have described it as blocked too. Flood water flowed swift and yellow over it. But men who regard such natural obstacles as belonging to the natural order of things are not much deterred by them, provided there seems a chance that noses and mouths can remain above water. The driver of the truck patiently removed both the fan-belt and the exhaust-pipe of his engine and then climbed back into the cab. He thrust his foot firmly down on the accelerator. The truck leapt forward, screaming.

"Quietly, quietly, for God's sake!" I shouted.

We went through as if we had been a landing-craft, with waves building up in a spearhead round us. As we staggered up the far bank the driver said: "You see?"

I was content to regard our crossing as an act of faith. Was this really the way to attack a flood? Perhaps it was, if you had faith and remembered to remove both fan-belt and exhaust-pipe.

*   *   *

I was to stay the night in Tank with the Assistant-Commissioner, and I found that the two little schoolboy sons of the Political Agent, South Waziristan, were there too, on their way up to Wana to join their father. Evidently an escort had been arranged to take them up next day—so the road must be open again. It was a lucky moment to have arrived.

Tank is horrible. Little foothill towns in the North-West Frontier districts can be horrible. Mostly their bazaars have been developed by small-time merchants anxious to fleece the tribesmen who come in from the hills, and anxious at the same time to remain living to enjoy the loot. They took a certain risk in the pioneering days, these merchants, but the gamble succeeded more often than not, even if something disagreeable happened occasionally. Such a combination of greed and a physical fear that is yet outdone by greed is as unpleasant as the bazaars that grew up in the shadow of it.

Dust, filth, squalor and the money-bags piling up in cellars. Part of the Tank bazaar area had fallen down, undermined by flood-water,

244

but it gave the appearance of having collapsed a very long time before. Now that Mahsud tribesmen have to all intents and purposes taken over, it is scarcely less horrible than it used to be, because Tank's soul is sour. The down-country merchants have gone—many were Hindus who fled to India after partition, in that bloody cross-migration of refugees between Pakistan and India: but very few Muslim refugees fleeing from India seem to have come to Tank to fill what ought to have been a vacuum, because the Mahsuds had already filled it first. The Assistant Commissioner told me something about the situation. He was an intelligent and well-educated young man, a member of the Civil Service of Pakistan that is the present-day equivalent of the old Indian Civil Service.

"The Mahsuds? They're accustomed to the loose political control we impose on them in the tribal areas—and, of course, to the special subsidies the tribes get from government in the form of allowances and the rest of it, to counterbalance their economic poverty. In due course the tribal areas will merge with the settled districts, naturally: but meantime the tribes need help. But it's different here in Tank. The Mahsuds who have taken over still think of themselves as tribal people to whom the privileges and 'allowances' of tribal life are due—and at the same time are making handsome profits from their businesses in Tank. They are shrewd, and quick-witted. But they can't expect to have it both ways. I must not, and don't, grant them special privileges here simply because they are Mahsud tribesmen. Nor do they need them. And so they come to me in a fury, demanding what they call their 'rights'. I have to tell them to go back to Waziristan if they want the 'rights' they refer to: or that they can remain in Tank, with my blessing, and accept the advantages that go with the peaceful, regulated life of citizens, together with the obligations that go with it too. They pretend to be affronted at my inhumanity."

He was very serious about it, and quite right to be, but when he had said this he remembered that it was funny at the same time, and grinned.

Next morning we were deposited, the two little Pakistani schoolboys and I, on the near side of a bridge that had collapsed when the river came down in flood. Then we tight-roped across a plank straddling the gap, and were loaded into another truck on the far side. We made for Wana, with a truckload of armed men following behind as escort.

*　　　　*　　　　*

To a good many soldiers and Scouts officers and political officers Wana is probably something to remember with affection, much as you might remember an uncle or a cousin: not very remarkable, perhaps, and in some ways rather a bore, but kindly—or so you like to think in retrospect. If Wana is part of your past, then it is a little bit sacred to the memory of whoever you may be. It had no such blood-ties for me. I had been there several times, but I was unable to pierce the plain exterior and reach to the heart of gold.

Wana lies in a high-floating parti-coloured plain in the country of the Ahmedzai Wazirs, whose relatives had been left, eroded and ill-tempered, up in the salient beyond Bannu. There are a few great big hills to the north, and a range that rises south and east, and to the west the land swells upwards to the Afghan frontier, less than a day's trek distant.

I was housed very comfortably indeed in the South Waziristan Scouts' mess. I had drinks on the lawn, the food was good, the bathwater hot, my companions were welcoming and delightful and the weather seemed set fair now. But I was soon told by the political authorities that the roads were all closed and likely to remain so for . . . how long was I thinking of staying, by the way? And had I not received their letter telling me all about the roads being closed? I had not received the letter, as it happened. I was here only by the accident of having run into the two schoolboys, and had thumbed a lift with them: but I did not press this point. When I said that in due course I hoped to leave South Waziristan by the Gomal Pass into Baluchistan, they said that that road was open, as a matter of fact. I was told a good deal about Pathans, also, and how they were really lambs in lion-skins.

Wana is the hub of things in this part of the world. People come in from all over the place, Wazirs, Mahsuds. How they were managing to get here at present, with all the roads blocked, was another matter—magic carpets, perhaps. Magic jeeps and trucks and cars and pack-animals and feet were to be seen leaving Wana, and others would come in, muddy but entire. I felt rather as I had felt in Kabul, all over again—but with a difference. In Kabul my Pakistani background had made me a suspect person. Here, back in the tribal areas of Pakistan, I could think of no reasons, even silly ones, for my being mistrusted.

It all seemed so stupidly pointless and I worried over it as I went mooning about 'the streets' of Wana.

'The streets' are like pathways in a suburban-villa garden: very trim, they are, and you have the feeling that you should keep within their neatly-kept boundaries and not walk on the grass or throw your cigarette-ends away, and that if you had a dog it should be on a lead. Wana had become a 'family-station' since partition. Wives made a difference to the atmosphere of the place, a difference I had not foreseen. Observing *purdah* themselves, and tending to hold their husbands in *purdah* with them, the Scouts' mess—which would otherwise have been the centre of social life—was for the most part deserted. Nevertheless officers would appear for a moment before luncheon, and a few more would be found playing squash-rackets or tennis when evening came, or, a little later, sitting on the lawn in a semicircle and listening to the Political Agent who was accustomed to paying a visit before dinner. At dinner there might be a bachelor officer in mess, and at nine or so perhaps a few would turn up dressed for a night-*gasht* with khaki knitted-wool caps rolled on their heads. They were most friendly and asked me if I would care to go with them. I like walking quietly on the mountain-sides, but I have no taste at all for patrols of this kind, tearing up an escarpment or slithering down one, all in the name of speed, efficiency and leg-muscles. They would laugh when I told them this, understanding perfectly. So I was mostly alone after dinner—the wrong sort of alone, and rather futile in this sleeping suburb. If I went walking in the dark, sentries would constantly challenge me, popping out from behind something—out of boredom, I dare say: and out of necessity I would find myself saying '. . . friend . . . friend . . .' and wondering if it was worth having travelled so far to make such mechanical little responses.

In the daytime I would wander a degree less disconsolately, away beyond the perimeter and beyond an orchard, to where a stream came down towards the camp and then swung right, under a tree-laden bank that it was gradually undermining with its pertinacity. Big sections of mud from the bank would plop into the water from time to time. I sat there, chewing grass and interesting myself in this, wondering at each repetition if it would be a bigger bit or a smaller bit, and if the river would fell a tree before I had to leave Wana. No one was there as a rule, but once a Pakhtun, in rough tribal clothes, came up and asked me a question:

"Who are you?"

"Don't get tired," I said. "I am an Englishman who is lost in Wana. Don't you get lost. But who are you?"

"I? I am Pakhtun."

"Of course. What kind of Pakhtun. What is your tribe?"

"I am Urmur."

The Urmurs are a little tribe who have got themselves rather mixed up with the Mahsuds. They are said to have been a bigger tribe, once upon a time, and to have occupied the Mahsud valleys in strength themselves, along with another tribe called Marwat. The Marwats have slid down since then, towards the plains and Pathan-hood.

"What are you doing here?" I asked.

"I have come to visit a friend in the *khassadars*. And you?"

"I have come to visit friends in the Mahsud valleys."

"Oh? Who?" He was interested now, and sat down beside me as I gave him the names.

"Ah, yes. They are my friends, too—except Fulana Khan, who is not my friend at all. You may please take me in your car as far as Ladha. It is on your way. You will also stay with me for a night or two, please. I will be ready to leave this evening, *Insha' Allah*, or tomorrow morning."

"I'm afraid I haven't got a car."

He looked surprised. "Have the English gone poor, then?"

"I have gone sad—because I don't think I will be able to visit my friends after all."

"Why not?"

"Because I am being told that all the roads are closed. Since I am asked to believe this, it would certainly be impolite for me to ask them, in my turn, to provide me with transport."

"Never mind. We will go together in a lorry. Or, if you like, we will send for your friends to come here and fetch you away with them."

"But I am unable to go. That is the point."

He put his hand on my shoulder and said softly, as if he were consoling a child: "Come at once to us, and you will not be sad any more. As a matter of fact you will be angry when you see the troubles that are falling on the Mahsuds."

And then, as he told me of the 'troubles', I began to see what stood like a screen between me and what I had come for.

The Mahsud companies in the *Azad Fauj*—the 'free army', of which I don't believe I had heard hitherto—were to be disbanded. The Afridi and the Wazir companies of the same force had been disbanded already, the man said. Now it was the turn of the Mahsuds and they were objecting loudly.

The year 1952 had been a bad one for Pakistan, as I knew—though the Urmur did not speak of this—a year of collapsing export markets for jute and cotton, a year of bad monsoon rains, of crops that failed, of belt-tightening all round; 1953 was not proving a much better year than 1952 had been, either. Something drastic had to be done. Pakistan's economy, so buoyant till now, had been seriously shaken. Fortunately, however, the threat of war with India had receded, though not so long before war had seemed almost inevitable and likely to involve trouble with Afghanistan in the north-west also. Economies of every sort must be made over the whole wide face of Pakistan and obvious amongst them would be the disbanding of these tribal levies raised against an emergency that—*Insha' Allah*—no longer existed. The *Azad Fauj* was inevitably marked with a cross. Except for one or two little incidents on the Afghan border which had caused more shouting than bloodshed, the *Azad Fauj* had never been called into action. It had just sat there, eating its head off, and to the tribesmen who drew their *Azad Fauj* pay, it was just an extra source of earned, or unearned, tribal income. Up in their valleys the Mahsuds were saying that the disbanding of the force was a crime against humanity—or whatever slogan it was that had taken their fancy.

There was nothing in the least shameful to Pakistan in all this, though for the moment it was, I suppose, annoying. Nevertheless I realized now that it would be an embarrassment to the local authorities to have me, or any other Pashto-speaking visitor, wandering about and sitting in *hujras* and being filled up with angry and ridiculous 'Unfair to the Mahsuds' talk. I felt, all the same, that they should have trusted me to understand. Instead I was expected to listen to pep-talks under a walnut tree, or to pore diligently over the statistics of school attendance, starry-eyed and admiring. I was deeply admiring of Pakistan and still thought of myself as Pakistani in part, and I was for that reason the more impatient. Moreover my eyes, as I have admitted, are like little flint-chips and not starry at all, and they kept glaring in the direction of Kaniguram and Ladha and the hamlets that cling to the mountain-sides, towards the Mahsud friends that I had come so far to see.

"Don't you want to come with me, then?" the Urmur asked me.

"I don't think they will let me go."

R

"But this is a free country, isn't it? It is not like the days when the British were here, and we were slaves!"

"Pakhtun slaves . . . ?" I suggested, smiling.

He smiled too and said: "I invite you. Therefore you are free to come."

"What is 'free'?"

Neither of us really knew. He said that 'free' meant doing what you liked, and I said 'free' was doing what you liked provided nobody else objected who had the right to object The Urmur could not agree to this, however.

"Then I think that 'free' must be something in the heart," I said finally, knowing that this meant nothing at all.

"Nonsense!" he exclaimed, taking up his first position again. "'Free' is free, and we will therefore start out together this evening or tomorrow, *Insha'Allah*. But at present we will go and take tea with the *khassadars*."

Together we made our way to the *khassadar* lines. They are outside the main camp, in a *serai*, and though they look like normal army barracks, rather grim and very ugly, the *khassadars* have made of the inside something very pleasantly indisciplined. They were sitting, close-packed on a haphazard arrangement of charpoys, as if upon logs jammed together at a bottleneck of a river. Somehow they made room for us. We chatted for a long time, drinking tea out of little chipped cups that were passed round, and someone had some old bits of 'biscoot' which were passed round too. I had cigarettes, but they disdained them. They preferred their chillums or *naswar*.

I would like to have heard more about the *Azad Fauj* but I did not want to bring up the subject myself and no one else did—no doubt because these particular men were not Mahsud, and Mahsud problems were consequently of no interest to them. The Urmur who had brought me had slipped away into a corner with whoever his friend may have been, and I could see them whispering and gesticulating. The Urmur did not look pleased, and the other, younger, man appeared to be saying 'no . . . no . . .' with monotonous obstinacy. Everyone has his troubles, I suppose. The men whose bed I was sharing had theirs too, though they were in the past now, and the first fine fury over them had dissipated itself.

"They cheated us, you see," they explained to me. "We are taking training in drill now, and we are of course very good at it—present

250

arms, quick march, don't talk there, round about and keep that chin in—all that business. We can do it very easily and well. Please do not think that we like it, but we can do it, and prizes are given. It is about the prizes that they cheated us."

They were not angry any more, but they had been extremely angry on the day of the passing-out parade when *khassadars* under training had been lined up and put through their paces, with the population of Wana watching. They had done well, and the climax was to be the distribution of prizes to the best platoons. The winners marched up to the tribune to collect their prizes. That was all right: what seemed wrong, of course, was that the losers received no prizes. The losers were shaking with rage and stumped off the parade-ground in protest. If this was the way they were to be treated after all that prancing about in the dust, then they would go to their homes and they would not come back again. It took a lot of cajolery to get them back and it was really not until a little anonymous sheep was brought into the camp for presentation to the Political Agent that authority knew the incident was closed—more or less closed.

"If a man has worked for his reward," one of the *khassadars* said pompously, "he must be given his reward. And if there is only one reward, then it is stupid that hundreds of men should work for it. What I am saying is sense, and everything else is nonsense. Do you agree, or do you not agree?"

I said: "I don't agree in this case. You see, it was a compet——"

He broke in: "I am not asking you if you agree or not, except from politeness. What I have said is *so.*"

"Exactly so," I said.

"Will you come to see us each day?"

"I am going away—at once."

"Where?"

"To Baluchistan, and from Baluchistan to Karachi, *Insha'Allah,* and from Karachi to el-Moghreb, back to the Moors."

The Urmur, who had rejoined our party by now and was standing beside me, said: "But you said you were going to stay with our Mahsuds."

"I had hoped to go to them, but now I see that I cannot."

The Urmur turned to explain to the others: "This man, whose name is Peter *ferangi,* says that he is not free to go to the Mahsuds, even with their invitation. He says that 'free' is in the heart. I tell him that free is free to come to the Mahsuds, and I do not know how he does not understand this."

*   *   *

But I was not free to embarrass the Pakistanis, who had always treated me with kindness and as if I too were part of themselves: nor was I free to embarrass my Mahsud friends by coming to them without authority and compelling them to choose between me, an unimportant guest, and the wishes of government.   There was only one way out, for me, and it led me from Wana to Baluchistan by way of the Gomal Pass.

Chapter 19

"'The world is a bowl . . . and . . .'" Said Akbar hesitated. "And then what?"

I finished the line for him: "'. . . and I an ant in it.'"

It was part of a Pashto verse that I had been reciting a day or two before, in Wana. It had seemed apposite then, but it was even more so today. We had emerged from the chasms of the Gomal and the world was indeed a vast, enclosing bowl. I felt a shrinking in of myself and an emptiness.

"'. . . and you an ant in it,'" he said.

"You too, Said Akbar."

He said something in reply but I suppose I was not listening—except to the empty echoes of my mind—so he jogged me with his arm. When I looked round at him he said: "There is no need to be sad. I am with you, and we are going to visit other friends." Then, in a different voice: "In Quetta, the guests of English friends, did you say?"

"Yes. Old and good friends. The Sakers."

"Who?"

"The Revenue Commissioner sahib and his family."

"Ah-h!"

He knew what the label meant, and it had a comfortably-important ring.

We were travelling with a *badragga* for the last time. There would be no need of escorts any more, and at Gul Kach ours turned back towards Wana and the true Pakhtuns. I watched them go, thinking: 'This story is finished for me now.' We could travel on as we pleased, without permits or escorts, now that we were in Baluchistan. Quetta was still two days ahead of us. The Zhob Militia, in their kindness, took us part of the way, offering us breakfast in the little fort of

Samboza and the hospitality of their mess that night at Fort Sandeman. The 'Scouts' picked their officers well: that was obvious: and it had been warming for an Englishman to see how zealously the old traditions were still maintained by Pakistanis—in Kurram, in Miranshah, in Wana, and now in Fort Sandeman.

"And the tribes?" one of the Zhob officers said. "You have noticed the change?"

"Indeed I have."

"For the better?"

"Very much so."

"Today we are all brothers in Islam—the tribes and the rest of us Pakistanis. Everything has followed from that. There's been a change of heart, you see."

I was thinking about this on my way to bed that evening when, outside my quarters, an old, old 'untouchable' whose task it was to tend the lavatories bowed over his broom and said: 'May you become Viceroy!' He must have said this in years gone by to a procession of Englishmen who for all his good wishes were to become nothing of the kind. Yet it was an ennobling thought and, even if too late and too ambitious, I gave him a penny for it.

We left next day for Hindubagh. Looking back from the lorry in which we had begged a lift I could see the mess of the Zhob Militia like a ship on the great wave of rock that bore it up, and then we turned away.

Yesterday the world had been a bowl. Today it had stretched itself out into a long, wide valley, as joyless as the moon and as empty. Nothing moved in it but the spinning columns of the dust, dust-devils that spun and turned and twisted, ceaselessly and without hope or purpose.

Hindubagh for the night—a little township in a ring of grey-green verdure—and on again: another truck, another stop for a meal that afternoon, Pishin this time, and on again: and so at last to Quetta.

Angela Saker was presiding over tea in the garden. There was something specially comforting about the scene—the trees, the filtered sun; Angela and their two boys; bread, butter, jam and home-made cakes. A Labrador lay in the grass with its tongue hanging out. Very soon Ken Saker joined us.

A tent in the grand manner

"We've put up a tent for you, Peter," he said. "Come and look."

I was very happy to see them again. The tent pleased me, too: a tent in the grand manner. It was lined with saffron yellow on which a hand-block patterning of flowers repeated itself. There was a bedroom, a bathroom and a little veranda. I stayed with Ken and Angela for several days and by the time I took train for Karachi I was in quite a rational frame of mind once more.

Part 4

EPILOGUE: KARACHI

Chapter 20

IT was my last day in Karachi.

I stood in my room staring towards the sea—the Arabian Sea. It was quite close, but invisible nevertheless behind a screen of its own spumy vapours. Mud-flats occupied the foreground and, from right to left along a highway that bisected them, a line of cars made for home, bumper to bumper, close-coupled as a train. It was about six in the evening. 'Home' on that highway could mean only the seaside suburb of Clifton, a half-mile farther south. The sands were blowing up from the beaches in the way they have, so I couldn't see much of Clifton except a beige blur.

The sun still hung about. It was a tin-foil disc these days. Streams of its nerve-racking silver brilliance came into my room, blinding me and banging about the walls. I suddenly realized that I was sweating like a horse because the window was shut. I opened it and a banging, blinding wind roared in. The evening paper took flight and flattened itself against the wall. My pores had already closed in self-defence.

I undressed and went into the bathroom for a shower, but by the time I came back I was sweating again, so I stood myself before the window, to dry off. After a while I heard the door opening behind me and the pad-pad-pad of biscuit-coloured feet.

"I've got to go to a party," I said over my shoulder. "A clean shirt, please."

It was Said Akbar, of course. I had meant to abandon him in Quetta with funds to carry him home to the North-West Frontier, but he had come with me to Karachi just the same. He handed me a shirt and then stood back, fanning himself with his own long, grey, *mazri* shirt-tails.

"*Ph-h-h-h-h-ew* . . . This Karachi! Again a party? Bobby sahib and the other Peter sahib are going again too. I know, because the bearer has told me."

"Yes, again. And now the trousers, please."

I put them on. Said Akbar watched despondently. After a moment he said:

Epilogue: Karachi

"Why did you not tell me that Karachi is like a sickness?"

"Come now!" I expostulated. I suppose I felt that I must defend poor Karachi, though I can't imagine why. "If it is a sickness, then it is a sickness that men survive, whereas Peshawar in summer . . ."

"We leave Peshawar in summer and go to our mountains, of course."

He was quite right. Karachi in summer is a low, recurring fever, an alternation of sweats and agues. People say it is nice, from a sense of loyalty or in order to hoodwink themselves: but it is nice in terms of what is unbearably nasty. Said Akbar was not obliged to live here or like it, and I told him so: "You could have gone home at once, if you'd wanted to."

"I have to remain here until you are put into the aeroplane. I have promised"

"Whom did you promise? Not me, certainly."

"People," he said. "Fateh Khan. And others."

"I see. *Insha'Allah*, your promise will be fulfilled tonight."

"Yes, *Insha'Allah*."

I was knotting my tie by now. Shirt, trousers, socks, shoes, coat, tie . . . what madness to give parties in such a climate—what madness to accept! A tie . . . it would certainly strangle me.

"And now the comb. And those brushes, please."

He handed them to me. Then, with an air of martyrdom, he closed the window. For this single instant of time, at least, my hair would stay respectably in place. The sweat broke out all over me again.

"The towel . . ." I whispered.

*　　　　　*　　　　　*

I was staying with an old friend—Robert Cochran. Another old friend, Peter Knox, was staying there too. But neither of them was ready yet, so I sat alone in the sitting-room, waiting.

The family of dachshunds eyed me from behind chairs. They were not resentful of my being there any more, so long as I sat quite still and did nothing to make them nervous. I was sitting quite still, in any case—legs apart, arms slightly raised from the sides, head held forward in the hope that a current of air would sweep in and out of my collar and cuffs and trouser-legs. After a time the dogs began tittupping about on the points of their sharp little claws, and moaning. I had

260

watched this performance before during the past days, and I knew what it meant. Time for another run over the mud-flats. I got up and poured myself a drink.

After all it was much cooler standing up than sitting down, and less creasing to the clothes. I stood by the window, glass in hand, and looked across the mud again. I saw that the train had been re-marshalled in Clifton and was now whirling back to town, from left to right, a solid line of cars. Clifton was going to the party, too. Almost everybody went to the party almost every night. The guests were hundreds of names on lists. Only the hosts and the rendezvous varied. Sometimes there would be alcohol to help the evening through: but on 'dry' nights, when the host was a Muslim, guests must rely upon curry-puffs and conversation. Tonight was to be 'dry'.

Bobby Cochran came in. "Time for a quick one," he said.

He looked wonderfully fresh and clean, whereas I was already a little creased, but now the dogs sprang into action and were squeaking and clawing at him, so I supposed that he would not long remain so neat. Actually he managed to beat them off before they could do any damage and a servant was sent for, to take them away. They were being taken out of the room in chains when Peter Knox came in. Directly they saw him they burst into tears and begged him to intercede, but he made straight for the drinks table and pretended not to have noticed anything.

"I see we have time for a quick one," he said firmly.

Both Bobby and Peter were feeling guilty about the dogs, I think. I was not. On the contrary I felt pleased that this evening it would be a servant, rather than ourselves, who would be calling hopelessly across the winds and the wastelands as dusk fell, a servant who would watch specks galloping like tiny rocking-horses over the horizon.

"You'd better have another, Peter," Bobby said.

"Me?"

"Well, both the Peters. All of us."

We all had another.

A few minutes later we were waiting in the car at the point where our branch road joined the highway. The 'Clifton Express' was still pounding by. Our driver's mouth was set. This was always a moment of tension.

Epilogue: Karachi

"*Now!*" shouted Bobby, and we all closed our eyes.

Shaken, speechless, but miraculously unscathed, we had jumped the train and were careering to the party along with all the other guests.

★   ★   ★

Down on the lawn guests were circulating with the air of experts. On the right, an unbroken fifteen-yard stretch of food: on the left an arrangement of Chesterfield sofas with a lot of ladies sitting on them. These would be mostly Pakistani ladies. The foreign ladies would be circulating with everyone else. At present I stood beside an unknown Englishwoman with a big, sweet, face.

"It's all so romantic," she was saying to me as she tweaked a bit of tulle over her shoulders. "I never seem to get tired of it. Never! It's so ... so ... well, so *romantic*, don't you think?"

"Yes, it is, isn't it?" I agreed, looking round.

Fairy signals, green and red and white, winked at each other from the branches of banian trees. Guests were bowing and passing and re-passing and bowing to each other, perhaps even to us, so we bowed again as well. It was stiflingly hot, except in the gap between the banian trees where a tin-foil gale screamed through.

"So beautiful," she said. "Beautiful and romantic—those are the only words to describe it."

"Yes," I admitted. "But perhaps we should stand back a little—just a few steps—because we seem to be ..."

The centre of the lawn was really for the privileged persons in whose faces all those flash-bulbs kept exploding. Lesser persons were expected to stay modestly out of focus.

"There! That's better," I said. "Now we can see everything beautifully."

"Yes. That's wonderful!" Her eyes made a complete circuit of the lawn. "I do think they do these parties wonderfully, don't you, Mister ... er ...?"

"Mayne. Peter Mayne. Yes, I think so too."

"So do I," she exclaimed. "Oh, I do so agree with you! And the colour of it all! I suppose it must be the artist in me or something ... those cannas, for instance!"

"And the ladies' *saris*!"

"Yes, and then the ... the ..."

"All those pink and green jellies and the rusty-gold of the *rossa-gullas*?"

"Of the what?"

"Those rusty-golden-syrupy things. Those cakes. Delicious, they are. Aren't they *rossagullas*, then?"

"Oh yes, I suppose they are . . ." she said, her voice tailing away.

"Shall I fetch you a *rossagulla*, Mrs. . . . er . . .?"

Perhaps if she had said 'yes' I would have left her, never to return, but she did not say 'yes'. Instead she said: "The name is Mrs. Bembridge-White. My husband is Number One in the Karachi Gas Corporation."

"Oh yes?" I murmured politely.

She smiled towards me in modest triumph. "Yes. He's burra sahib of the Gas Corporation. And you, Mister . . .?"

"Me? My name is Mayne."

"Yes, yes, you told me that. But what are you in?"

"I'm not in anything."

"Not in anything? Then what are you doing in Karachi?"

I started to tell her and she nodded once or twice, but her eyes were looking vaguely at a number of other things. I suppose that my attention must have wandered too, because in retrospect I seem to hear my voice faltering and my mind creaking to a stop. For a while we stood there, side by side, in a vacuum, neither of us knowing what to do about it. After a bit I became aware of a face passing nearby. A thin face. At first nothing registered particularly, and then there was a click and I saw that it was the Pathan I had met and talked with in Dean's Hotel garden, months before. I called out to him. He stopped, turned and started towards us, and I must have taken a step or two to meet him, leaving Mrs. Bembridge-White behind in the vacuum.

"Peshawar, wasn't it?" the Pathan said as he came up. "In June?"

"Yes. Do you remember?"

"Very well. I talked a lot, didn't I? How did you get on with the Pakhtuns? Did you enjoy yourself?"

"Yes . . ." I began—and the word suddenly sounded so alone that I added to it: "Yes, enormously."

He was looking at me with a curious expression. "And 'no', too, do you mean? Yes *and* no?"

"Mostly 'yes, enormously.'"

"Hm-m," he said. "I see. I wonder what you expected to find that you didn't find."

I was watching his eyes, wondering in my turn what he meant exactly, and whether he would laugh at me if I said: 'me.'

He didn't laugh. Instead he said, very gently: "Of course. And you were nowhere to be found."

A voice broke through the little silence that followed, a voice with a slightly petulant edge to it: "I think perhaps, if you would be so kind, Mr. Mayne, I *will* have a *rossagulla* after all."

Mrs. Bembridge-White was with us once more.

Lightning Source UK Ltd.
Milton Keynes UK
UKHW030630250419
341590UK00006B/626/P

9 781179 403106